MW01199795

ACROSS THE BLOODY CHASM

CONFLICTING WORLDS
NEW DIMENSIONS OF THE AMERICAN CIVIL WAR

T. Michael Parrish, Series Editor

ACROSS THE BLOODY CHASM

THE **CULTURE** OF **COMMEMORATION** AMONG **CIVIL WAR VETERANS**

M. KEITH HARRIS

LOUISIANA STATE UNIVERSITY PRESS

BATON ROUGE

Published with the assistance of the V. Ray Cardozier Fund

Published by Louisiana State University Press
Copyright © 2014 by Louisiana State University Press
All rights reserved
Manufactured in the United States of America
First printing

Designer: Barbara Neely Bourgoyne
Typeface: Sina Nova
Printer and binder: Maple Press, Inc.

Library of Congress Cataloging-in-Publication Data

Harris, M. Keith, 1967–
   Across the bloody chasm : the culture of commemoration among Civil War veterans /
M. Keith Harris.
      pages cm. — (Conflicting worlds : new dimensions of the American Civil War)
   Includes bibliographical references and index.
   ISBN 978-0-8071-5772-5 (cloth : alkaline paper) — ISBN 978-0-8071-5773-2 (pdf) — ISBN 978-0-8071-5774-9 (epub) — ISBN 978-0-8071-5775-6 (mobi) 1. United States—History—Civil War, 1861–1865—Veterans. 2. United States—History—Civil War, 1861–1865—Social aspects. 3. Veterans—United States—History—19th century. 4. Veterans—United States—History—20th century. 5. Veterans—Confederate States of America—History. 6. War memorials—United States—History. 7. Collective memory—United States—History. 8. Memory—Social aspects—United States—History. 9. Reconciliation—Social aspects—United States—History. 10. Social conflict—United States—History. I. Title.
   E491.H33 2014
   973.7′1—dc23
                                                                          2014011006

For Coni

CONTENTS

ACKNOWLEDGMENTS ix

INTRODUCTION 1
Enemies and Americans

CHAPTER ONE 15
The Memories of Those Days

CHAPTER TWO 42
"The Greatest Conspiracy of All Times"
Union Veterans Commemorate the Suppression of Treason

CHAPTER THREE 66
Unrepentant Rebels
Commemorations and Confederate Reconciliation

CHAPTER FOUR 90
The Enduring Work of the Republic
Commemorating Freedom in the Era of Reconciliation

CHAPTER FIVE 114
Calumny Masquerading as History
Rebels' Response to the Emancipationist Cause

EPILOGUE 139
Legacies under Pressure

NOTES 145

BIBLIOGRAPHY 185

INDEX 213

ACKNOWLEDGMENTS

At long last, I am honored to sit down and thank those who helped breathe life into this book. I suspect that anyone who reads such monographs will understand that the research, writing, and revision process is a long one. My study is no exception to this. The process, as it were, began for me on the Gettysburg battlefield during a University of California, Los Angeles, undergraduate travel study program in 2001. There, Joan Waugh introduced me to the field of historical memory. I would like to thank her for this and for suggesting that Civil War veterans' commemorative efforts would be a worthy topic for future study. As it turned out, they were.

Since then, I have amassed more debts than I could possibly enumerate. This insurmountable task notwithstanding, I wish to thank specifically those who made the most significant contributions. As a graduate student at the University of Virginia, I was privileged to work with some of the finest scholars I have had the pleasure of knowing. In particular, I wish to acknowledge the tireless efforts of Gary W. Gallagher. While serving as my dissertation adviser, he offered me wisdom and guidance that amounted to more than I could have ever expected. A decade later, and gallons of red ink used, my work reflects the influence of an exceptional historian. Thank you.

I would especially like to thank University of Virginia professors Joseph F. Kett, Joseph C. Miller, and Peter Onuf for encouraging me to take the consensus to task and for instructing a novice in the art of historical writing. You may recognize more than a few of our conversations within these pages. My classmates at Mr. Jefferson's university made Charlottesville a happier place. I would especially like to thank Cynthia Nicoletti, Kanisorn "Kid" Wongsrichanalai, and the entire Cavalier Civil War Caucus roster, a supportive crew all. Our conversations at Casa Gallagher, in post-conference restaurants and bars from New Orleans to Birmingham, and on road trips around the upper South (and lower North) were most satisfactory. Any scholarly discourse that transpired along the way was at once enlightening and a whole lot of fun. We were indeed a merry band.

I would also like to express my gratitude to the gifted scholars Caroline E. Janney and Barbara A. Gannon. Both read manuscript versions of this work and offered invaluable suggestions. They helped me better understand the nuances of veteran commemorations beyond what I initially discovered. I am eternally indebted to both for their frank and candid critiques of my work. At the Louisiana State University Press, T. Michael Parrish offered his vast expertise and ultimately helped turn this into a better book. I was always happy to find the copies he sent of books and journal articles in the mailbox during the last series of revisions. They were all of great help. It has also been an especial pleasure to work with Rand Dotson at LSU Press. His thoughtful critique of everything from content to cover art has in all ways eased the final stages of this work. Copy editor Jo Ann Kiser saved me from embarrassment more than once, and two anonymous readers provided some first-rate suggestions in regard to context and analysis. I could not have completed this book without the munificent support of the Archibald Craig fellowship at the University of Virginia, the Gilder Lehrman Institute of American History, and the Andrew W. Mellon Foundation. Their fellowships afforded several weeks of focused research in Charlottesville, Virginia; Madison, Wisconsin; New York, New York; and Richmond, Virginia. I trust you will find that your money was well spent. Archivists and library staffs across the North, South, and Midwest were extraordinarily helpful. Your patience and knowledge helped me weave together a great number of loose threads. In particular, those at the Veterans Museum in Madison, the Virginia Historical Society in Richmond, and the New York Public Library in Manhattan were especially obliging.

If scholarly writing has always been something of a collaborative effort, then the advent of the Internet has made it all the more so. For years I contributed to the blogosphere with meditations on the Civil War era at Cosmic America. I am now the creator and host of Keith Harris History, a multimedia American history online network (keithharrishistory.com). Through this platform and the social media juggernaut Twitter (@mkeithharris), I have met and talked shop with academics and the informed public alike. Many have gone well beyond the call of duty—adding depth and context to my work. I thank them all and look forward to many more years of engaging discourse.

Finally, I dedicate this book to my beautiful wife, Coni Constantine. No one single person has been a greater inspiration or has offered more support in all of my endeavors, scholarly or otherwise. She has listened patiently while I prattled on for hours (years, really) about Civil War veterans. She knows their songs, their sentiments, and their ambitions nearly as well as I. It would be difficult to reduce to mere words exactly how much you mean to me. Suffice it to say, you made all the difference.

ENEMIES AND AMERICANS

[An] estrangement developed until it gave to the people of the
North and the South the aspect of two races, manifesting towards
each other all the antipathy with each other's standpoint.

—GEORGE L. CHRISTIAN, Virginia veteran

"We are ready to forgive," Union veteran W. T. Collins affirmed in the nation's capital in 1869—only a few years after the smoke from America's Civil
War battlefields had cleared. "But we will never consent to public national
tribute to obliterate the wide gulf which lies between principles for which
we fought... and those for which the rebel armies banded together." Forty-
one years later in Austin, Texas, Confederate veteran William R. Hanby remarked that in the future "whatever passions and prejudices that once may
have animated us will be forever buried." Still, he noted, "We today must
hear the fife and drum, must feel the deep-seated, intense commotion of
that period."[1] Neither man was opposed to national reconciliation—indeed,
they embraced it. Yet they were both, over a time spanning four decades,
resolutely unwilling to disregard memories of the causes for which so many
had sacrificed. In their reluctance to forget, veterans from both sides of the
Potomac undermined the broader reconciliatory message tacitly—often
explicitly—endorsed by a nation.

Across the Bloody Chasm is the story of the confluence of national reconciliation in the wake of the Civil War and veterans' efforts to preserve
and commemorate the war's memories. While death was busy thinning
veteran ranks, former soldiers of the Union and Confederate armies commemorated national memories denoting American valor and fealty. But
more important, they worked tirelessly to preserve sectional memories

that advanced one side over the other and conjured fear, anger, and resentment among formerly warring parties. From a Union perspective, reuniting the nation had been the driving reason to fight, and veterans of northern armies overwhelmingly embraced the concept both during and after the war. Former Confederates had little choice in the matter. An inconsolable few left the country, but the overwhelming majority of ex-Rebels reclaimed their citizenship in a reunited nation. What veterans felt about past enemies was indeed diverse, but the plain fact of reunion impelled veterans to edge toward some kind of reconciliatory message.[2]

One can easily blur the distinction between "reunion" and "reconciliation."[3] The two words are related but not interchangeable. Reunion simply meant the coming together of individual states, previously united under one government, subsequent to a protracted war. It was a reality sealed by the final surrenders of Confederate national armies, the dissolution of the Confederate government, and the forced suppression of a domestic rebellion. Reconciliation, in contrast, was an experiential action undertaken by the participants of that war. The word conveys sincere forgiveness, but in the context of Civil War veterans, refers more pointedly to an acceptance that those once-warring parties were again fellow citizens. The promotion of reconciliation acknowledged a sense of past unity. This abstraction is precisely the idea to which veterans were reconciled. They accepted the vision of countrymen standing side by side under the same flag with a shared connection to the nation's past, its founding documents, its heroes, its villains, its enemies, its religion, and its language. Veterans willingly, often enthusiastically, committed to embracing an all-encompassing national identity on these terms—an identity as Americans, one and all. Ultimately, national politics depended on reconciliation; economic expediency rested on it. So veterans from both sides of the bloody chasm set out to craft this particular message of reconciliation from the scattered shards of disunion. But in so doing, they preserved the memories of their sectional ideals, their trials, and their respective causes.[4]

How could veterans' memories at once promote reconciliation and serve to widen the chasm between sections? Resolution of this tension rests with an acknowledgment of veterans' layered perceptions of the past. Like W. T. Collins, many veterans may have been ready to forgive, but genuine forgiveness was contingent on an unlikely consensus. Civil War veterans, both Union and Confederate, built the framework of Civil War memory and their understanding of reconciliation on the foundation of very different perceptions of an imagined past. Differing memories of, and even nostalgia for, decades-old national identity in the image of the founding generation is precisely what informed the memories of their lived past: the sectional crises that tore the country apart; the wartime experiences and the causes that motivated them to kill their fellow countrymen. One should not underestimate the power of veterans' imagined past—a past where sections came together under one constitution guided by the wisdom of the founding fathers. Veterans were thus reconciled to the abstract notion of "America," or more specifically, their perceptions of the early republic. This is how veterans such as former Confederate artillerist William Gordon McCabe could so forcefully embrace reconciliation in the late nineteenth century while holding steadfast his genuine appreciation of the founding generation—what informed his commitment to the Confederacy. Such recollections were the very "mystic chords of memory" to which Abraham Lincoln referred in his first inaugural address. An imagined past could reflect ties to the founding generation, the spirit of fraternal camaraderie, the merits of compromise, American exceptionalism, or any number of perceived American traits and virtues. Though they were only part of the many strands of national memory, it was the sectional perceptions of the original intentions of the founders that informed the thinking of commemorating Civil War veterans. What it meant to be "Americans one and all" differed greatly depending on veterans' sectional allegiances. But most important, what it meant to be American would move Gordon McCabe and countless others to such utterances as "the enemy was posted there . . . I mean our friends, the enemy."[5]

We Are All Americans

Veterans remembered the war primarily through commemorations. Their speeches, parades, monument dedications, and literature reflecting on the war provided the means through which they articulated visions of reconciliation—visions that in essence mirrored the causes for which they had fought. Veterans' reconciliationist views were in fact colored by their experiences of war, the issues that had been at stake, and the respective causes for which they fought. They both promoted reconciliation and reminded their audiences that only one side had been right. Their challenge was how best to situate former enemies within these commemorative contexts. The story of reconciliation and Civil War memory is thus a story of competition, negotiation, and contestation. Fueled by controversy and sustained by argument, veterans constructed their visions of reconciliation on the foundation of their most contentious memories. Though they expressed spread-eagle paeans to postwar unity and often styled themselves as "reconciled," veterans recalled their former enemies as base perpetrators of lies who carried with them the spirit of treason or the spoils of tyranny.

In light of such vituperative commemorative language, one could observe a disingenuous quality to veterans' reconciliationist rhetoric. Evidence suggests that this is unlikely. Ultimately, veterans' efforts fell short of unmitigated forgiveness. But the historical record is replete with veterans from both sides clearly conjuring the spirit of Americanness and a desire to be in league with all countrymen. They issued such statements in both public and private consistently across time and place. Ultimately, the memories of their lived past stood between veterans' desires and reality. While they did not set out to intentionally hinder reconciliation, their words often did exactly that.

Modern observers often emphasize consensus rather than conflict. They perceive Civil War veterans' commemorative cultures changing over time from sectional and divisive to national and generally benign. They likewise conceptualize the postwar period as a clearly delineated transition away from a fragmented collection of regional loyalties to a new national unity thus signifying veterans' commemorative activities and their memories sweeping along with the vastly changing national commemorative ethos. The movement to a distinctively new national era necessarily suggests the reconfiguration of commemorative traditions. A common way to contextualize this transition is to accent the broader shift in Americans' nationalist vernacular. In modern popular culture, 40 million television viewers warmed to this idea in September 1990 via the folksy wisdom of novelist Shelby Foote in Ken Burns's epic nine-part documentary *The Civil War*. Viewers learned that prior to the war, citizens referred to the United States in a plural sense, as in "the United States are ..." Only after the war did the singular "the United States is . . ." come into fashion. "That's what the war accomplished," Foote informed a nation of viewers, "it made us an is."[6]

Within the context of shifting traditions, the war with Spain in 1898 looms large as a culminating point in the reconciliatory process. Undeniably, the "splendid little war" offers a telling landmark in the broadly defined story of reconciliation—one embraced, celebrated, and commemorated by a national citizenry. Northerners and southerners alike reveled in their self-congratulatory national commitment and sent their sons by the thousand to fight under a single banner. Even a few veterans of Rebel armies dusted off their sabers and committed themselves to the unified nation's war effort. Appearing as living monuments to reconciliation, former Confederate generals Joseph Wheeler, Thomas Lafayette Rosser, and Fitzhugh Lee—now well beyond their prime—donned the blue uniforms of the United States Army and led the sons of a reconciled nation against a foreign foe.[7]

Most troubling, a "reconciliation premise" fundamentally informs the modern interpretive framework. Recognizing that profound racial inequalities coincided with an extensive support for reconciliation, many use this era as a vantage point from which to define and lament a moment forgotten in historical memory—a lost chance for the nation to capitalize on the promises of Union victory. A powerful narrative illustrating a dichotomy between the reconciled and unreconciled places historical actors in analytically limited categories. In this narrative, a clear distinction emerges between one-dimensional reconciliationists and the few who flatly refused to accept reconciliation—bloody shirt-waving Yankees and unreconstructed Rebels alike. The overwhelming majority of those who survived disunion agreed to remember selectively war events bolstering the distinctly American virtues of Union and Confederate fighting men. This conclusion obscures the tense, often vituperative negotiation processes of a nation's formerly warring sections suddenly thrust back together, each staking claim to a reconciliationist spirit.[8]

Further analysis of the reconciliation period as a movement founded on the marginalization of black people is of limited utility. Civil War veterans from both North and South shared in their racist sensibilities. But while the participants were undoubtedly racist, emphasizing veterans' reconciliatory impulses solely as efforts to commemorate a "white only" war runs the risk of obscuring veterans' intentions.[9] Veterans did not calculatingly contribute to historical amnesia along racial lines in the name of reconciliation. It is true that from the point of view of most veterans, reconciliation seemed the soundest course of action. Yet the memories that informed the terms of reconciliation suggest that Civil War veterans acquiesced to reaching across the bloody chasm only so long as their former enemies accepted their respective arguments—a scenario that seldom transpired. Rather than ignoring the issues of war, veterans exploited them. Invoking the unnecessary destruction of civilian property and treatment in prisoner-of-war camps, sectional ideology, and slavery and emancipation, veterans wrote the terms of peace to the detriment of their former enemies. United States victory secured reunion; reconciliation was far more fragile.[10]

"The story of the great conflict will never diminish in interest."

Civil War veterans who took the time to contribute to the historical record usually promoted reconciliation. But how exactly did they perceive forgiveness in light of observable and extensive bitterness? Most veterans endorsed reconciliation in ways that suggested certain conditions first be met. These conditions more often than not involved the proposal of a national commemorative ethos that favored one section. Not surprisingly, veterans from opposing sides were unwilling to concede to former antagonists' terms. From the perspectives of both northern and southern veterans, former enemies' efforts to author a national Civil War memory in sectional ways held little merit. Instead, veterans would respond to sectional memories with memories of their own. Despite their genuine reconciliatory rhetoric, letting "bygones be bygones" was often the furthest thing from veterans' minds.[11]

Aging veterans were working within a broader national commemorative experience. Nonveterans, who in many cases came of age after the Civil War and thus did not share veterans' sectional commemorative framework, authored much of this commemoration. National events scripted specifically to convey unity of purpose such as the World's Columbian Exposition in Chicago in 1893 essentially ignored past conflict in favor of the marvels of progress, American ingenuity, and national prowess. The "White City" in Chicago was a national monument to a new era. Even national events mentioning the war, such as the tercentennial celebration at Jamestown Virginia in 1903, sought to establish distance from past discord and instead illuminate modernity and unity. At such events, the war passed from lived memory to myth and offered a nonthreatening—and indeed sentimental— window into the past. Civil War veterans fought not only among themselves but also against a changing national commemorative ethos that increasingly redirected commemorations away from a divisive past and toward progress, expansion, and a modern unified nation.

Against the backdrop of commemorative change, most veterans disdained an overly sentimentalized memory of the Civil War. They did not contribute in any significant way to the whitewashed memory of the war. What then, did they do? Veterans organized in the postwar years. They formed groups, kept meticulous records, attended celebratory gatherings, held meetings, made speeches, and corresponded with one another and their leaders. They did so not to forget the hardships of their years at war, but to do precisely the opposite. Veterans' objectives were to remember; they labored to make sure that they were honored in their lifetimes and that future generations would understand exactly why they had gone to war. Commemorative efforts were not simply whitewashed stories of bravery, but recollections of issues and instances—often painful, but vitally important to those who had lived through them and now sought to contribute their experiences to the national identity.

Veterans' sentiments are remarkably consistent over time. Their devotion to issues and memories of the war years appeared as sharp in the late nineteenth and early twentieth centuries as they had in 1865. Most used precisely the same language and expressed the same views late in life as they had as young men. This alone could refute the conventional wisdom that veterans' memories gradually faded. Careful consideration of veterans' speeches, publications, and organizations' records reveals that while their words remained constant, the intensity and frequency with which they used them increased as they grew older. Veterans understood that as time passed and their numbers dwindled, the memories of their respective causes faced the danger of disappearing. Accordingly, they redoubled their efforts late in life to insure that this disappearance did not take place. While their messages remained consistent, the zeal with which they communicated these messages grew (relative to their diminishing numbers) as the years passed. Schoolchildren and various "sons" groups became the focal point for preservation, and veterans on each side worked diligently to illuminate both the "right" and the "wrong" versions of Civil War history. While their words remained constant, they worked to impart their experiences within the contexts of the changing world around them.

Most veterans returned to peaceful pursuits after the war and contributed little to the historical record. Those who had the means may have attended reunions or turned out for patriotic events in their communities, but seldom did they offer words to attest to their postwar sentiments. They made known their continued commitment to their causes by attending public events, joining veterans' organizations, and subscribing to groups' publications. Veteran leaders—prominent individuals who were active in commemorative efforts and among the most prolific authors of commemorative literature—spoke for the majority of their comrades. These men shared many traits. Most had enlisted for service as young men, and a significant number lived well into the twentieth century. Many were professionals in civilian life both before and after the war, and as their wartime letters attest, while their morale ebbed and flowed, they were fiercely patriotic. They often held prominent positions in their communities and in the postwar nation. Veteran leaders included politicians, doctors, attorneys, industrialists, businessmen, ministers, planters, and educators. While the years following the war saw the nation riddled with divergence of opinion, political infighting, and vast disagreement among the white population, prominent veterans who had fought under the same flag would generally concur when it came to sectional memories of the war.

The places veterans chose to gather are perhaps the most significant in terms of Civil War memory. No matter who was speaking or in attendance, no matter what they were saying, their surroundings offered much in the way of symbolic gestures to their causes. The Gettysburg battlefield is without question the most important site of memory in this regard. But this battlefield functioned in multiple ways. On one hand, nationalists used the battlefield to promote the broader national commemorative culture. In July 1913, for example, veterans of the United States and Confederate armies, along with thousands of civilians and those not of the war generation, gathered in Gettysburg to commemorate the fifty-year anniversary of the Civil War's bloodiest and most famous battle. The four-day "Blue-

Gray Reunion" featured parades, reenactments, and speeches from a host of dignitaries including President Woodrow Wilson. Striking among the event's activities was the lack of a comprehensive remembrance of the war's causes and consequences. Veterans and other public figures highlighted only the virtuous aspects of soldiery such as courage, valor, and selfless devotion. Thousands of spectators enthusiastically approved of President Wilson's remarks to former Yankee and Rebel alike: "Valor? Yes! Greater no man shall see in war; and self-sacrifice, and loss to the uttermost; the high recklessness of exalted devotion which does not count the cost."[12]

In 1938, President Franklin Delano Roosevelt voiced a similar sentiment before a comparable (although much smaller) gathering of veterans from northern and southern armies and other American citizens. In a speech dedicating the Eternal Light Peace Memorial and celebrating the seventy-fifth anniversary of the battle, Roosevelt concurred with Wilson's statements denoting shared valor. Further, the president reminded Americans that the veterans were "brought [to Gettysburg] by the memories of old divided loyalties, but they meet here in united loyalty to a united cause which the unfolding years made it easier to see." In words conspicuous for their lack of sectionalism, Roosevelt perhaps summoned Lincoln's "better angels" by noting, "All of them we honor, not asking under which Flag they fought then—thankful that they stand together under one Flag now."[13] The words of both presidents typify those of one particular nonveteran commemorative culture—that which offered little substance concerning the war's causes or consequences. These were not generally the veterans' sentiments, but rather those of a reconciled nonveteran citizenry far removed from the war by time. While much of the nation's citizens in the early twentieth century (many of whom were born after the war) embraced a celebratory message speaking to the power of progress and unity, veterans held fast to their memories of conflict and their loyalty to sectional interpretations of the most significant event of their lives.

In fact, messages colored with sectional hues more often informed commemorative events at Gettysburg and elsewhere. Blue-Gray reunions, while noteworthy, were unusual events when compared to the typical veteran commemorative experience. Rarely did veterans meet face to face with their former enemies when revisiting wartime memories. Veterans' reunions, whether celebratory, in memoriam, social, or any combination

of the three, were nearly always defined by exclusivity. Veterans came together in the postwar years along the lines of company, regiment, army,
or some other shared experience. Accordingly, the messages delivered at
veterans' reunions varied significantly depending on audience. In this case,
Gettysburg assumes a very different meaning in Civil War commemorations. Union veterans more frequently used the battlefield site as a way to
promote some of the most heated and controversial arguments involved
in the contest to write the terms of peace. Here it was mainly northerners
who articulated a commemorative message that veterans of Union armies
could embrace. These veterans dedicating monuments and staging reunions
reminded Americans that they welcomed peace between countrymen, but
only with the acknowledgment that their cause alone deserved accolades.

Late in the nineteenth and early in the twentieth century, former Confederates also used Gettysburg as a place to voice their version of war memory.
But the occurrence of Confederate events at Gettysburg, as evidenced by the
paltry number of Confederate state monuments on the battlefield, paled in
comparison to the thousands of Union speeches, dedications, and reunions
held on the famous ground. Former Confederates had to look elsewhere to
voice their particularly southern commemorative culture. And there were
many places ready and available. Some of the sites of Lee's most storied
victories saw regular postwar visits from the Rebel veterans who gathered
simultaneously to promote the Confederate vision of reconciliation as well
as recall their account of the war. The battlefields at Chancellorsville, Fredericksburg, and Manassas were perfect venues for former Confederates
who perpetuated the Rebel cause in the postwar years. Just as in the North,
veterans' speeches at Confederate reunions resounded with sectionalism—
especially when there were no Yankees around to hear them.[14]

The phenomenon of speaking one's mind in front of friends took hold in
places beyond the battlefield. In this regard place proves even more significant. When it came to commemorative efforts, veterans' meeting halls were
particularly hot with sectionalism. The relationship between speaker and
audience took on a significant meaning in the confines of veterans' posts.
Posts offered places where veterans could freely express themselves in ways
they may not have been comfortable with in front of nonveteran civilians in
step with the broader national commemorative ethos. Shared experiences
and a general acceptance of their respective country's causes suggest that

veterans speaking in such places were far more likely to articulate genuine feelings. Post minutes and records of speeches and discussions often reveal a sectional commemorative culture infused with the terms of a conditional reconciliation emanating from both sides of the Potomac. They also suggest a stark contrast to the changing nationalist commemorative culture around them.

Veterans' writings functioned in similar but more public ways. Personal reminiscences and memoirs were hardly benign treatises on the war's central issues. In fact, the authors of these works tended to provide specific points of view—often envisioned for friendly audiences. Many of their works lauded the virtues of all American fighting men. Yet they likewise accented the shortcomings of their former enemies and did so in ways that defined reconciliation in sectional terms. Their periodicals and other newspapers also provide information regarding veterans' activities and attitudes during this period. Former Confederates added their experiences of war and its aftermath to such publications as *The Southern Bivouac, The Land We Love,* the *Southern Historical Society Papers* (a publication that worked effectively as a collection of various sources including unpublished speeches and newspaper articles) and most significantly, the United Confederate Veterans' widely distributed monthly, *Confederate Veteran.* Former Union soldiers published periodicals as well and contributed greatly to the veterans' postwar commemorative record. Particularly through published testimony and various other "war papers," as well as the foremost publication of the Grand Army of the Republic, *The National Tribune,* Union veterans added their views of the war.

One of the most underutilized resources in the commemorative record is the regimental history. Although regimental histories may not supply the most accurate account of the war or may tend to show the regiment in question in only the brightest of lights, regimental histories reveal a great deal about what veterans were considering at the time of writing. Between 1865 and the early twentieth century, and most especially in the late nineteenth century, when former soldiers came together specifically to encourage the publications of their war records, veterans published scores of histories recounting the unit's formation and the various battles engaged. They also highlighted commanders and prominent members of the regiment. But most importantly, they mused over the cause(s) of the war and the issues at stake. The authors' purpose, as noted by one former Connecticut soldier, was clear: "To transmit to posterity [the] glorious record of heroic service freely given to their country . . . to perpetuate in remembrance the brave deeds . . . [and to] stimulate the fire of patriotism." Not always, but frequently enough to merit attention, these works suggest a clear conflict in how veterans remembered the war, how they commemorated it, and how they promoted reconciliation.[15]

Across the Bloody Chasm underscores the sectionalism infused in veterans' reconciliatory efforts. Chapter 1 discusses the "atrocities narrative"—veterans' recollections of cruel treatment in prisoner-of-war camps and harsh measures inflicted upon civilians and private property. Former Civil War soldiers were extremely concerned with their legacies and how future generations would remember them. As they aged they increasingly reminded citizens of their heroism, trials, and tribulations between 1861 and 1865. Northern and southern veterans' concerns regarding textbooks, patriotic instruction, and the formation of veterans' fraternal groups show a clear commitment to memory preservation; and Civil War veterans situated bitter memories of the war in the forefront of their commemorative efforts—in essence setting a bitter commemorative tone. While their aim was to guarantee that all wartime memories would not fade with time, war-related atrocities, in ways that might have surprised veterans, are what primarily took hold in the broader national commemorative context.[16]

Chapter 2 examines northern veterans' commemoration of the Union cause. The ideological commitment to the Union's preservation rang true throughout the reconciliation period. While modern scholars have gone as far as to suggest that during the war, "preserving the Union [was] a goal too shallow to be worth the sacrifice of a single life," northern veterans nearly unanimously agreed that Union was a primary motivational factor (among several) behind the decision to enlist and fight for four bloody years. In postwar commemorations, veterans did not imagine Union in vague amorphous ways but rather in quite specific ones. While preservation of Union implied reconciliation, undercurrents of sectional bitterness ran throughout northern commemorative efforts that defined reconciliation in sectional terms. Northern veterans never let the nation forget that one group of Americans had committed the highest crime of treason. Calls for punishment may have subsided over the years, but the simple fact that some Americans had shouldered muskets to destroy the Union, as set forth by the founding generation, resonated throughout the period.[17]

Chapter 3 addresses former Confederates' responses to such allegations. Unwilling to tolerate accusations of treason, ex-Confederates insisted that their cause was both just and in accordance with the ideals of the founders. Union victory did not suggest the triumph of principles. These men distanced themselves from the fight to preserve slavery, but nevertheless resuscitated Confederate ideology in the form of state rights and the right of secession, all the while emphasizing that the Confederate war was a fight against tyranny. Claiming to have been carrying out the traditions of their fathers, many balked at the term "Rebel" and insisted that northerners had strayed from the national virtues laid out by such southern notables as George Washington, Thomas Jefferson, and Patrick Henry. While some of these views represent the foundation of the Lost Cause argument, a significant number of former Confederates denounced the Lost Cause, arguing that such sentiment functioned as an "apologetic whine."[18] Most former Rebels grudgingly accepted the fact of reunion. And soon many turned from simply accepting defeat as a fact to openly promoting reconciliation on their own terms. Within this number, a prominent and vociferous group of former Confederate soldiers insisted that defeat by a force of arms did not wash away the core principles of the Confederate States of America and publicly endorsed and commemorated Confederate ideology.

Meanwhile, former Union soldiers insisted that the defeat of a slavocracy and the destruction of the institution of slavery not only assured unparalleled progress for a reunited nation but also provided a moral high ground from which to celebrate a truly righteous cause. While few had enlisted with the goal of freedom in mind, many nevertheless embraced emancipation during the war as a way to punish Rebels and undermine the Confederate war effort.[19] Union veterans reiterated their commitment to freedom through postwar celebrations and emphasized the moral dimension. Chapter 4 accents former Union soldiers' positions on slavery and emancipation. Those wedded to the reconciliation premise emphasizing exceptional events and implying extensive rejection of the causes and consequences of the war obscure these important features of northern Civil War memory.

Individual former soldiers and groups of white northern veterans singled out the sectional conflict over slavery as the fundamental origin of the war and praised emancipation as its righteous consequence.[20]

Finally, chapter 5 examines the many ways in which former Confederates worked to challenge Union emancipators' haughty claims of moral superiority. These challenges ranged from considering postwar racial policies "Yankee meddling" to countering assertions from the North that the war had had anything to do with slavery. But rather than restating how ex-Rebels set out to prove to the world that the slavery issue was incidental to the bloody struggle, this chapter will show how Confederate rebuttals to Union claims reinforced sectionalism. While scholars have recognized how former Confederates constructed bizarre arguments ignoring abundant evidence identifying slavery as fundamental to the Confederate bid for independence, they have overlooked the ways in which former Confederates attacked northerners for making such accusatory statements. When contentions stirred along racial lines, many drew on memories of northern abolitionists and the war for emancipation. Former Confederates did not hold African Americans responsible for racial unrest in the South, but white Yankees.[21]

This account of the reconciliation era emphasizes contention and continuity among former enemies. The wounds of their lived past festered well into the twentieth century, and those veterans who took part in the commemorative efforts of the period harnessed the bitterest of memories to make their points. So long as veterans lived, their memories of disunion remained vibrant. "Those there are who say 'let bygones be bygones,'" avowed Union veteran Joseph W. Morton as the nineteenth century drew to a close, "[but]not those whose life-blood watered the gory field—not those who went promptly to the front when danger threatened, ready to sacrifice life or limb upon the alter of patriotism. We know the war is over; the strife has ceased; the victory has been won; but the story of the great conflict will never diminish in interest, and the tales of veterans will always command respect and attention. Whatever is worth talking about is worth writing; and whatever is worth writing is worth publishing."[22] And publish they did—the historical record is replete with their testimony. But the purpose of veterans' words—to contest the terms of reconciliation within the context of a shifting national commemorative ethos—has been lost. This study seeks to recover their intentions.

CHAPTER ONE

THE MEMORIES OF THOSE DAYS

We have indeed sad memories of the past, which we cherish,
and he is but a tyrant, and no friend of man or liberty, who would
seek to prevent us from cherishing those sad memories.

—REVEREND DR. MITCHELL, Texas veteran

A massive demobilization of military forces followed quickly on the heels of
Union victory. After four years of bloody war, citizen soldiers of the United
States resumed work on their farms and in their factories, shops, and firms
across the reunited nation. For Federals, an army that had once boasted
over 1 million men shrank in size to eighty thousand. The peacetime army
soon numbered fewer than twenty-seven thousand soldiers.[1] Confederate veterans also returned to civilian pursuits. In certain respects, fortune
smiled on the defeated Rebels. At Appomattox, Ulysses S. Grant offered
generous terms of surrender to the remaining soldiers of Robert E. Lee's
battered Army of Northern Virginia. Grant allowed Confederates to return
home unmolested. Union commanders duplicated Grant's terms across
the South as the final days of war drew to a close and, with few exceptions,
guaranteed former Confederate soldiers amnesty. Defeated Confederates
returned home to a devastated economy, destroyed infrastructure, and social system completely dissimilar to that of 1861. But despite these hardships, the overwhelming majority of former Confederate soldiers faced no
imprisonment, no mass executions, and little punishment from the United
States government.[2]

Gracious gestures went far in terms of crafting a peaceful reunion. But
if any sense of brotherly affinity developed in the early postwar years, it
quickly ran aground on the rocky shoals of veterans' lived past—particularly

when it came to remembering wartime atrocities. Of these, two salient points deserve attention. First, the matter of prisoner-of-war camps, notorious in the North and South for reprehensible conditions and staggering death rates, numbered most prominently among the many issues veterans recalled with sulfurous language. Second, destructive hard-war strategies leveled at civilians and private property stirred flames of resentment. The development of veterans' organizations were key to the preservation of these experiences, and the growth of veterans' groups testifies to the heightened sense of urgency many felt when it came to preserving distressing memories. Prisons and dubious military tactics had little direct bearing on either country's ideology, but memories of such matters were nevertheless some of the essential elements bolstering the view that only one side, be it Union or Confederate, could claim moral superiority. Veterans' generally bitter sentiment would set the tone of conflict and inform the ideological and political arguments they would add to their respective commemorative cultures; illuminated moral deficiencies would enhance claims to the ideological foundation of the nation. Former enemies, each side would argue, not only perverted the national vision as set forth by the founders but also cast away their moral imperatives.[3]

"We can never forget."

Within months of April 1865, soldiers of the Confederate and United States armies transformed themselves into armies of veterans. These veterans wasted no time commemorating their wartime experiences. But as each side asserted moral supremacy in war, so too did they claim it in peace. Former enemies, as veterans would claim, lacked the moral virtues of their ancestors. Foundational in veterans' commemorative cultures, reminiscences of Elmira, Libby, Andersonville, and other prisons, as well as recollections of the burning of Atlanta, Columbia, Darien, Chambersburg, and elsewhere, exacerbated the troubling confluence of veterans' commemorative efforts and national reconciliation. Such remembrances worked to frustrate a national movement. This suggests that commemorations were less about letting "bygones be bygones" and more about empowerment. Whoever could write the terms of reconciliation would have an upper hand in dominating the veteran commemorative culture. And they hoped their ideals would inform a reunited national celebratory ethos—the future was at stake. But in April 1865, the side that would hold the moral high ground and write these terms remained to be seen. So veterans drew from a wealth of war experiences—many conjuring the bitterest of memories—to ensure that one side or the other would dictate exactly how the world would view American unity.

Bitterness notwithstanding, reconciliatory rhetoric found a welcome home in veterans' posts, civic gatherings, and reunions. Frequently, veterans celebrated their place in the postwar national fold in ways that seemingly overshadowed any past differences, some resounding "the American soul shall go marching on—marching on forever,—under the flag of Union" while others noted the "ties of a common history, the recollection of a common peril." Such sentiment imparted nationalist feeling reminiscent of the revolutionary generation and perhaps enlightened the consciousness of many American citizens. This was handy rhetoric, particularly when drawing on images of unification to support reconciliatory impulses. Unknowingly foreshadowing the American war effort against Spain, individuals such as former Confederate Bradley T. Johnson used commemorative speeches to bolster not only a southern but also an all-inclusive commitment to American unity. "If it should happen that this country should become involved in foreign war, the veterans of the Army of Northern Virginia and of the Army of the Potomac would show to the younger men the way to the front. That is the force of Americanism." As such, this particular veteran's pronouncement reverberated the notion of growing American prowess in the world—a hallmark of late nineteenth-century nationalism embedded in the broader commemorative culture.[4]

Such sentiment sometimes found its way into commemorative speeches. More often, opposing veterans or groups of veterans viewed commemorations as the means to articulate their sectional positions as reconciliationist movements took hold across the nation. Since veterans deemed nothing honorable about the enemies' mistreatment of prisoners of war or the destruction of civilian property, many saw to it that commemorative efforts were heavily weighted with negative imagery. One group of Union veterans, the Union ex-Prisoners of War Association, emblazoned their banner with apparent contradictions. Their flag's message, on one side depicting a Union prisoner under attack by a Confederate guard dog, incongruously offered an inscription illustrating members' desire to forgive. Still, the principal theme of the banner reminded Americans "We can never forget." These men were not minimizing an overall national commitment to reconciliation. They were, however, illustrating the memories of former enemies' brutality and thus ensuring that any "brotherly" spirit would favor one section over another.[5]

Most veterans organized precisely with this thought in mind. For Union veterans, commemorative activities began in spring 1865. The Military Order of the Loyal Legion of the United States (MOLLUS) came together while a few scattered Confederates remained under arms. Many other veterans' groups followed shortly on their heels. Within thirty years of Appomattox, groups such as the Soldiers and Sailors National Union League, the Society of the Army of the Tennessee, the Society of the Army of the Cumberland, the Society of the Army of the James, the Society of the Army of the Potomac, Union Veteran Legion, Union Veterans' Union, the Society of the Burnside Expedition, the Union Soldiers' Alliance, and the largest and most powerful Union veterans organization, the Grand Army of the Republic (GAR) reunited hundreds of thousands of former soldiers who commemorated union and their fight to suppress the rebellion.[6]

The growth of veterans' groups during the last third of the nineteenth century greatly enhanced veterans' commemorative efforts. For many groups, including the GAR, members' enthusiasm ebbed and flowed in the earliest years. In some cases, membership rosters dwindled, forcing chapters to close their doors permanently. Suspicion of military orders and an economic panic in 1873 contributed to a low point in veteran activities during the 1870s. Moreover, controversy, infighting, regionalism, envy among various groups, and difference of opinion within organizations also plagued veterans' societies. But despite these troubled beginnings, Union veterans' groups eventually thrived. Organizations had many stated purposes but all seemed to have one goal in common: the preservation of wartime memories. This unifying objective fueled veterans' commemorative efforts. The vexing concern that memories might be forgotten by civilians or future generations increased the membership rolls and the efforts of many organizations. By 1890, the Grand Army of the Republic alone boasted nearly five hundred thousand members.[7]

Unlike their northern counterparts, Confederate veterans did not organize on a large scale immediately after the war. Before 1870, women managed most commemorative activity under the watchful eyes of occupying Union forces.[8] The death of Robert E. Lee in October 1870 initiated a heightened sense of urgency regarding the organization of veterans and the commitment to the preservation of Confederate memories. The previous year, veterans had formed a few scattered groups such as the Confederate Survivors' Association of South Carolina, the Confederate Relief and Historical Association of Memphis, and the Southern Historical Society (SHS), located in New Orleans. But interest in such groups quickly waned. The SHS's presence especially declined during its first year due to the group's geographic isolation and what cofounder Joseph Jones called a lack of "material support from the Southern people."[9] The Confederate Survivors' Association and the Confederate Relief Association did little in terms of rallying veterans to the colors and closed their doors permanently within a few months of their formation.

Lee's death revived interest in Confederate commemorations, and plans soon got under way to memorialize the Confederate chieftain. Efforts undertaken by white southerners to enshrine Lee as the definitive American hero progressed despite his image in the northern states as a traitorous rebel. Such endeavors were significant in terms of the establishment of an antagonistic Confederate commemorative tradition. First, the SHS moved from New Orleans to Virginia, where prominent unreconstructed Virginians such as Jubal A. Early gained control of the organization. Second, veterans including Maryland's Bradley T. Johnson proposed the formation of a Society of the Army of Northern Virginia. This new group, later named the Association of the Army of Northern Virginia (AANVA), dedicated itself to preserving the memories of the cause and most importantly, erecting a monument to Robert E. Lee worthy of the commander's stature in the South. Together, these two groups established a long-lasting precedent. Both societies were dedicated to preserving their memories of war, however distasteful they might have been to Americans in the North.[10]

Members of the United Confederate Veterans (UCV), the largest and most powerful of the Confederate groups, followed cues set by earlier organizations. Formed in New Orleans in June 1889 by prominent veterans from

various groups and states, UCV leadership emphasized the preservation of
the history of the Confederate war effort. The early organizers, following
the lead of the GAR, sought to establish an all-inclusive national group
and called together members of the AANVA, the Association of the Army
of Tennessee (AAT), and a group of veterans organized as the Confederate
States Cavalry to draw up a constitution and appoint a commander-in-chief.
The UCV flourished early on and grew quickly. By 1892, over 188 camps
belonged to the group. This exponential growth stemmed largely from an
aggressive advertising campaign undertaken by UCV leadership. However, independent groups seeking to join the organization also supplied
the swelling ranks with more veterans. The well-known R. E. Lee camp
in Richmond, for example, joined forces with the UCV and changed its
designation to Lee Camp #1, UCV.[11]

"I blush for it in sorrow."

The earliest commemorative activities on either side invoked the prickly
prisoner-of-war issue. Veterans' assessment of prison atrocities threw open
the most basic question regarding former enemies: were they morally depraved? Memories in answer powerfully shaped the commemorative climate
North and South. Veterans described the horrors of prison life, often in
sharp detail, via three general commemorative forms. First, the popular
regimental history medium not only chronicled a particular regiment's
war record but also revealed the author's opinion on various events and
circumstances—including life in an enemy prison. Second, organized veteran group activities and writings specifically ventured down these commemorative paths. Group leadership took the lead in promoting the memories of prison life, and their prominence ensured that citizens across the
nation heard their message. Finally, commemorative gatherings, whether
for regimental reunions or monument dedications, tended to illuminate
controversial subjects. Speakers at such events would often support their
recollections of bravery under fire with stories of fortitude and perseverance while in the hands of enemy captors. Overall, these stories—enduring
throughout veterans' commemorative period—had a combined result. They
bolstered the idea of soldierly courage in the face of adverse conditions.

They also highlighted the deficiencies of the enemy and thus claimed moral victory for one particular side.[12]

Three detailed histories reveal the bitterness one might expect soon after the war. In 1866, veteran Winthrop D. Sheldon offered typical statements concerning the treatment of Union prisoners. In the regimental history of his unit, the 27th Connecticut, he specified the realities of prison life. Overcrowding, disease, exhaustion, food shortages, and general mistreatment colored Sheldon's recollection of his time in Libby prison. That same year, Osceola Lewis remarked in his history of the 126th Pennsylvania that those confined to Confederate prisons had served their "term of misery." Pennsylvania veteran William Watts Hart Davis would have agreed. Again in 1866, he made certain to note the "forlorn appearance" of prison survivors in his history of the Keystone State's 104th regiment. Davis would continue to chronicle the details of suffering that would become commonplace by the end of the century and generalize about "the enemy" in harsh terms. Rebel captors, he pointed out, offered no assistance to wounded [prisoners] and no food.[13]

Like those by Sheldon, Lewis, and Davis, many early regimental histories are filled with resentment toward Rebel captors. So soon after the war, veterans understandably harbored animosities while memories of prison life remained fresh in their minds. In the latter half of the 1860s and throughout the 1870s, while Reconstruction Era politics distracted the national population, veterans continued to circulate their Civil War stories. They reached an extensive audience. William Henry Locke, Thomas H. Parker, and Charles H. Banes, all Pennsylvania veterans, added to the growing body of regimental histories during this early commemorative period. All three men commemorated the war by accenting prison atrocities. Coupled with the long lists of comrades who died at Andersonville, Libby, and elsewhere, their words were formative in terms of building a postwar anti-Confederate sentiment. Tales of lingering in confinement, at last dying of disease or starvation, peppered their volumes and contributed to a consensus among northern veterans regarding the mistreatment of Union soldiers.[14]

If early regimentals were filled with umbrage concerning prison life, the later volumes overflowed. Veterans' written recollections seldom closed without at least one moving prisoner-of-war story. With few exceptions, veterans' animosities in the 1880s, 1890s, and the early twentieth century mirrored that of the years immediately after the war. These histories are strikingly similar to the earliest commemorative efforts regardless of the changing nature of commemorative/celebratory efforts undertaken by the nonveteran population. Commemorative efforts at the World's Columbian exposition in Chicago in 1893, for example, left no room for resonating wartime bitterness. But such efforts were meant to heighten the strength of the nation and bolster national progress. Veterans, who in many cases stood behind the notion of national prowess and progress in the late nineteenth century, nevertheless refused to part from their memories of the late conflict. "War has written on its ghastly pages no blot so dishonoring to humanity than that traced by rebel hands in their treatment of Union prisoners," wrote Ezra D. Simons, chaplain of the 125th New York Infantry Regiment. "No fair words can mitigate the cruelty of withholding bread from a hungry enemy."[15] For those who would see the virtue in fighting for a cause, however misguided, authors of regimental histories offered a brisk response. Many would censure former Rebels' "high-toned sense of honor" that was taking hold in the South as Confederate veterans' organizations developed their own commemorative culture late in the nineteenth century.[16]

Union veterans who recognized that Confederates had trouble supplying their own men in the ranks and thus were incapable of attending to all the needs of prisoners of war failed to absolve their former captors of any wrongdoing. It made little difference to survivors of prison camps and their comrades that Rebels had had troubles of their own. Most would find no palliating circumstances under any condition. Adding additional insult to injury, Union veterans suspected a miscount concerning Union deaths at the hands of Rebels. Correspondence with the editors of the *National Tribune* suggests their suspicions were correct. In June 1896, the *Tribune* replied to one of many inquiries. "The facts warrant the belief that the actual number of deaths of Union troops in the prison pens of the South very greatly exceeds the number shown by the records."[17]

By the 1880s, Union veterans had developed a commemorative script that nearly always included the obligatory prison story. Regimental histories authored by such individuals as Illinois veteran Charles Clark, Rhode Islander George Lewis, New Yorker James Harvey McKee, as well as the reminiscences compiled by Mary Genevie Green Brainard, reflect a consensus and confirm the degree to which veterans held on to distressing memories of the war in their commemorative literature. These stories—forming part of a powerful "atrocities narrative"—were particular to neither place nor time and appeared throughout the commemorative literature. Incensed veterans used language denoting the "horrors of the brutal prison," the "long sufferings," and the "unspeakable hardships" to describe places like Andersonville and Libby prisons. Most of these regimentals failed to reach a national audience but rather spoke to the localism of much of the commemorative activity. However, viewed together, the resounding similarities among the many regimental histories suggest an extensive acknowledgment of deficient Confederate morals. Recollections of Andersonville, for example, as a "hell-hole … a God-forsaken place not fit for cattle" functioned as necessary, permanent, and powerful components in the overall Union commemorative culture.[18]

While regimental histories spoke to citizens on a state or community level, veterans' organization leadership reached out to a national audience. Some of the most influential Union veterans took up the cause of remembering the sordid details of the war on a broad commemorative stage. In 1867, founding GAR commander John A. Logan admonished his countrymen on the dangers of forgetfulness in an address to Congress. Logan was among the most prominent Union veterans in the nation. During the war, he showed his skill as a commander, rising through the ranks to command the XV Corps in the Carolina campaigns of 1865. His postwar civilian life was equally distinguished. Serving as a member of the House of Representatives and then senator from Illinois, he would eventually run for vice president in James G. Blaine's 1884 presidential bid. As early as 1867, Logan was perfectly willing, even eager, to welcome southerners back into the national fold—provided that the nation recognize the mistreatment of Union soldiers at the hands of former Rebels. His deep-seated apprehension concerning the likelihood of national amnesia came through in a systematic attack on forgetfulness that included tributes to those who had suffered in Andersonville and elsewhere. "I could give my friend (addressing a Mr. Robinson—a political opponent) illustrations of individual suffering that would make his hair stand on his head, the blood freeze in his veins, and curse spring involuntarily to his lips."[19]

None of Logan's reconciliationist leanings tempered his commitment to remembering the grisly details of suffering in Confederate prisons. Logan's General Order No. 11 officially proclaimed May 30, 1868, Memorial Day, and these first observations at Arlington National Cemetery included honoring of Union *and* Confederate dead. But despite such heartfelt reconciliatory gestures, the GAR commander-in-chief was remarkably consistent over time when it came to noting Rebel shortcomings. According to Logan, Confederates, morally depraved because of their attachment to the institution of slavery, were naturally inclined to promoting suffering among their prisoners of war. "It is the savage spirit of this Institution," he wrote in 1886, "which starves the Union prisoners at Richmond ... and which fills up the catalogue of wrong and outrage which mark the conduct of the Rebels during all this war."[20]

John G. B. Adams followed in Logan's commemorative footsteps. An admired hero in his home state of Massachusetts, Adams had had an unblemished war career. He proved his gallantry by saving the regimental colors and rallying his comrades at Fredericksburg, an act for which he won the Medal of Honor. Promoted to captain, Adams commanded a company at Gettysburg, was severely wounded, and recovered in time to see action in the battles at the Wilderness, Spotsylvania, and Cold Harbor, where he was captured. Adams served the rest of the war imprisoned at Libby in Richmond, Virginia, then at Columbia, South Carolina, and finally at Morris Island. In civilian life, he served in numerous civil service positions including postmaster and sergeant-at-arms in the Massachusetts State Legislature. Always active in veteran activities, Adams also served as a department commander in the GAR and eventually as the organization's commander-in-chief.

Adams's commemorative activity focused heavily on prison memories. In addition to his work with the GAR, he also served as president of the Association of Survivors of Rebel Prisons, an organization that boasted many prominent members. Similar to other organizations such as Ex-Prisoners of War Association, the Survivors of Rebel Prisons' members wrote prolifically of their prison experiences, recalling the malevolent policies of the Confederate government. They did so throughout the period generally defined as having a unified commemorative spirit. Members' works published late in the nineteenth century, including Adams's regimental history published in 1899, described barbarous and inhumane treatment of Union soldiers by Rebel authorities.[21]

Those who shared the sentiments of organizational leadership found several outlets to perpetuate prison memories. By the end of the nineteenth century, veterans' reunions were extremely popular. Prison images frequently framed the topics of discussion at such gatherings, and reports of gruesome details stood out among the reminiscences. Despite the move away from issues of contention in the national commemorative ethos during this period, veterans' commemorations remained consistent on this theme. It was quite typical for veterans to describe prison experiences with vivid accuracy, particularly when they were among other veterans who would understand the suffering. Comrade Jones of Minnesota, entirely out of step with the late nineteenth-century national commemorative spirit of national progress and unity, noted to his fellow veterans in 1891 that "some of you can well remember the time when we could see men with their arms and feet rotting from their bodies, bones protruding through the skin for want of attention in the terrible prison."[22] Even those who applauded the reconciliatory efforts of Union men reminded Americans of the suffering endured at the hands of Confederates. "I am proud that our government showed such magnanimity. I am proud of it as an American citizen," professed GAR comrade Halstead of Minnesota in 1892, "but it is there, a part of history, this terrible, terrible, terrible record of the scenes at Andersonville, at Millan, at Belle Isle and Libby. They are there in our history and will remain there permanently, and I blush for it in sorrow."[23]

Themes of barbarity, deprivation, and suffering provided veterans with materials to keep bitter memories alive for other veterans. Articles running in the *National Tribune* and similar publications catering to Union veterans continually reminded readers of Confederate cruelty. Not only ruthless commanders, but guards and others associated with prisons faced the wrath of angry Yankees. One such article, authored by an unnamed Union cavalryman, illustrates perfectly the thoughts shared by thousands of survivors. Describing his captor as a "lying son of Belial," he painted a vivid picture of the hardships suffered by himself and his fellow prisoners at several prisons. The cavalryman attacked the punished and unpunished perpetrators of evil and used such evocative imagery as the bloodhound chase, summary executions, torture, and intentional starvation.[24]

Gatherings at meeting halls and other reunions usually had at least one source to turn to for a graphic look at life in Confederate prisons. In 1896, Union veteran and GAR comrade Edward P. Kimball of Massachusetts compiled a pictorial history of his post's meeting place, Brimley Hall. Among the trivial and mundane facts, figures, and anecdotes, he placed a vividly brutal portrayal of prison life. Along with descriptions of maggots, exposed wounds, filth, gangrene, and the lack of medical attention, Kimball described the captors as "haughty and remorseless" and the scene as a "Barbarous atrocity of those who sought to destroy the Union."[25]

The prison leitmotif accelerated as the nineteenth century drew to a close. In the 1880s, MOLLUS Commanderies began publishing a series of "War Papers" and other talks. These papers were made available to veterans, libraries, and other public repositories. Organized by state, the papers offered a comprehensive collection of war memories complied into easily accessible volumes. By the early twentieth century, MOLLUS War Papers were widely dispersed throughout the nation. Forthright in this prevalent commemorative literature and appearing in nearly every volume, veterans referred to places such as Libby as the "death camp of the dark loathsome prison" and the soldiers at Andersonville as being "herded and packed together like so many swine."[26]

Language such as this was not uncommon among MOLLUS companions. By the 1890s, the prison leitmotif was firmly entrenched in veterans' commemorative literature and was thus available to a wide veteran audience. MOLLUS Commanderies, including those of Illinois, Minnesota, and Ohio, all published accounts of prison life, including entire chapters dedicated to stories of soldiers "suffering from sickness, hunger, heat, and filth" in various "dismal prisons" such as Andersonville and Libby. The mere discussion of "vengeful prisons," as one survivor branded them, struck an echoing sour note with most Union veterans. Prison memories even moved one veteran to suggest, "The dread of a prison gives one wings, almost." But all of this amounted to more than mere bickering or the recitation of a list of grievances. The prison commemorative theme offered proof of moral depravity, further illuminating the characteristics of a southern populace that could attempt to sunder the nation.[27]

While images of the suffering of Union soldiers in places such as Andersonville distressed northern veterans, former Confederate soldiers absolved themselves of any culpability. They blamed General Grant and Secretary of War Edwin M. Stanton's policies of refusing to engage in customary prisoner exchange. Confederates reasoned that because United States officials placed a moratorium on prisoner exchange in 1864, the want for scarce supplies in the South led directly to the unintended hardships of Union prisoners. In reality, Grant had halted prisoner exchange until the Confederates agreed to honor the terms of paroled Confederate prisoners and end the draconian policies levied against captured African American soldiers. Despite these details, often missing from Confederate diatribes against Grant and Stanton, former Rebels placed the blame of Andersonville, Libby, and elsewhere squarely on Union shoulders. One Confederate veteran argued succinctly that the "suspension of exchange" did more to harm Union prisoners of war than did any Confederate policies.[28]

Former Rebels also voiced grievances against the treatment of Confederate prisoners of war. Mistreatment in Union prisons meant little more than malicious cruelty. Confederate veterans reasoned that the United States, unlike the Confederacy, had more than enough to care for prisoners of war. Why would they inflict such unnecessary punishment? Such protests represent the Confederate side of two distinct commemorative cultures clashing during a period characterized by veteran organizations' tacit, if not explicit, reconciliatory underpinnings. While the Confederate government, many argued, had no choice but to deprive prisoners of the basic necessities due to shortages, they considered Union policy wantonly cruel and immoral. During the war's final months, thousands of captured Confederates from the Petersburg front found themselves in Union prison "bull pens" near City Point and at Point Lookout. Veterans such as Charles T. Loehr, of the 1st Virginia Infantry Regiment, described prisoners' harsh treatment. "The water was all brackish, the food was wholly insufficient. There was little or no medicine for the sick. Over 6,800 men died at this prison." Despite the reconciliatory wishes of Union high command, this former Confederate noted, "it was not until the middle of June [1865] that the United States government saw fit to release us. A more miserable looking set of men could hardly be produced on an exhibition."[29]

Numerous pieces in publications geared specifically to commemorate the Confederate war experience attest to a legacy of animosity toward Yankee captors. Episodes of brutality and humiliation, for example, colored

several reports of prison life and cast a dark shadow over the flowery reconciliationist writings appearing elsewhere.[30] The editor of *Campfires of the
Confederacy*, an 1898 compilation of anecdotes, songs, and poems written
by Confederate veterans, dismissed themes of peace, good will, and nationalism when he invited veterans such as L.T. Dickerson to recount their
experiences as prisoners of war. Any all-inclusive celebratory sentiment,
typical during a nationalist period when much of the country was rallying
against a foreign foe, found no room in this volume. Dickerson instead recalled brutalities and especially noted that "negro troops" working as guards
at Point Lookout, Maryland, "heaped indignities upon the prisoners that
were almost unbearable" and "enough to make a Southerner's blood boil."[31]

Members of one veterans' group in particular perpetuated the animosity
shared by many former prisoners. The Society of the Immortal 600, a group
of former Confederate officers who had been intentionally placed under
fire while held as prisoners of war, gained a great deal of attention from
the southern populace.[32] Veterans of the 600 had served time in various
northern prison camps including Sandusky, Ohio; Fort Delaware on Pea
Patch Island in the Delaware River; and ultimately Morris Island, South
Carolina—where they found themselves used as human shields in a stock-
ade placed before the Union batteries conducting the siege of Charleston.
These practices along with the allegedly harsh treatment carried out by
Union Colonel Edward N. Hallowell and his command of African American
guards led many to direct anger northward—a practice that never subsided.
Veterans glossed over one important point. The 600 found themselves in
harm's way as a retaliatory measure undertaken when Confederates moved
Union prisoners from Andersonville to Charleston—a city frequently bom-
barded by Union gunboats and nearby batteries. In essence, Confederates
were guilty of the same crimes but emphasized only Yankee atrocities.

At late as 1910, surviving members of the 600 voiced their animosity in
ways suggesting little had changed since 1865. Thomas Coleman Chandler,
a former officer who had left the Virginia Military Institute in 1861 to enlist
with the Tyranny Unmasked Artillery, recalled his hardships after an early
twentieth-century trip to Morris Island. This aging veteran, who had been
wounded several times and captured at Spotsylvania, addressed his fellow former prisoners with imagery as vivid as it was filled with animosity.
Chandler focused on a number of troubling aspects. "Suffering men" typical

of most prison reminiscences formed the foundation of an argument attacking the Union commander and especially the "Negro guards" at Morris Island. These particular points most certainly would have stirred emotions among Confederate veterans reminded of the "brutal laugh of Hallowell and his niggers as they gloated over your suffering."[33]

The frequency with which Confederate veterans published reminiscences of their prison experiences illustrates yet another way the 600 and other former prisoners remained in public view. Their works added to the popularity of survivors' groups. Recognition of the official Immortal 600 veterans' organization gained steam in the early twentieth century when John Ogden Murray, a captain with the 11th Virginia Cavalry and member of the society, began compiling information on the group with the purpose of publishing the first book-length paean to the 600. Funds generated by such a publication would be set aside to finance a monument to the group on Morris Island. His bitter tale illustrated for all American readers the degree to which Confederate officers needlessly suffered at the hands of their Union captors. In a powerful work intended to "give the world a true history of the wanton cruelty inflicted upon helpless prisoners of war, without the least shadow of excuse," Murray vividly recounted how his Union captors "hated everything southern." Murray presented incidences of the officers' transfer to Morris Island and their subsequent incarceration with a decidedly bitter tone.[34]

While proceeds fell short of the funds necessary to construct a monument, Murray's book nevertheless created a stir in the South and saw several printings. The popularity of this publication illustrated white southerners' desire to commemorate the 600 and revealed the influence of the atrocities narrative in the former Confederate states. Seizing the commemorative reins, the Virginia state legislature recognized appeals to honor the 600 and appropriated necessary funds for the monument in 1910. Making sure to point out that any such monument would pay tribute to those "inhumanely treated by the United States Government," Virginia legislators kept lingering hostilities in the forefront.[35] So too did a number of authors who had served in the Confederate ranks. Arguing that Edwin M. Stanton and others in the federal government simply acted out of vindictiveness, veterans Yates Snowden of South Carolina and McHenry Howard of Maryland agreed that Union policy regarding the 600 constituted the "[worst] sort of retaliation.

For alleged ill treatment of Union prisoners [the 600] were put, and for a long time kept, on slow starvation rations." Noting that "their story has been told and retold at Confederate reunions," neither man suggested that any of the surviving 600 or their former Confederate supporters had moved beyond these experiences. Demonstrating persistent efforts to perpetuate such memories, *Confederate Veteran* published as late as 1922 soldiers' reminiscences of "the weeks of hardship, wretched food, sickness and death . . . all aggravated by the humiliation of being guarded by a negro regiment."[36]

The moving stories of 600 survivors echoed the sentiments concerning other Union prisons voiced at veterans' gatherings, including those of the AANVA and the UCV. Members frequently lambasted the United States government for their treatment of Confederate prisoners of war at notorious places such as Illinois's Alton prison and New York's infamous Elmira prison. Offering an example typical of those made by prison survivors throughout the postwar decades, one former Confederate remarked in 1912 that his stay in Elmira was "nearer Hades than I thought any place could be made by human cruelty."[37] Like GAR comrades, Confederate veterans recorded and published the speeches, toasts, debates, and other minutes from their regional and national meetings. Holding their first national meeting in 1890, UCV members incorporated precisely the same language as their northern counterparts when it came to prison experiences. Stories of smallpox, starvation, and other afflictions peppered veterans' speeches voiced at ordinary meetings and large reunions alike.[38]

Prisons were not the only things that rankled former Confederate soldiers. Veterans frequently recalled episodes of the destructions of private property and treatment of civilians by Union troops. Memories of the shelling and occupation of Fredericksburg in December 1862 especially riled those who saw Yankees as ruthless invaders. Again the commemorative literature questioned the moral attributes of an invading force—those who waged war beyond conventional means. Reminiscences concerning the battle of Fredericksburg illustrate two important themes. First, the familiar idea that Confederates outsoldiered a better-equipped and much larger army ran through most veterans' speeches and writings. Veterans had a solid base of evidence from which to make such claims. Images of regiment after regiment of Union soldiers falling before Confederate defenders appeared often in publications such as *Confederate Veteran* and the *Southern Historical Society Papers,* as well as at monument dedications on the battlefield.[39] But another theme, intensely important to veterans, involved Yankee malevolence. Southern authors suggested that the Union army, commanding general Ambrose Burnside in particular, deliberately launched an attack on noncombatants despite knowledge of their presence in the historic town. Pointing out that many civilians were compelled to remain in Fredericksburg, one author described the scene of the bombardment as a "stormy and distressing time" in which civilians lost their lives. But beyond illustrating the danger involved for those who remained, this Confederate lashed out at Federal soldiers who ransacked the houses of those who did flee Burnside's guns. "The thieving soldiery of the Federal army" populated an otherwise heartening (for his intended audience) story about Confederate perseverance.[40]

The issue most pressing among the many witnesses at Fredericksburg concerned the differences between civilized and uncivilized warfare. Claiming that Burnside "assuredly knew of the wide destruction which would follow his order" to bombard the town, former Confederates such as James Dinkins averred that "the necessities did not warrant the destruction of that city, and we regard it as a savage act.... The bombardment was kept up for over an hour, and no tongue or pen can describe that dreadful scene." Whether or not Dinkins felt anyone capable of describing the wrath of the Union army, many tried. In fact, veterans carried with them scenes of destruction so vivid in their memories that they were compelled to tell and retell their stories. Often as a response to accusations that Confederates practiced unconventional warfare, former Rebels retaliated by enumerating the crimes against southern citizenry. Veterans reminded southerners of the burning of Darien and Rome, Georgia, the towns of Williamsburg and Hamilton, North Carolina, and especially the burning of Columbia, South Carolina. "The memory of those scenes," Dinkins argued, "will be hard to efface."[41]

But while some veterans might have attempted, however unsuccessfully, to move past the destruction of so many Confederate towns, few would even try to put Sherman's Georgia campaign behind them.[42] Memories of the destruction left in the wake of General William T. Sherman's 1864 campaign through Georgia and the Carolinas perhaps fueled more bitterness during the postwar years than any other single incident. Those who recalled how Sherman laid waste to a wide swath of the Confederacy voiced their animosities frequently, and more important, in commemorative forums. In 1882, one Confederate veteran responded to an article in the *Cincinnati Commercial* in which a former Union soldier argued that the "male natives of the South have ceased to bear animosity to the grim old warrior." Calling this assertion into question, this bitter Rebel recalled that "Sherman went beyond his legitimate duties to tyrannize over helpless women and children; he went out of his way to exercise heartless cruelty." In language reserved for the most despised, the Rebel concluded that Sherman lacked "the decency of a well-bred dog."[43]

Such inflammatory language typified Confederate reminiscences of the burning of Atlanta and Sherman's subsequent march. Harsh criticisms of Sherman (and Sheridan's handiwork in the Shenandoah Valley) underscore the fact that many Confederates infused unpleasant memories into their commemorative literature. Perhaps to add validity to the recollections of those removed from the events by time, publishing houses reprinted wartime diaries and letters using similar language. Years after the event, these pieces served as reminders of the hardships overcome by the Confederate population in 1864 and of the sentiment expressed by those soldiers who faced the northern onslaught. Words such as "bloodthirsty" described a commander who "totally disregard[ed] all the laws and usages of civilized warfare.... Attila, Geiseric and Alaric were not more cruel to the conquered Romans, than the brutal Sherman has been to the defenseless, utterly helpless old men, women and children of pillaged and devastated Georgia." Postwar animosities resonated as loudly as they did during the war. "Amid agonies and sorrows indescribable," veterans recalled how citizens, especially the elderly, women, and children, suffered "terrors and anxieties" as they faced the Yankee invaders.[44]

Much like prison memories, recollections of Sherman's march took hold as a central theme in Confederate commemorative literature. Whether noting atrocities, war crimes, or any other wicked deeds, former Confederates secured Sherman's place among the principal villains in the overall war story. In fact, memories of General Sherman often proved to have more animus than those of Lincoln or even Grant, both of whom could be respected for their magnanimity. Sherman was the Confederate trump card when it came to proving beyond a doubt (to other white southerners) that Confederates had faced a ruthless invasion undertaken by individuals lacking in any moral decency. If the Yankees had stories of Andersonville, former Confederates had the war levied against civilians waged by the leader of the fiercest army of mercenaries that the North could muster. In part because Sherman himself took credit for "making Georgia howl," he proved an easy target and served as the very best case to illustrate the moral shortcomings of the Yankee invaders. Moreover, former Rebels attacked the general for falsifying history. When Sherman claimed in 1881 that the "rebels were notoriously more cruel than our men," he elicited a sharp response from the editors of the *Southern Historical Society Papers*. They reminded readers of the chimneys of burnt houses serving as "sentinels left to guard the scenes of [Sherman's] vandalism" and concluded that Sherman himself confessed to the widespread destruction and he "should not care a straw" for further accusations.[45]

Former Confederates seethed at Sherman's boasts and "historical fabrications," and their words informed a host of authors in the late nineteenth and early twentieth centuries. Many mirrored veterans' words and helped further irritate the festering wounds left in the wake of Sherman's march. By the turn of the century, histories favoring the Confederacy more or less reflected the commemorative recollections of former Confederate soldiers. The attack on civilians especially moved the authors of various historical works, and they frequently pointed out that Sherman's conduct was condemned by an extensive group of people, including some in the North. "All the balderdash which has been written and spoken about this vaunted 'march to the sea,'" suggested one author, "can never, in the clear light of history, cover up or excuse the lack of dash and the want of military skill betrayed by General Sherman." Other notable individuals agreed. In 1896, celebrated author, folklorist, and journalist Joel Chandler Harris—a Georgian best known for his collection of Uncle Remus stories—pejoratively deemed Sherman's activities as nothing more than utter "chaos and confusion."[46]

Reducing northern testaments to union to "cheek, gall, impudence, brass and falsehoods in a few words," Colonel R. J. Harding, president of Hood's Texas Brigade Association, admonished southerners who seemed too eager to join hands with their former enemies. "Chronic reconcilers who are over-hasty to forgive their enemies, are quick to forget them. But to forget, then, indeed are our minds gone." Bearing distinct similarities with testaments issued during and immediately after the war, this early twentieth-century speech shows how memories of war atrocities remained paramount. "Your mothers, wives and sisters and children suffering for life's necessities, and insulted by foreign hirelings and Yankees; want and poverty everywhere. Your hope of salvation almost ground out of you under the iron heel of the military boot." While the atrocities narrative rarely appeared in the broader national commemorative ethos, it retained a strong sectional presence. It fact, this strand of commemoration proved to be the most powerful of veterans' memories to inform the general public's understanding of the war for decades to come, at least on a sectional level.[47]

Harding went on at length regarding Yankee soldiers' "crimes" against the southern people. Specifically, he singled out the shelling of Fredericksburg and the devastation of Georgia and the Shenandoah Valley. Ultimately, however, Abraham Lincoln figured as the key criminal. "Lincoln ordered Burnside to 'shell the town [of Fredericksburg]. Burnside telegraphed the town was full of women and children and non-combatants. His order was to shell the town, and the old city was knocked into brick dust and laid in ashes." Turning to the Valley campaign of 1864, he continued, "When Sheridan was ordered to devastate the valley of Virginia so that a crow could not fly over it without carrying his rations, Lincoln thanked him for doing so well." Closing by redirecting his focus beyond Virginia, Harding added, "When [Sherman] made that march from Vicksburg to Meridian he boasted that he had destroyed 2,000 homes. When he made the march from Atlanta to Savannah, Ga., he boasted again that he had destroyed $98,000,000 worth of property and appropriated $2,000,000. None of this was necessity, but meanness begot of hell-born hate. Lincoln telegraphed the thanks of a nation."[48]

Although former Confederates possessed a wealth of evidence from which to recount stories of looting, destruction, and the general abuse of civilians, they did not hold a monopoly on stories of uncivilized warfare. Because the war unfolded almost entirely on southern soil, nearly all combat-related incidences took place in the Confederacy. However, Union veterans capitalized on the few stories of Confederate atrocities carried out on northern civilians and turned the tables on the embittered former Rebels. The burning of Chambersburg, Pennsylvania, on July 30, 1864, reminded loyal citizens of the United States that Confederate civilians were perhaps not the only victims of war they so often claimed to be. When citizens of

Chambersburg could not, or would not, pay a hefty ransom demanded by Confederate general Jubal A. Early, the cantankerous Rebel ordered the town fired. Union veterans described the violent scene. Confederates kicked in doors, stole private property, and threatened the townspeople with weapons. Many claimed that Rebels executed their orders with vicious glee, destroying the town while in a drunken state of rage. In June 1905, one GAR veteran described the aftermath of the Rebel invasion according to his commander-in-chief. Utilizing new technology, Comrade H. L. Burnell recorded the speech "phonographically" describing the horrors of the "terrible scene" including unburied dead and the sick lying unattended on the sidewalk. It was a drama narrated publically and recorded for posterity that few who heard would ever forget. Some considered Rebel atrocities the spark that ignited the final push against Confederate forces in the Valley. "The boys in blue," suggested one Union veteran in 1881, "frenzied by the sight of homeless, weeping women and children, again charged upon the foe, never allowing them to stop for a moment."[49]

Old Jube essentially absolved himself of any wrongdoing by defending the burning as a retaliatory measure. Early had been incensed by the mistreatment of Confederate civilians—especially women—in the Shenandoah Valley and was particularly angered when accounts of the misdeeds were "heralded forth in some of the Northern papers in terms of exaltation, and gloated over by their readers."[50] This bold lack of remorse did little to appease Union veterans. In the hands of former Federal soldiers, the Chambersburg story grew in intensity by the twentieth century. While nowhere near as angering as the Andersonville stories, Chambersburg nevertheless numbered among the many "rebel atrocities," "increasing acts of barbarity," and "deliberate acts of vandalism" perpetrated by the Union veterans' former foe. Veterans acknowledged that during the war the incident caused a "considerable civilian panic" and "attracted the anxious attention of the whole country." Most remained aggravated by the "destruction ... caused by a public enemy" and recalled the acts of insolence, theft, and violence alongside the Union battle cry: "Remember Chambersburg!"[51]

The notion of Rebel atrocities extended to the traditional battlefield as well, especially when recalling the acts committed against soldiers of the United States Colored Troops (USCT). While white Union veterans certainly conformed to the racist proclivities of the era, they nevertheless looked negatively on clear acts of murder committed against comrades wearing the Federal uniform—regardless of their race. Memories of the incident at Fort Pillow in April 1864 where Confederates under the command of Nathan Bedford Forrest executed surrendering USCT soldiers, exemplifies GAR veterans' attitudes toward Rebel cruelty on the battlefield. In 1869, at a Memorial Day ceremony in Chicago, GAR comrade Collyer noted, "For Fort Pillow, and all other murder and torture, I feel an unutterable loathing. Such things can only be done by the very spawn and refuse of the pit."[52] By the early twentieth century things had not changed. Veterans continued to recall the atrocities at Fort Pillow—and in fact viewed them in conjunction with other Rebel crimes. At a 1903 GAR national encampment in Michigan, Vice Department Commander Dan J. Wilson spoke of a gamut of evil Rebel deeds, suggesting the "pages of history were destined to chronicle the dark pages of Ft. Pillow, Libby, Andersonville, Belle Isle, and Columbia."[53]

Former Confederates accused northerners of harboring ill will toward southern citizens. At a monument dedication in Alexandria, Virginia, in 1889, Fitzhugh Lee argued that northern outsiders hampered the noble reconciliatory efforts of former Confederates. "Let me say here that it remains for the people of the North to make this a homogeneous and harmonious nation. Let us hope that in the near future impertinent intermeddling of one section with the domestic affairs of the other will cease."[54] Others perceived that the rest of the country scorned former Confederates. Northerners, many white southerners would suggest, extended a peaceful hand provided former Confederates admitted guilt for attempting to destroy the nation. William C. P. Breckinridge, speaking before a gathering of veterans of the Army of Northern Virginia in 1892, took a stance familiar to those in the South who claimed they had always supported the Union created by the founders. "I sometimes hear that the South in these days is to express some sort of added patriotism—a greater amount of patriotism than any other part of the country; that we are under some sort of a cloud which requires us to give some additional bond of security for good behavior. I claim for the South that she has always been equal in her duty." Underscoring a problem that necessarily impeded the strengthening of sectional bonds, he saw no way out of this troubling situation in the immediate future. Turning to future generations, Breckinridge argued: "The problem how diverse speaking people, with different traditions and separate religions, can by representative government so unite themselves that their local interests, being protected by themselves, will not find hostility but friendship in the powers of the Federal government, remains to be solved by our children hereafter. Let us not add to the labors of our children by handicapping them with improper reverence for us by teaching them that the war settled that question in any of its aspects."[55]

Former Rebels thus concentrated their efforts on preserving their memories specifically for the indoctrination of white southern youth in ways that revealed so-called northern manipulation of the truth. In 1913, Confederate veteran W. W. Ballew summarized the palpable anxiety felt among many in the South when it came to school-age children. "The sons, and daughters of the South should, as bravely imitate the examples of their ancestors." Ballew objected to inciting sectional battles, claiming, "We do not want to arouse the prejudice of the South against the North." However, his stern words seemed to advocate exactly that. Ballew directed all of his anger northward and left few people there blameless in his verbal assaults. "We want to repudiate the infamous slanders that have been heaped upon the South for more than 60 years, by Northern Writers, politicians, Clergy, poets, newspapers, and alleged historians." Roughly a year later, an unnamed Confederate veteran recorded in his organization's minute book the happenings of a reunion of the Surry Light Artillery. Somewhat less vituperative but just as adamant, this man made a point to mention the large gathering of young people associated with the veterans' group. It must have been a relief that so many southern youth had taken an interest in the old veterans. The recording officer resounded with hopefulness and confidence, stating, "The assemblage was composed in by the largest part, of young people—the sons and daughters of the Confederacy, upon whom must now soon fall the sacred task of continuing the patriotic sentiments and feelings that inspire these meetings, and which we trust, will ever fill the bosoms of all true Virginians."[56]

Such writings mirrored the work of many of the more incensed Confederate veterans. George L. Christian, for example, often referred to the preservation of Confederate history for the sake of posterity in his speeches and writings. In 1898 he warned a group of Virginian veterans that their children were clearly in danger of being misled by vindictive Yankee liars. "It must command the attention of Confederate soldiers and their descendants for all time to come," he pronounced. "I fear that some of our children, misled by the false teachings of certain histories used in some of our schools, may have some misgivings on this all-important subject." Christian then aimed a few irate jabs at his former foes, revealing in 1898, a year of national exuberance, that sectional tension remained alive and well. "The shrewd, calculating and wealthy Northerners realized the importance of trying to impress the rising generation with the justice of their cause . . . 'all the blame' is laid on the South." With a surprising twist, Christian concluded his tirade of taunts and accusations with a reconciliatory note. While it is unclear exactly how the audience interpreted these seemingly conflicting messages, Christian's words suggest a man who supported reconciliation, so long as he could continue disparaging Yankees. "And I want to say, in conclusion, that to think and feel, as we think and feel about the Confederate cause, does not mean that we are disloyal citizens of our now united and common country. But on the contrary, it is just in proportion as we are true and loyal to the cause of the South, that we will be true and faithful citizens of our country to-day." Finally, addressing the children of the audience directly, Christian added one last point showing exactly how former Confederates viewed their responsibilities in regard to the education of their children. "Yes, my young friends, this cause, which is thus, as I think, *established to be right,* is the one for which your father fought, and your mothers worked and wept, and prayed. They *thought* they were right then, they *know* they were right *now.*"[57]

Union veterans hardly stood by while former Confederates wrote, rewrote, and created their own history. Although a few stories painting Rebel soldiers in an honorable light made their way north, most Union soldiers balked at any indication that Confederate history was taking hold across the nation. Union men were painfully aware of the possibility of national amnesia when it came to the American citizenry's remembering the sacrifices endured to save the country. Union veterans vented their anger accordingly. The *National Tribune,* for instance, published articles coinciding with a broad GAR campaign to eradicate Confederate-leaning sectional histories from southern schools. Arguing that such volumes were treasonable, GAR comrades waged a bitter war against Alexander H. Stephens's *War between the States* and other books available to southern schoolchildren.[58]

A division of the GAR, styled "Patriotic Instruction," functioned to relieve veterans' anxieties that schoolchildren might forget the trials endured by northern soldiers and the issues central to the conflict. Schoolchildren's essays submitted in 1910 to GAR chief patriotic instructor Hosea W. Rood, a veteran of the 12th Wisconsin Infantry Regiment and member of the prominent Lucius Fairchild post in Madison, illustrate exactly how northern school children understood the Civil War. Above all else, union served as the principal ideal that motivated northern soldiers. One fifteen-year-old summed up his comprehension of the war in short remarks. "Some people may say 'What did these boys in blue and gray fight for?' Why! to preserve or dissolve the Union, according to which side they were on." He added that northern soldiers also fought with emancipation in mind. 'What did they want to dissolve or preserve the Union for, and was this all they were fighting for?' No! It was shall there be slavery or not in the United States. After many hard years of struggle the boys in blue won and slavery was abolished."[59]

Schoolchildren recognized slavery's significance. One twelve-year-old summed up his understanding of the war in two concise sentences: "About this time there were negro slaves in the south owned by southern planters. Abraham Lincoln set them free by the War." Similarly, a ten-year-old observed, "The people in the cotton growing states believed that by this election that the North were going to pass laws to deprive them of their slaves so six of the southern states withdrew from the Union." In the respect of teaching children the lessons of a war for union *and* emancipation, Union veterans succeeded. Wrote fifteen-year-old Stephen Wise, "Children should be taught how necessary it is that they should begin to know why we observe Memorial Day."[60]

Despite Rood's successes, the prospect of forgetfulness remained ominous to many Union veterans—especially when children were concerned. "The Union men of this nation," suggested MOLLUS companion Lymon G. Wilcox, "are determined to transmit the National Union and Constitution unimpaired to their children, or they will transmit to their children's children, and to posterity, an eternal war." But in so doing, veterans found it impossible to handle history with kid gloves. Rebellion and all its trappings proved the principal villain in the story of the war for Union, and in transmitting the National Union, veterans felt no qualms about shedding light on Confederate shortcomings. Especially as time passed, Union veterans seemed more determined to perpetuate the memories of the war for future generations, even calling on the young to take up the banner of preservation. James Addams Beaver, a former brigadier who had lost a leg at Ream's Station in 1864, insisted that the youth preserve for "this generation and for generations to come the deeds of the Companions" before they "pay the great debt to which they owe to nature."[61]

"Such self-sacrifice should never be forgotten."

Veterans from both armies feared that time could wash away the memories that told the noble story of loyalty, patriotism, and perseverance in the most adverse conditions. Just before the dawn of the twentieth century, Virginian veteran John Lamb voiced his fears in an address given to members of R. E. Lee Camp, Sons of Confederate Veterans, on the popular topic of the Battle of Fredericksburg. Lamb was in every way typical of prominent veterans. He enlisted in the Confederate army as a young man, served with honor for three years, and successfully pursued business and political activities in civilian life. He lived out his days loyal to the Confederate cause and passed in 1924 having gained the respect of former soldiers throughout the South. But on this day in 1899, he could easily have been speaking for all Civil War veterans, North and South: "Such self sacrifice should never be forgotten; such love of country should live forevermore.... The saddest thought in the life of every soldier, martyr, or patriot is the fear that some day he shall be forgotten; that some day those that follow after him shall forget his name, and remember not his deeds."[62] Like Lamb, other veterans were gravely concerned about their place in history. In many cases, they resurrected wartime bitterness specifically to ensure that citizens of the United States would remember the war—in all its glory and all its horror.

But if veterans held tightly to their bitterest memories, how can modern observers come to terms with the discrepancy between veterans' embracing reconciliation on one hand and galvanizing into opposing sectional sides on the other? The answer lies in an analysis of the battle over meaning. Deeply embedded sectional perspectives sustained the war for independence for the Confederates and the preservation of union and emancipation for the Federal veterans. How these perspectives would convey in a push for reconciliation and what they would mean in terms of Civil War memory remained the work of those who had fought and who now took up the mantle of commemoration. In this respect, the war of words assumed a character founded on bickering over prisons and the dubious practices of armies and their commanders as well as accusations of moral depravity. And it was this bickering that made a lasting impression on the nation at large. American nonveteran citizens could agree in part with former soldiers when writing the great progressive American story. But unlike their veteran contemporaries who made sweeping claims against the enemy, nationalists found and chastised specific villains. They preached valuable lessons against individual errant soldiers such as Henry Wirz or William T. Sherman for moral depravity while leaving the majority of soldiers alone. Meanwhile many nonveterans displaced the divisive issues at the heart of the conflict in favor of a teleological story of national progress. But for veterans, worldviews remained at stake during the postwar years. Veterans' efforts at reconciliation most often rested not on forgetting but on assurances that certain sectional ideologies—perceived as the original intent of the founding generation—remained intact and informed the present.

CHAPTER TWO

"THE GREATEST CONSPIRACY OF ALL TIMES"

UNION VETERANS COMMEMORATE THE SUPPRESSION OF TREASON

We thank Thee for the preservation of our National life and unity,
in spite of all treasonable efforts to sunder and destroy it.

—REVEREND W. C. WAY, former chaplain, 24th Michigan Infantry

Nothing stirred the hearts of Union veterans more than their memories of southern treason. Despite undeterred commitment to national unity, they generally shared the notion that Confederate soldiers, politicians, and even civilians who supported secession and the Confederate cause had committed heinous acts against the nation—deeds that were unforgivable. Union veterans were willing to welcome former enemies back into the national fold. After all, they had fought to preserve national unity. Embracing reconciliation seemed the logical next step. But while their epic story of reunion had its heroes, it also had its villains. One need only recall veteran Union cavalryman and Illinois orator Robert Green Ingersoll's famous diatribe against the Democratic Party (read: former Confederates) in 1874, which conjured images of treason and noted that "every scar, every arm that is lacking, every limb that is gone, every scar is a souvenir of a Democrat." One might also look to the famous "Doorkeeper Controversy" of 1878—Benjamin F. Butler's nomination of aging Union veteran James Shields for doorkeeper of the United States House of Representatives—to underscore the sectional tone of the 1870s political environment and the heated arguments that ensued. These events reveal the lingering animosity in national politics that reflected veterans' memories despite a genuine reconciliatory movement. But reconciliation notwithstanding, many Union veterans who had lived through the tumult of the 1860s were unwilling to cast any shade of honor on their former foes' cause. "The Rebellion," argued Edward

McPherson before a gathering of Michigan veterans in 1889, "had not a redeeming feature. It was wholly bad. It was organized as a conspiracy, by stealth. It had its origin in passion, not reason. It was based on a pretense, both false and fraudulent in fact. It was carried on in heat, not with the deliberation which befits a great movement for vindication of rights or redress of wrongs."[1]

McPherson, a Gettysburg politician who had served the Keystone State as Republican congressman during the war, and whose farm west of town had been hotly contested ground on the first day of battle in July 1863, did not stand alone in his convictions.[2] Former prisoner of war C. L. Sumbardo, a captain with the 12th Ohio Infantry Regiment, likewise condemned his past adversaries. Sumbardo wrote extensively in the 1890s on the Union's invincibility due to "that higher courage brought into action for the intelligent defense of . . . a Republican form of government." He also made certain to note precisely who was right and who was wrong in the conflict. "The firing upon Fort Sumter," he stated, "was an act of audacity prompted by treason as damnable as can be found in the world's history—an act that never will and never should be condoned, but be held up for the everlasting execrations of a civilized world!"[3] These men underscored a prominent theme embedded deep within late nineteenth- and early twentieth-century Union commemorations. Those favoring a nationalist spirit reminiscent of the Revolutionary era, one that included white southern Americans, determinedly upheld the premise that Confederates had tried to destroy the "last best hope on Earth."[4]

From the perspectives of many Union veterans, Confederate flag-waving former Rebels, worshiping before the altar of secession and state rights and paying homage to Robert E. Lee, Stonewall Jackson, Jefferson Davis, and the rest of the Confederate pantheon, were unwelcome additions to the national image. Union men found no places in which the celebratory contributions of their treasonous former enemies could enhance the national commemorative ethos with any real validity. After all, according to Union veterans, the appearances of former Rebels, many of whom continued to don Confederate gray and parade in military style, resurrected the memories of a period where Americans had tried to destroy the United States—a cause hardly worth celebrating. The prevalent culture of reconciliation did not dissuade Union army veterans from harsh critiques of their quondam enemies. Grudging nods to benign commemoration such as parades and reunions sponsored by Union and Confederate veterans together were both infrequent and awkward. They were staged, scripted, focused almost entirely on shared courage, and hardly reflections of veterans' broader commemorative sentiments. How could northerners honor any vestiges of the Confederate cause, asked the *National Tribune,* commemorated by "organizations of the very men who did all in their power to destroy the Government, and whose only bond of Union is comradeship in that terrible disloyalty?"[5]

Union veterans could not. Commending a soldier's courage was one thing. Honoring his cause was something altogether different. Rather, they commemorated the suppression of treason. The themes these men employed were as varied as they were adamant. The notions of truth and right, their connections to the founding generation, the principles of law and order, the creation and celebration of national holidays, the rejection of Confederate imagery, and the concern that Confederate heroes and other Rebels garnered far too much praise in a nationalist context all informed a highly contentious commemorative text. Union veterans wrote and spoke often of what they would have termed southern "crimes" against national integrity. While they could acknowledge the bravery and fortitude of southern soldiers, many were unable to console themselves with this simple fact alone. As the nation's dissolution infuriated Union men in 1860 and 1861, so too did the memories of disunion. When voicing their grievances, Union men saw no contradictions in at once promoting reconciliation and damning the actions and cause of their former adversaries.

Union veterans commemorated the war against a backdrop of reconciliation. Yet they did so while peppering their commemorative forms with clear expressions of sectional allegiance and resentment toward former enemies; they infused the reconciliationist façade with sectionalism. Rather than overlooking former discord, they amplified the salient issues of the early 1860s. Their lived past was thriving in the present—indeed, it helped shape it. This point was not lost on aging veterans. But as their ranks thinned with time, the work veterans undertook to preserve their memories grew in importance. "The past is grand with the recollections of the glorious work performed by our comrades of the Army and Navy of the Union, in the cause of universal liberty and right," remarked George W. Johnson at an annual gathering of the Department of Maryland, GAR. Illustrating how veterans redoubled their efforts as more and more veterans passed, Johnson continued, "The survivors of the war are growing fewer and fewer each year; the comradely spirit—the linking of the past with the present in the minds and hearts of the Veterans—more intense."[6]

The passage of time did not seem to affect the understanding of precisely what "discord" Union veterans had in mind. Accenting southern malevolence and Confederates' perversion of national principles as set forth by the founding generation functioned as a dominant theme in Union commemorative literature. Very late in the nineteenth century, Luther Tracy Townsend, author of the 15th New Hampshire's regimental history, offered a typical example regarding the sum of southern evils. "We need not proceed in this review of what then appeared, and appears still, to be Southern treason," he claimed as he tendered his final words on the subject." "Southern theft, Southern deceit, and Southern outrage on both a small and large scale" all worked to provoke animosities among Union veterans, even though so much time had passed since the close of war. "The recollection of these things make one knit the brow," he argued, "though nearly forty years have intervened." Despite concerns that veterans were "passing down to the sunset of life," memories remained crystal clear. Townsend's work was typical among the numerous regimentals published in the last decade of the nineteenth century—written with explicit passages disregarding the passage of time when it came to wartime memories. Rather than veterans' quietly putting the past behind them, this surge of publication indicates that they grew more vociferous on the subject as they aged. While their sentiments remained constant, their voices grew even more forceful.[7]

Specifically, Union veterans insisted that they were on the right side of history. Charles L. Holstein, an Indiana veteran who after the war studied law at Harvard University and eventually became a popular poet, noted, "Glory has been the common heritage of soldiers in all wars, in all ages. Such glory we are quite willing to share with our late enemies, for they too were soldiers." But, Holstein added, "we believe that there was something more involved in the late war than the mere bubble, reputation, which was won at the cannon's mouth." He went on to illustrate a weighty point that most veterans held dear. "The war for the Union was a conflict between right and wrong—between truth and error. The Union soldier stood embattled on the side of right and truth. The Confederate soldier was arrayed on the side of wrong and error." As if speaking of veterans across the nation, Holstein concluded with words that could easily explain the roadblocks inherent in the drive to reconcile formerly warring sections, namely that "right and wrong cannot be reconciled." Holstein was perfectly willing to praise the valor of the Confederate soldier—he even advised his comrades to do the same. But like so many of his fellow veterans, he was absolutely unwilling to surrender "not one jot or tittle" of the cause for which he fought and won.[8]

Holstein's idea is not a difficult one to imagine—the victorious party naturally recognized that their side was right and the other wrong. Revealing deep-seated perceptions of the nationalist vision rooted in sectionalism, Union veterans would indicate that northern sensibilities had for some time been the only course for the nation at large. Many would retrospectively argue that the North had abandoned the earlier notion of the right of secession and that the South had so "cherished the heresy, until it became a fixed political belief, poisonous and pernicious" based on which the strife went on until, as one unnamed journalist phrased it, heresy culminated in "most unjustifiable, revolting, and most wicked attempt to overthrow our central government."[9] Those who noted Confederate bravery did so while underscoring southern crimes against national integrity. One veteran, speaking before a group of Pennsylvanians, summed up this sentiment in a succinct fashion: "[The Confederate] cause was lost—a nation's gratitude is not bestowed upon them. To their surviving comrades there remains only regret. Great as may have been their valor, their memory goes down in history linked with rebellion, no matter how much we may forgive and forget."[10]

"Victory to the Rebellion meant death to the Republic."

Rallying around the notion of "Truth and Right," Union veterans infused their commemorative literature with nationality, patriotism, and ultimately an interpretive premise suggesting inevitable victory. One veteran remarked of victory with poetic flourish, "as the battle closed a shower came up, and on the eastern sky was painted by the hand of God a beautiful rainbow; it was a remembrancer of his promises to the world; that Truth and Right should triumph among men, that our country should prevail in its struggle for Nation and Liberty."[11] While Union veterans may have realized a certain variance in terms of the war's meaning, they near unanimously underscored how one side was in error. From a Union veteran's perspective, controversy between sections would continue unless all Americans recognized the rightness of the Union cause. "However much we may indulge in disputation and controversy concerning the events of the past," suggested Illinois veteran William Henry Newlin in 1890, "fact will remain unchanged. Controversy *must* cease and truth *will* stand."[12]

From a Union perspective, the twin ideals of Truth and Right worked as a direct connection to the founding generation and their ideals of unity and a democratic republic. This connection—a significant component in the commemorative literature—championed union while highlighting their opponents' treasonous aims. Two examples serve to illustrate this commemorative trend. At the Twenty-Third Annual Encampment Department of Maryland, Grand Army of the Republic, held in February 1899, the department chaplain, J. L. Grimm, reminded an approving audience, "We battled during the sixties for the rich heritage bequeathed us by our patriot fathers." Although Grimm left that "heritage" largely unexplained, connecting the two wars in this manner suggests continuity between the Civil War and Revolutionary War—both waged to establish and perpetuate a particular vision. Nine years later, a letter from the national GAR patriotic instructor confirmed such sentiment. Considering the significance of Flag Day, GAR officials wanted to be sure comrades properly honored the "flag under whose folds more than one hundred thousand of the young men of the nation laid down their lives in its defense, and for the perpetuation of the Union as it had been handed down to them by their fathers."[13]

What veterans referred to as a "daily recurring lesson of noble patriotism and self-devotion" at once proved Union mettle on the battlefield and connected northern men to the Revolutionary generation. Soon after the war, Union veterans reminded readers that northerners from all walks of life were "never faithless to the patriotic instincts of her Revolutionary sons." Winthrop D. Sheldon, former Union lieutenant and author of the 27th Connecticut's regimental history, suggested that northerners, in this case Yale university professors and students, were simply carrying out the work of the founders and rallying behind their deep revolutionary heritage.[14] By the 1880s, the self-proclaimed inheritors of the republic of 1776 believed

Lincoln, as well as the northern soldiers who would later lead the country, were the true links to the founders. Veterans promoted this idea to ensure future generations would see the connection clearly. "In you," suggested one veteran at a Pennsylvania reunion, "[the youth] see the living links between the old war for constitutional liberty and the war of twenty years ago for the preservation of our national life." Decades later, veteran Robert M. Green had strikingly similar opinions. Editor of a compilation of records put together with a history of the 124th Pennsylvania Regiment, Green saw it necessary to underscore the moral deficit of the late rebellion by reprinting the words of a late GAR post commander, Ross C. Duffy. "There was one war in all of history as worthy as the war in which you fought. That was the war of the American Revolution." Duffy's comparison was clear. "As at the end of that war there was no one to gainsay what our fathers fought for, so at the end of that great conflict in which you took so conspicuous and so honorable a part, there was no one who was not thankful for its result." Duffy's words would have alarmed former Confederates, but this day he addressed Union men—men who clearly saw their victory as a legacy of the revolutionary generation.[15]

For Union veterans, those who had intentionally broken from the founders' designs had disrupted law and order. Among the many stated purposes of the Grand Army of the Republic, the perpetuity of union and law and order numbered among the most important. "Every reader of history knows," argued one veteran, "that the immediate cause of the war was the violation of the laws of the land." Veterans underscored this departure as the secessionists' primary violation both in war and in peace. Noting that "votes govern better than rebel tyrants," many veterans concluded that secession went against the grain of the republic. According to the bylaws of the Nebraska GAR as well as GAR departments from many other states, the primary objective for forming such patriotic associations was to promote "allegiance to the U.S. based on respect for and fidelity to its Constitution and laws." Further, recalling a war fought against traitors to the country, veterans aimed "to discountenance whatever tends to weaken loyalty and to incite, insurrection, treason, and rebellion."[16]

Abraham Gilbert Mills, a prominent New York businessman and commander of the Lafayette Post, Department of New York, GAR, uncompromisingly referred to former Confederates as "enemies of the Union and law and order." Mills, veteran of Duryea's Zouaves, better known for his tenure as president of National League of Professional Baseball Clubs, understood sectionalism to be alive and well in the postwar Union. Early in 1894 he bemoaned the activities of former Confederates and the "spirit of disregard for law and its peaceful modes of administration . . . who are constantly indicating their ignorance of the true meaning of 'liberty of speech' and assume that 'freedom' means to do just as one pleases." For Mills, union and law were synonymous and those who acted to sunder these ideals in any way were traitors. Late in the nineteenth century, Mills and the other comrades of the Lafayette Post agreed that the men of the GAR were best suited to stand between enemies of the republic and national integrity. Citing law as the "steadying balance of the American citizen," he was ready and willing to "quell the spirit of disloyalty" he saw thriving in the former Confederacy.[17]

Mills and his contemporaries firmly believed that had the Confederates proved victorious, they would have not only destroyed the country, but everything that the republic stood for on a global stage. What many recognized as an experiment in republican government had triumphed and illustrated to the world how law, order, and even progress could prevail under such a system. "Unlike other revolts against constituted authority," Mills observed, "this rebellion was not an endeavor to throw off a tyranny or to secure a larger scope of human action; but it was organized to resist the progress of beneficent ideas."[18]

Mills's colleagues repeated this sentiment in veteran halls across New York. In so doing, they sometimes revealed the ease with which veterans could promote reconciliation on one hand and assert sectional contention on the other. State GAR department commander John H. Maxwell, a devout reconciliationist, nevertheless did precisely what many other reconciliationists did and indicted former Confederates in May 1907 by pointing out just how profound the Union fight had been. "The bitterness and animosity engendered by the war have happily almost passed away" he confirmed with enthusiasm, "yet we must remember that victory to the Rebellion meant death to the Republic." The Union soldiers had prevented such a death, and the republic lived as a beacon of democracy bolstered by the "verdict of the world." Maxwell's idea that the republic had to survive for the sake of the "civilized world" was remarkably similar to the recurring theme offered in regimental histories written over the previous two decades. The story of the 20th Connecticut, wrote veteran John W. Storrs in 1886, "is no longer a story of weary marches, sleepless nights, battle, danger, and death, but it is, on the contrary, henceforth to be honored as among the saviors not only of their country, but of this world of humanity."[19]

Further suggesting that American free institutions and republican liberty stood as the vanguard of world progress and invoking the rhetoric of American exceptionalism, Mills interpreted the victory over the Central Powers in the First World War within the context of Union triumph in the Civil War. Addressing the Lafayette Post in February 1919, Mills connected Union victory to an inevitable victory over all oppressive governments. "If the Union Soldiers of the Civil War had gone down to defeat in the days of '61 to '65," he argued, "the savage, bloodthirsty, hun would now be bestriding the world like a Colossus, and that when the story of [World War I] is written, and the contributing causes of our final triumph are fully appraised, foremost among such contributions will be found the triumph of the armies and navies of the Union in that historic struggle."[20]

"At last Jeff Davis is dead."

The celebration of Memorial Day offered the perfect opportunity for Union veterans to voice their sentiments concerning treason. The official "first" celebration took place in Waterloo, New York, in May 1866—a day promoted by GAR founder John A. Logan soon thereafter. Logan, in 1868, issued a proclamation stating, "Decoration Day" should be observed nationwide and annually.[21] Many believed that while Memorial Day honored all American soldiers across the states, former Confederates were necessarily excluded from such tributes (former Rebels had organized their own memorial day, with varied dates or celebration and origin). Rather, northerners who celebrated the holiday insisted that they esteemed only those who had fought to preserve the nation, not those who had tried to destroy it. Such obvious nose thumbing at southern Americans would seem to have pushed sections further apart, and in many cases, although most embraced reconciliation, Union veterans' activities hindered reconciliatory efforts. Orders dating to June 1869 from Grand Army of the Republic headquarters in Washington, D.C., clearly stated, "[W]e strew flowers on the graves of our comrades, and prevent them being strewn in the national cemeteries at the same time on the graves of such rebel dead as may be buried therein, not because we cherish any feelings of hate or triumph over our individual foes, but because we seek to mark the distinction and manner the feelings with which the nation regards loyalty and treason."[22]

The recognition of southern courage—a prominent refrain in reconciliatory rhetoric—did not preclude the acknowledgment of southern treachery. "They were brave," observed GAR Adjutant General W. T. Collins, "but mere courage never ennobled treason." Such words provided a lasting text from which Union veterans could draw. As time passed, Union men echoed the sentiments of the immediate postwar Memorial Day celebrations—indicating an intense commitment to unity that by and large focused on the sacrifices and patriotism of northern soldiers. "We may join with them in extolling the heroism of the people of the South," suggested Massachusetts GAR post commander Joseph W. Thayer, "but we must not be asked to countenance or to palliate the gigantic crime which they committed in seeking to destroy the Union, or to allow the attempts to distort the facts of history to go unrebuked."[23] Thayer's remarks concerned the dedication of a Confederate monument in Chicago's Oakwood Cemetery. Although both Union and Confederate veterans participated in the dedication services—meant to honor Confederate soldiers who died in Chicago area prisons—many GAR men condemned not only the construction of the monument and Union veteran participation but also the conspicuous dedication date: Memorial Day.[24] Such activities on northern soil incensed Union men. First, they found the statue erroneous in appearance, arguing that the depiction of a ragged Confederate suggested mistreatment at the hands of Union captors. But more importantly, Union veterans were perturbed by the lauding of treason on the most sacred of Unionist days. "The blood of our martyred Lincoln," declared one Union veteran, "cries out in protest against this blasphemy."[25]

Northern opposition to Confederate monuments in Chicago and elsewhere persisted well into the twentieth century. As late as the 1930s, after Congress debated a series of House Resolutions concerning the monuments commemorating Confederate soldiers killed in battle, Lucy S. Stewart, secretary of the 31st Ohio Regimental Association, summarized the thoughts of the few remaining Union Civil War veterans in her state through an open letter to the "patriotic citizens of America." Members of the association were chiefly concerned with the expenditure of money earmarked to aid Confederate groups or fund Confederate monuments. The lending of supplies to the UCV by the War Department or even allowing the Marine Corps band to play at Confederate functions triggered rejoinders from Union men. But the congressional movement to sponsor Confederate monuments throughout the South especially irritated loyal Unionists. These resolutions, if passed, would have cost the federal government "*many* thousands of dollars, each, for there are scores or hundreds of such cemeteries all over the South, in which are buried many thousands of such rebel soldiers." Money, however, was not the principal issue. These Ohioans were more concerned with the idea of the United States honoring the Confederacy. "By this manipulation of markers into monuments," Stewart announced, "the markers, which it was claimed a humane government should place at the graves of these misguided men, would become monuments of glory to the traitors who tried to establish a Slave-holders' Confederacy on the ruins of the Union. It is an insidious scheme."[26]

The numerous Confederate soldiers' monuments appearing across the South deeply troubled many Union veterans. If Confederate commemorative activity in general fostered the likelihood that Union men would verbally issue some sort of condemnation, this activity in particular only acted as an accelerant. Such flagrant veneration of rebel traitors was not only unseemly but also cause enough for some sort of official action. By the 1880s, Confederate commemorations had increased dramatically, moving from cemeteries to public arenas such as courthouse lawns and town squares. The sudden increase in commemorations suggests a steady rise in the collective power of the former Confederate voice in the South. Many Union veterans would certainly agree with GAR comrade Castle, a Minnesota veteran who observed in 1892 through a toast to the old soldier, "It is a marvelous delusion that inspires the vanishing generation of traitors to monumentalize their own infamy."[27]

Denunciations from the North did not deter former Confederates. They proceeded to honor their former leaders through statuary and other forms. As Confederate efforts progressed through the 1880s and 1890s, Union veterans simply redoubled their efforts and attacked both the Rebel cause as well as the pantheon of southern heroes. From their perspective as victors, the ex-Rebels made easy targets. "Neither the living nor the dead of a great and holy cause can be confounded with those who fell in the wretched struggle to destroy a nation or erect a system of government false to the great principles of liberty," suggested MOLLUS companion and Massachusetts native Charles Devens to a group of Ohioans in the spring of 1890. An attorney and veteran of the 15th Massachusetts Infantry, wounded at Ball's Bluff in 1861, Devens was not prone to subtlety. "Nor shall we fear [the great tribunal's] verdict can be otherwise than that it was the cause of order against disorder, of just and righteous government against rebellion." What angered Devens most, however, were the tributes to former Confederate president Jefferson Davis. Union veterans counted Davis among the most deplorable of all traitors—the "archfiend of this bloody carnival . . . who [wore only] a mask of patriotism" wrote another MOLLUS companion. By 1890, merely a year after his death, plans to memorialize the Rebel executive in bronze and marble were well under way across the South.[28] Devens responded sardonically, asking: "Was Mr. Jefferson Davis the patriot he has been somewhere lately eulogized, and we, and the brave who offered their lives with us, but successful traitors?"[29]

Antagonism notwithstanding, the legality of commemorating the Confederacy was never really in question. Such actions would have been delicate at best, considering that ex-Rebels were once again under the purview of the Constitution and had a right to praise whomever they wished. Constructing a monument was not against the law. "I recognize that it is impossible for this Department to prevent the dedication of Confederate monuments," noted GAR comrade L. H. B. Bebe, "but I trust that it is not impossible for this Department to express its disapproval." Union veterans accordingly called for an official stance at the organizational level and issued a number of reproving resolutions. One such resolution, read before the annual encampment of the Department of Minnesota, GAR, pleased veterans who "most earnestly protest against the erection or dedication of monuments to the rebel dead on Memorial Day." Union veterans recoiled at the idea that certain Confederates would ever be elevated to the level of Union heroes. "Look one moment at Abraham Lincoln," one veteran observed, "the embodiment of all that was great and noble, the embodiment of human liberty, progress and nobility of character, and shall the time come when the when the day set apart and held sacred to his memory, that some one shall come along and on that day erect a monument to Jefferson Davis? No, no! It ought not to be. It can not be. It can not be if we are true to our principles."[30]

At the end of the war, many had called for the trial and execution of Confederate president Jefferson Davis.[31] Although cries for retribution had subsided by the time of Davis's death in December 1889, Union veterans still found him unappealing in every way. In October 1887, Union veteran Asa B. Isham, a cavalry officer who had spent seven months as a prisoner of war and would eventually write extensively of his experiences with Custer's Wolverine Brigade and life in Confederate prisons, suggested before a group of Ohio veterans that "upon Jefferson Davis and his advisors rests the fearful weight of responsibility for the ruthless sacrifice of [Union] men." Knowing full well that Davis continued to enliven the patriotic spirits of former Confederates, perhaps perpetuating the spirit of treason, Isham attacked, "Jeff. Davis still lives, a phenomenal monument to the mercy of a benignant government and a long suffering Providence. He chews the cud of bitter disappointment, a thousand-fold intensified by the unscrupulous efforts he put forth to achieve success."[32]

Celebratory attacks on Davis multiplied after the former Confederate executive's death. Claimed one Union veteran, "He [Jefferson Davis] became the embodiment of political bigotry and prejudice. He has passed away. Thank God." Veteran publications such as the *Grand Army Record* declared, "At last Jeff Davis is dead.... We are finding no fault with the Lord on that account." Back in 1896, the periodical had reminded its readers that Davis was not merely a belligerent, but a Rebel, lest anyone's opinion of the traitor had softened as national celebrations moved away from contention. This sentiment numbered among other prominent themes in veterans' publications confirming, at least for Union men, that Confederate leaders were traitors to their flag and country. Union veterans would generally resuscitate this theme in the pages of the *Grand Army Record* and the *National Tribune* as acts of protest, particularly upon the death of a prominent Confederate or when southerners proposed to create national holidays honoring their heroes.[33]

The reputation of Confederate general Robert E. Lee likewise suffered at the hands of Union veterans. In the early 1890s, while tributes to Lee flourished in the South, Union veterans attacked the Rebel commander as a traitor to his country. Erecting monuments to Confederate generals made treason and loyalty equally commendable. As such, commemorating the former was intolerable. In 1891, the *Grand Army Record* passionately objected to the "saintly slopping over Robert E. Lee," and others agreed. In fact, GAR protests against Lee helped create a lasting thread in northern commemorative literature. In 1910, one Union veteran wrote, essentially expressing in the same breath how some might find Lee both virtuous and reprehensible, "Though in his Confederate uniform [Lee] may possess all the culture and personal worthiness he had before he thus clothed himself, this badge of disloyalty—of rebellion—so characterizes him that by it he must be judged." As late as 1922, a variety of groups continued to honor the veterans' legacy by protesting in "unmeasured terms" the organizations that celebrated the Rebel chief, arguing that treason should never be forgotten, much less rewarded.[34]

Late in the nineteenth century, especially as controversies stirred over the publication of southern-leaning textbooks, veterans circulated condemnations of such authors as D. H. Montgomery and his *Leading Facts of American History* and *Beginners' American History*. These books, Union veterans argued, portrayed Lee far too favorably, considering him a noble combatant while overlooking his traitorous acts. Members of GAR posts in Massachusetts and New York petitioned to have the books banned from state schools but eventually dropped their cases when the publishers made significant changes. Still, although adulation of the Rebel general found a place among northern civilians who perhaps sentimentalized or romanticized the genteel South and all that the Lee family embodied, Lee's standing among Union veterans never reached the heights the general obtained in the South. "No Grand Army man," offered one Union veteran, "can honorably lend his name to any movement which shall dignify to posterity the name of the traitor Robert E. Lee, or shall make him the equal of the loyal, victorious Grant."[35]

In fact, Lee's legacy suffered a long and enduring attack at the hands of his former adversaries. Union veterans remained determined to praise only the Union heroes, who *saved* the country, rather than a Rebel who had tried to destroy it. The praise allotted to the Rebel chieftain wore Grand Army veterans particularly thin. One *Collier's Weekly* article citing Lee as America's most "noble citizen" especially drew fire from the GAR's patriotic instructor, Robert Kissick of Iowa. "If Lee was all you claim, then the men I represent were wrong in fighting to preserve the nation he fought to destroy." Further arguing that "Lee did not follow his state out of the Union," but rather, "his state followed him," Kissick lambasted the Confederate hero and heaped much of the blame for upper South secession on Lee's shoulders. As decades passed, few Union veterans could stomach the praise of Robert E. Lee. In 1922, when the American Legion veterans of the Great War attempted to honor Lee's birthday, veterans of the Pennsylvania GAR shuddered at the idea that anyone would "place a premium on Disloyalty to the Flag and our Country."[36]

"I confess a regret that we did not burn them up 40 years ago."

Attacks on the personifications of treason went hand in hand with attacks on Confederate symbols. A revealing episode concerns the drive undertaken by politicians in the upper echelons of the Democratic Party to return captured Confederate battle flags to members of their former units. Spearheaded in 1887 by President Grover Cleveland, the only Democrat elected to the White House between James Buchanan's election in 1856 and the election of Virginia-born Woodrow Wilson in 1912, the plan suggested a reconciliatory gesture on the part of the federal government. Cleveland was already at odds with Union veterans—especially with the comrades of the GAR. Having avoided military service by purchasing a substitute—a Polish immigrant named George Brinski—Cleveland spent the war years practicing law safely in Buffalo, New York. This did not sit well with veterans who had faced death on the battlefield. Further, suspecting corruption within the veterans' pension lobby, Cleveland vetoed a number of allegedly dubious pension bills, actions that did not win him support from the veterans of the GAR, MOLLUS, or any other Union veterans' organizations. But nothing rankled the veterans more than Cleveland's proposal to return Rebel flags to the South. Members of the GAR, including Commander-in-Chief Lucius Fairchild, turned vicious. Cleveland even received threats of physical violence. In June 1887 a group of Ohioan veterans resolved that the order to return Confederate flags was "a Dastard outrage and Disgrace to all Patriotic American citizens."[37] Although Cleveland eventually reconsidered his plans, he could not turn back the clock. Quite possibly, considering the narrow election results in 1888 and the number of voting GAR comrades, Cleveland's actions in this regard might have cost him reelection.[38]

Any indications that Confederate flags, considered treasonous emblems by most Union veterans, would be returned to southern states fueled bitter opposition. A few disparaged the flags' very existence. One Union veteran even suggested destroying the banners. "I confess a regret that we did not burn them up 40 years ago," he lamented, "They are about as valuable as confederate money."[39] Early in the twentieth century, when President Theodore Roosevelt and reconciliationist members of Congress once again proposed reuniting former Confederates with their captured colors, GAR men and other veterans fired away with bitter rancor. One collection of post minutes suggest discussions in unanimous agreement concerning what many considered no less than a diabolical scheme to honor treason. Reporting on an address given to Brooklyn Post, 233, Department of New York, by department commander Alan C. Baker, the post recording officer noted in March 1905 that the congressional bill supporting the return of Confederate flags "was in every way a most reprehensible thing to carry out." For an organization where "no discussion or controversy of partisan political character, or of nature to impair harmony [was] permitted," these veterans took a decidedly partisan stance.[40]

Five days subsequent to the commander's visit, in a letter to William Sears, assistant adjutant general of the GAR, Adjutant B. William Ennis of the Brooklyn post voiced his concern regarding the matter of Rebel flags. Embittered remonstrance clearly overshadowed any shades of benign reconciliation. He reminded his fellow veterans of the old Republican slogan, "Let Us Have Peace," but noted also that "loyalty and treason cannot harmoniously march 'elbow to elbow' in the same column under 'Old Glory' and the 'Secesh' emblems." Ennis directed his concern toward future southern generations, who he feared would have their minds fired by what he termed "false admiration." He thought in terms of preservation for the sake of the memory of his mistaken foes' courage, but without exhibition of "maudling sentiment that would apparently place treason and loyalty on level." Much to the consternation of comrades of the Brooklyn Post, and although "the adjutant's letter to Department Headquarters relative to return of the rebel flags, was discussed and approved," GAR headquarters did not quite warm to their complaints. Posturing matter-of-factly, a reply stated that a "law has already passed Congress, and the flags have already been returned." GAR leadership appeased angered comrades somewhat by at least stating that no Confederate flags would ever be paraded side by side with the Stars and Stripes; they would only be retained only as "relics to the lost cause."[41]

The Brooklyn post's dialogue concerning Rebel flags was not an isolated incident.[42] Across the nation, at veterans' gatherings both large and small, mentions of the flagrant use of treasonous symbols propelled Union veterans into states of palpable anger. In fact, GAR leadership forbade comrades from even appearing in places where the flag might be displayed. In a resolution read before the annual gathering of the Department of Minnesota in 1892, one veteran identified only as Comrade Thomas scorned the Rebel flag as an emblem of "a false and treasonable government." Further, he heartily endorsed the late order of Commander-in-Chief John Palmer relating to comrades marching or appearing in public gatherings where emblems of treason such as the Confederate flag were in any way displayed. Adopted unanimously to great cheers, the resolution deemed any comrade of the Grand Army of the Republic who would recognize that emblem of traitors and disloyalty by so marching or appearing, as "untrue to his obligations as a member of the Grand Army."[43]

Combining a commitment to thwart any attacks on the American "way of life" with their work in suppressing the rebellion, Union veterans associated other "disgraceful" emblems with the flag of the Confederacy. The exponential increase of immigrants arriving from foreign shores went hand in hand with the influx of other political ideologies—some considered antithetical to republicanism. By the turn of the century, the number of immigrants arriving at United States ports such as Ellis Island had nearly tripled since the previous decade. In 1898, Minnesotans once again lashed out at their former enemies by associating the Confederate emblem with the flag of anarchy. Commander-in-Chief Ivan N. Walker, an Indiana native who rose to the rank of colonel before spending a year suffering in Libby prison, offered these words of comparison to his GAR comrades. "While we hold open the doors of this great country for the entrance of all loyal people of Europe, and welcome those who come for the best intentions to better their conditions, we have no use for those who come to teach and practice anarchy in this country." Amid great applause, Walker concluded, "The red flag, like the rebel flag, is a menace to this country, and it is time that both should go." Although Walker's comparison was stretched a bit thin, his point was clear nevertheless. Symbols conceived in opposition to the government of the United States were unwelcome.[44]

"TREASON, *deep, dark, and damnable.*"

Union veterans generally agreed that the creation of a dubious Confederate nation constituted an act of treason. "Treason" was no abstraction—it needed little definition beyond what was made apparent by secession. Long after the war's end, the experiences of suppressing treason remained deeply etched in veterans' collective memory—and thus dominated their commemorative literature. Commemorating its demise took on several forms, each adding to the collective commemorative ethos expressing an overall celebration of victory. One such strand of memory justified the killing of one's own countrymen. Orlando B. Potter, a prominent New York politician and Manhattan real estate developer, for example, noted in 1888, "It has been said that the battles and victories of the late war ought not to be celebrated, because they were battles against and victories over our own countrymen." Potter chose not to mention who might have desired this course of action. "I cannot agree with this sentiment," affirmed Potter; "they were battles for the supremacy and preservation of our constitution and government . . . for the overthrow and annihilation of the fatal heresy of secession."[45]

Others focused on the Confederate dead. Rebel graves served symbolically as the physical representations of treason. Then men entombed in southern cemeteries and unmarked graves by the thousands had given their lives to ensure that treasonous intentions had been carried out. Living ex-Confederates at least had the chance to (attempt to) argue their way out of such accusations. The Rebel dead did not have such liberties and thus from a Union perspective, made easy targets. Members of Post #11, Wisconsin GAR, were particularly dismayed by national debates concerning a military salute over the graves of Confederate dead—a movement initiated by some in the interest of cementing fraternal bonds between the GAR and UCV. Most Union men maintained that such gestures should be reserved for the Union dead. Although members of this post mentioned that "the veterans of both sides of the Civil War are coming to be very friendly in their relations with one another," they recognized how honoring their former enemies in this manner could tarnish their own image. "It was moved that the custom of firing salute over the graves of the Confederate dead be discontinued," noted one veteran, "which is not the proper thing to be done." After a bit of discussion, the motion was carried, noting that firing over Confederate graves was tantamount to bestowing military honor upon traitors.[46]

Only a few years earlier Pennsylvania veterans reunited at Gettysburg concluded a similar debate. They decided that any graves of the Confederate dead at Gettysburg were to be kept at a distance from those of the saviors of the Union. While many recognized that the bitter embers stirred over the right of southerners to honor their heroes should be left alone, Unionists demanded that the graves of traitors and patriots not be mixed. Likewise, they demanded that no Union activities take place among the graves of Confederates, even though the veterans expressed reconciliatory concerns. "The flag is the flag of all, and the country is the country of all," argued one Union veteran, "yet thinking people cannot forget that the Confederate soldier fought to destroy the Republic and that our country and its flag was only preserved by those who fought for the Union."[47]

These thinking people must have also been acutely aware of the delicate situation in the border states. They chose to commemorate the suppression of treason by noting how populations of states such as Missouri and Kentucky especially remained split when it came to sectional allegiance. These states sent men by the thousands into both the Union and Confederate armies. Further, sectional loyalties in these border regions pitted Confederate sympathizers against loyal citizens resulting in brutal unconventional warfare. While border state commemorations could be interpreted as the epitome of reconciliatory celebrations in a reunited nation, conveying a sense of a "brothers' war," as did the Maryland state monument located behind Ziegler's grove at Gettysburg, Union veterans were just as likely to emphasize the treasonous activities of Rebels in loyal states. In fact, GAR posts across the North welcomed loyal men from border states and honored them for their perseverance in the face of an enemy who made little effort to disguise his traitorous actions. GAR comrade Mark D. Flower remarked before his post in 1898, "We have in our midst today a comrade who enlisted from the border state of Kentucky, where treason stalked abroad at high noon unabashed, and where union sentiment was rewarded with death." Flower, a Minnesota veteran and the state's adjutant general, needed not to hide his bitterness nor mince his words in the presence of his fellow veterans.[48]

But while some veterans highlighted the juxtaposition of loyalty and treason in border states, many others were far more likely to condemn the Confederate cause by detailing the point where treason reached its zenith. Union monument dedications on the battlefield at Gettysburg serve as the principal site of this commemorative theme. Memories—even the most bitter—were not likely to fade in the presence of hundreds of monuments to the Union cause. Veterans who believed that in 1861 "secession lifted its hydra head, and rebellion threatened the integrity of the Government" could channel their distaste into a celebration of the victories of 1863. Gettysburg stood out prominently as a battle worthy of observance; for many, treason suffered a mortal wound on the fields of Pennsylvania. "The rebellion that was inaugurated at Charleston in 1861 culminated at Gettysburg in 1863," noted A. M. Mills.[49] Adding a sardonic twist to his speech concerning the memories of the war, Union veteran William Glenny, who had sustained severe wounds at the Battle of Fair Oaks, eventually to be brevetted brigadier general for 'conspicuous gallantry," announced at Gettysburg on the twenty-seventh anniversary of the battle with more than a hint of sarcasm, "The next time you are met with [a] disloyal and insinuating phrase, ask the individual in what regiment of the Confederate army he served; or, if it meets the case better, say: 'How are you, my erring brother? Yes, the war is over. Have you just returned from Canada, and have you been there since 1861?'" Humor aside, Glenny admitted, "It is not likely that this Union [would] be again disrupted or thrown into bloody strife." Nevertheless, he insisted, "the flag of treason should be suppressed, for the reason that it is a constant menace to perpetual peace."[50]

In similar fashion, Michigan veterans focused on Gettysburg as the commemorative epicenter of the fight against treason. We claim it to be our solemn duty," argued Clinton Spencer, a veteran of the 1st Michigan Infantry, "here above this hallowed dust to proclaim and reiterate, that disloyalty to the old flag *was, is and always will be*, TREASON, *deep, dark, and damnable,* and the survivors of the Old 1st Michigan Infantry do not believe in palliating or shading in the least degree that definition of the term." Highlighting the significance of the battle of Gettysburg, Spencer underscored the problematic nature of honoring Union veterans and former Confederates with an equal emphasis on American virtues. "If so," asked a troubled Spencer, "what mockery to mark the place where heroes fell. What lesson would it teach the sons of the North and South if we say the other side simply erred in their construction of the Constitution?"[51] The "high tide of the Confederacy" worked not to salute the efforts, fortitude, or bravery of Rebels, but to point out their treasonous aims. One Captain Miller, a Union veteran who drew his sword not at Gettysburg but rather with the Army of the Cumberland under the command of George H. Thomas, nevertheless pointed to the meaning of Pickett's Charge and its culmination at the Angle in his very northern interpretation of Civil War history. "It was high tide there! And as the crest of Pickett's terrible rush was stayed and its ruins flowed back, the tide of treason changed. From thence onward to the end it ebbed and ebbed till, at Appomattox, it was at rest."[52]

These expressions were typical. Grand Army veterans especially recounted the day when Union men "hurled back the high tide of treason and rebellion at Gettysburg" at annual reunions and other gatherings. Gettysburg loomed large as the pivotal turning point for many Union and Confederate veterans. But while southerners tended to remember the defeat as the beginning of a long and valiant struggle against unmatched resources, Union veterans recalled Gettysburg as the beginning of the inevitable victory over treason. But ultimate victory was not without Herculean effort. Many veterans noted this point—implying that the rebellious soldiers clung to their treasonous aims long after hope for independence had been lost. In 1919, New York veteran and GAR department commander Clarendon E. Adams recounted scenes of soldiers "rushing on and ever onward, amidst the roar of cannon, the rattle of musketry, the groans of the wounded and dying, onward and onward to victory, unwilling to give up until the last vestige of rebellion and treason was pulled up and the Southern Confederacy was no more."[53]

Adams's address mirrored earlier statements regarding the Confederate "high tide." This commemorative theme was as prevalent in many Union speeches and writings as it was among the former Confederates. Both sides interpreted the High Water Mark as a profoundly significant place; both sides recalled the fighting around the area as the culminating moment in a political movement. But in contrast to Confederate views of a lost moment for independence, Union veterans saw it as the furthermost achievement of a treasonable people. "While traitors in high places plotted treason," recalled I. M. Cravath in 1869, "[Union soldiers] stemmed the high tide of rebel victories and rolled back defeat on the foe at Gettysburg . . . and carried our 'Spangled Banner' from the Wilderness to Richmond." Forty-five years later, when a new war in Europe captured the attention of most Americans, this sentiment was just as prominent at veterans' gatherings. "You swept back the tide of disunion and rebellion," argued New Jersey GAR comrade Cole in September 1914; "you kindled alight again the fires of liberty that has almost been extinguished, you swept back the rebel horde on the field of Gettysburg, and buried for all time rebellion, treason, slavery, and the degradation of human labor." From churches to the halls of Congress, notable citizens repeated the theme of turning back rebellion at Gettysburg. At the Old Dutch Church's two-hundredth anniversary in Tarrytown, New York, in 1897, Theodore Roosevelt, noted for his reconciliatory rhetoric, acknowledged those GAR men in attendance who "saw the high tide at Gettysburg and fought until at last the country was once more made a Union indeed." In 1903, Republican representative Charles Dick of Ohio demanded that the United States continue to honor Union veterans' pension claims, noting that it had only a "rear guard remain[ing]" of the men who had turned back treason and disunion that had "reached a high flood at Gettysburg." If loyal citizens needed a single spot to illuminate the fight against disloyalty, Gettysburg easily filled the bill.[54]

But Union veterans did not necessarily need a prominent, nationally recognized place to develop and articulate their commemorative culture. Local meeting places often provided adequate venues. As part of many GAR and MOLLUS posts' orders of business, meetings would characteristically open with a reading of the previous meeting's minutes, followed by readings of national general orders. A few words were then offered for veterans who had recently died. Recording officers then made note of veterans' comments when the floor was opened for general discussion. These discussions worked as a commemorative form on par with public activities, but often more vehement. Records of New York's Lafayette Post are typical in this regard. The post's stated purpose, in fact, was to "discountenance whatever tends to weaken loyalty, incites to insurrect, treason, or rebellion." Members were well acquainted with post concerns that "no miscreant fraud, no treachery with assassin heart, [and] no sullen and vindictive treason ought to live." To be certain, even Lafayette Post members' most reconciliatory messages were laced with admonitions against disloyalty. "We will send forth the inspiration [of the GAR]," stated one member, "until every heart shall again be warmed by the vital principles of loyalty, and every remnant of treason be driven from the land."[55]

MOLLUS veteran Thomas H. McKee would have agreed. He spoke of South Carolina's Governor Francis Wilkinson Pickens, who, when his state seceded from the Union, had stated that Palmetto and Confederate flags "would float forever in defiance." McKee, who served with the 1st West Virginia Infantry and later wrote extensively on the "test of loyalty" in Virginia during the war as well as a biography on Edwin M. Stanton, referred to the governor's words as a "false prophecy of treason and his insult to the flag of his country." As late as 1906, McKee remarked that the few remaining remnants of Confederate Charleston were nothing more than the "ashes of desolation and treason" and Montgomery, the site of Jefferson Davis's inaugural speech as the Confederacy's president, the "seat of the greatest conspiracy of all times."[56]

Repeated condemnations of southern treason undertook an important cultural work. By the early twentieth century, a distinctly Union culture of reconciliation took hold in the loyal states and formed a pillar of northern commemorative activity. This allowed veterans of the United States' armies to honor the preservation of union by underscoring the treasonous aims of their misguided countrymen. Federal soldiers saw no contradictions when infusing their reconciliatory messages with bitter words. Union veterans created this culture complete with a story of paramount struggle. They accented a moment when all that was great about the republic could have been lost. They likewise celebrated a momentous triumph over fanaticism and evil. But former Confederates did not stand idly by while the victorious North assaulted their cherished cause. As time and change distanced the attentions of many Americans from the events of war and Reconstruction, and as the federal government loosened reins of control over the defeated states, Confederate veterans emerged in public with their own visions of how a reconciled nation should appear—to American citizens and the rest of the world. In many cases, these men combined the symbols of rebellion with professions of loyalty to the United States—in seemingly contradictory ways. However conflicting such imagery may have been, former Confederates, now claiming their place in the nation as proud Americans, flaunted their Confederate heritage in public ceremonies, often sporting Rebel gray and waving the Confederate battle flag. While Union veterans fought to preserve their memories, former Rebels did the same—frequently stirring up bitter fires in the process—and in turn, creating their own Confederate culture of commemoration.

CHAPTER THREE

UNREPENTANT REBELS
COMMEMORATIONS AND CONFEDERATE RECONCILIATION

The issue of battle never yet established a *principle,*
it can only determine a *policy.*

—JOHN HERBERT CLAIBORNE, Surgeon, 12th Virginia Infantry

For Confederate veterans such as Thomas Neville Waul, postwar commemorations served as reminders of disunion. Waul, like many of his contemporaries, was intent on "fighting his battles o'er again." At an early 1880s tribute to Hood's Texas Brigade in Austin, Texas, he reminded former Confederates "to great cheers" that "we cannot forget the war; we do not want to forget it and he who was a soldier, and pretends to forget it, is a hypocrite and a traitor." At the same gathering, Reverend J. W. Stevens, former chaplain of Hood's Brigade, fueled his invocation with reminders of the war. The soldiers of the Union army were not worthy foes, but rather part of an "onslaught of an insolent, invading host, whose battle cry was devastation and hatred, and whose line of march was marked by the smoke of devastated homes and burned towns and cities."[1]

But as ex-Rebels had once had a stake in Confederate independence, they now had a stake in a peacefully restored Union. Coloring their speeches in reconciliatory hues, many veterans would readily agree that "we are proud of our great country, and as true Americans we look on the bravery and valor of the Confederate soldiers as reflecting honor and glory on our whole country." But reconciliationist sentiments notwithstanding, unrepentant Rebels commemorated their Confederate experiment by conjuring the spirit of disunion. Speeches, parades, monument dedications, and other veteran gatherings were all part of a collective vindication—clearing Confederate veterans from northern accusations. They were vindicating their honor. In so doing, they commemorated their war effort on their own terms.[2]

Former Rebels added to the commemorative culture by resuscitating Confederate ideology. Some, who took an apolitical stance in public, nevertheless conveyed a commitment to the Confederacy in private correspondence. Others felt compelled to offer their sentiments publicly—to all those who would listen. They suggested that although Federal armies destroyed the Confederate nation by force of arms, their cause was far from lost so long as former Rebels remained resolute in their convictions. They articulated these convictions through a number of commemorative forms. Of these, among the most important was a commitment to the principles of the founding fathers. Defining these principles from a Confederate perspective, veterans claimed that they were one and the same with those of the Confederacy, that they were undermined by northern fanaticism and victory, and that they ought to be actively pursued in the reunited nation. Former Rebels accepted defeat on the battlefield. But their memories of cause remained intact and prominent—and fueled bitter reflection. Anger coupled with reconciliationist sentiment may have made strange bedfellows, but it was precisely the antipathy present in southern commemorations that made the Confederate reconciliation unique in a reunited nation. Their memories served to inform the distinctly Confederate brand of reconciliation former Rebels could embrace. The business of reconciliation left little room for forgetfulness.

"I do not believe that we fought in any 'Lost Cause.'"

In the spring of 1865, United States armies realized victory and thus reunited the nation by force. While this event was cataclysmic for Confederate nationalists, the reuniting of the several states was a reality. As such, former Confederates were faced with multiple choices as to how best to respond to this matter of fact. Some simply left for Mexico or Canada. Jubal A. Early, one of the most notorious of the unreconstructed Rebels, did exactly that, if only for a time. He traveled to Mexico, Cuba, and finally to Toronto before returning to Virginia in 1869. Some fled to Brazil and attempted to establish a quasi-Confederate system. Others stayed in the United States but remained resolutely unreconstructed. This relatively small group counted among its numbers Old Jube (after 1869) and a few other prominent former Rebels. A third group made their way in the postwar nation the best they could. The overwhelming majority of former Rebels belonged to this group. Many were silent on the war and returned to their peacetime pursuits. Their precise sentiments on the war, defeat, and reconciliation are mostly elusive, primarily due to their silence on the matter. But one meaningful way to gauge how these silent thousands felt about the Confederacy is their participation in commemorative events. Those who did weigh in on the war and its aftermath spoke and wrote frequently concerning their place in the reconciled nation. They accepted reunion and embraced reconciliation. Yet their testimony reveals a paradox. While generally reconciled individuals, these men were both unrepentant and unwilling to dismiss the issues that had sustained their four-year Confederate war. These unrepentant Rebels belonged to an extensive, influential, and powerful network of former Confederates who articulated the principles embedded deep in the foundation of the Confederate States of America. They traveled the former Confederacy and delivered addresses before other veterans, civic groups, ladies associations, historical societies, and anyone else who would listen. They worked tirelessly, more so as time distanced the former soldiers from the war. They carried their profoundly politicized set of Confederate values and ideas framing a fundamental definition of citizenship with them in the present and worked to cast it into the future. "A people forgetful of their past," argued one such veteran before the Pegram Battalion Association in Richmond, Virginia, early in the reconciliation period, "would proclaim their own degradation in the present and their doom for the future."[3]

Unrepentant Rebels were prominent, well-respected, and influential men who remained committed to the Confederate principles of the 1860s. The public sought them out and attended their speeches and lectures. Presses churned out their books, and various periodicals printed their articles. Indeed, some of the most fervent ex-Rebels contributed an unbalanced share to Confederate memory—and created a prominent Confederate reconciliationist leitmotif. The guiding objective of commemorating the Confederacy within a reunited nation was proving that the cause was right and justified. There is no other way to account for such widespread resonant hostility in a supposedly reconciled nation than to illuminate the ways in which former Confederates felt the pressure of history weighing heavily upon them from outside of the South.[4]

In public settings, some former Confederates might have suppressed the sentiments they would otherwise voice privately. Soon after the war, Robert E. Lee fostered a conciliatory public image based on sectional healing and made several statements showing his inclination to set an example of moderation. Lee offered his own "submission to authority" as a model for the success of the South's educated. He felt it necessary to "avoid all controversy, to allay passion, [and] give full scope to reason and every kind feeling" in order to restore Virginia's place in a peaceful Union. Lee judiciously maintained an image of accommodation by not participating in public discussion of controversial political or war topics. In 1867 he informed former general James Longstreet, "I have avoided all discussion of political questions since the cessation of hostilities. I have in my own conduct, and in my recommendations to others, endeavored to conform to existing circumstances."[5]

Lee instructed others, such as former subordinate Jubal A. Early, in the delicate art of public speaking. He cautioned Early against making "epithets or remarks calculated to execute bitterness or animosity between different sections of the country." Nevertheless, Lee himself privately "understood [such] feelings" and maintained an indignant attitude. In correspondence not intended for publication, Lee revealed his resentment of harsh Reconstruction measures implemented by Republican politicians in Washington. "[The United States Congress] has shown unfavorable disposition," he wrote to former general Cadmus M. Wilcox; "I fear the South has yet to suffer many evils." Lee's opinion of both the legality of secession and how the war irrevocably diminished the position of southern states in the Union amplified his postwar bitterness. In a letter to Lord John Dalberg Acton, an English moralist, historian, and philosopher known for his opposition to the "evil state" and his aphorism "absolute power corrupts absolutely," Lee invoked Washington and Jefferson to support his opinion on centralization of power and despotism. He maintained that these American leaders "had always asserted the right of secession," and even the "leading state in hostility toward the South [Massachusetts] supported secession at the 1814 Hartford Convention." Lee insisted that this had been "the doctrine advocated by the leading men of the country for the last seventy years" and lamented the loss of a war waged to protect this right. "The judgment of reason," he argued, "has been displaced by the arbitrament of war, waged for the purpose of maintaining the Union."[6]

Many of those who would follow Lee's example of moderation and accommodation in public speeches or through published materials revealed similar attitudes of lingering bitterness in their private writings and correspondence. In the third decade of the twentieth century, prominent United Confederate Veterans member and Fredericksburg attorney and judge John T. Goolrick published *Historic Fredericksburg: The Story of an Old Town*. In this work, he favorably described Civil War commemoration during the 250th anniversary of his "own beloved town." Goolrick celebrated a festival where one could witness "the Blue and the Gray riding side by side," where "ground was consecrated by the blood of armies of the North and the South," and where both "The Battle Hymn of the Republic and Dixie with its ever inspiring melody were sung." Yet Goolrick's private correspondence reveals a different man altogether—one who harbored a stubborn sectional animosity despite his public record of forgiveness. In a letter to William Berkeley written only a few months prior to the publication of *Historic Fredericksburg,* Goolrick complained, "I hear a great deal now about forget and forgive. I am one who will never forget nor forgive the vile-heartless-and-cruel treatment of the South."[7]

Among the many ex-Confederates who pursued a life of politics, both Fitzhugh Lee and John Warwick Daniel also embraced public conciliation. In an 1876 address delivered to a group of Confederate veterans shortly after a trip to Boston meant to foster sectional harmony during the nation's centennial celebration, Lee approvingly announced to his former comrades, "The 'crust' of separation had been 'broken at last' and 'men of the North and South' could now see each other 'face to face.'" Similarly, in a 1907 speech before a contingent of Confederate veterans, Daniel praised the conciliatory efforts of the old soldiers, approvingly noting how his fellow veterans had given Federal veterans a "cordial welcome." Although Daniel was aware that some former Confederates would condemn reconciliatory gestures as "treason," he maintained his public position and followed Lee's example of "noble magnanimity."[8]

Despite their overtly conciliatory positions on the public stage, both politicians voiced private resentment regarding the outcome of the war

and their former foes. When Jubal A. Early criticized Fitz Lee's participation in Boston's celebration of the national centennial as an obvious ploy
to gain political favor in the North, Lee responded that he would not have
gone to Boston if he had know there would have been a "demonstration"
for him. Furthermore, he condemned one particularly Unionist speech for
its "horrid taste" and proclaimed he was "no *repentant rebel*." Suggesting a
persistent loyalty to the Confederacy, he went on to argue, "If Virginia had
not seceded in 1861, [he] would have deserted her to help the Southern
cause." Daniel similarly revealed his sectional loyalties. When prominent
southerners suggested in 1909 that a monument commemorating Robert E.
Lee belonged among other American military figures in Washington, D.C.,
Daniel made mention and resented the northern inclination to "miscall"
Lee "the world's greatest Rebel."[9]

Were these men being disingenuous when it came to reconciliation?
They were generally not. But they insisted that they and their comrades craft
reconciliatory efforts on very specific terms—those that reflected the ideals
set forth by the Revolutionary generation and adopted by the Confederate
States of America. In their imagined past, the founders had maintained the
rights of states to resist federal authority. It was this very principle—the
right of secession in the face of tyranny—that fueled reconciliatory rhetoric in a reunited nation. This defining ideology had not been lost on the
battlefield.

Confederate veterans were unlikely to distinguish and precisely de-
lineate the present from the war years in the name of benign reconciliation. Such an action was problematic for many who had had a stake in
the Confederate experiment and similarly had a stake in the realization
of Confederate ideals after the war. John Randolph Tucker, an attorney
from Winchester, Virginia, who had served as the state's attorney general
during the war, summed things up for those who found dismissing Confederate principles for want of a contention-free reconciliation troubling.
Tucker, a former Washington and Lee University law professor who would
eventually find his way to the presidency of the American Bar Association,
outlined in a few words the resonance of the Confederate past and outlined
a nexus between the old and new. He admonished those who supposed
the past should be buried and its memories and ideas discarded because
a revolution turned its society upside down. Tucker worked to guarantee

that "political virtue" was not deemed "worthless *débris* to be cleared away to make place for a new order of ideas, principles, and faith."[10]

Like Tucker, many Confederate veterans thought benign public expressions of reconciliation reduced Confederate commemorations to sanguine sentimentalism. Such commemorative activity was indeed unsettling, particularly the idea that the Confederate cause was best remembered simply as a "cause thought right." This somewhat trite expression in all its variations functioned well for those who wished to honor the virtues of Confederate soldiery free from controversial ideological convictions—implying to postwar southern whites that their bid for independence had been an honorable but doomed, perhaps even misguided, experiment from the beginning. This sentiment smacked of an act of contrition—a "half apology" in the words of one cantankerous veteran of the Maryland Line, who voiced no subtlety when he trumpeted, "we fought for what *was* right." Unrepentant Confederate veterans chastised individuals who couched "Lost Cause" commemorations in terms of an "apologetic whine." Even those who stated that "bitter memories [were] softened by time's tender hand" insisted that "we fought for what was right—only God ruled that we should not become an independent nation."[11]

"The Southern cause was just and right," affirmed Confederate veteran G. B. Harris Jr. in the early twentieth century. "Defeat is not the test of righteousness of a cause. Right is right." This theme resonated throughout all Confederate commemorative forms. Hunter McGuire's work offers a typical example of this theme prevailing in general written treatises of the war. McGuire, a prominent physician and educator, was a battle-hardened veteran who had served as an infantryman with the 2nd Virginia and as surgeon in Jackson's Corps of the Army of Northern Virginia. In 1904, four years after his death, he was honored with a statue on the grounds of the Virginia State Capitol. His coedited publication *The Confederate Cause and Conduct in the War Between the States,* published posthumously in 1907, made note that all the men of the Confederate armies "were well satisfied now as they ever were that their cause was just."[12] McGuire stated in the book's introduction that "[Confederates] had not lost their manhood, and they had not surrendered their self respect and honor." But he further elaborated to include the principles for which Confederate soldiers had fought. They had lost nothing of their "faith in the right and justice of their cause,"

he argued. Even in the twentieth century, former Rebels held fast to perceived American ideals such as the right of secession, self-government, and
the abhorrence of a centralized state, while living in—and even embracing—
a reconciled nation. That these ideals fell on deaf ears outside the South
did not seem to bother McGuire or the host of other former Confederates
who shared his beliefs.[13]

George L. Christian was among the most prolific and vociferous of these
former Confederates. A prominent Virginia attorney who had been horribly
wounded at Spotsylvania, losing part of one foot and all of the other, he
hobbled around the former Confederacy speaking before a variety of audiences. At a tribute to Confederate general Jubal A. Early in 1894, he claimed,
"The man whose soul is so dead that he is not proud to have been a part of
[the Confederate] army, battling not for what he thought was right, but what
was right, is too contemptible, in my opinion, to be by any human power
raised to the level of brute." Four years later, Christian, in one of his many
appearances throughout the former Confederacy, would remind the people
of the South that "whilst the cause for which [Confederates] fought is a 'lost
cause' in the sense that they failed to establish a separate government within
certain geographical limits, it is only lost in that sense. The principles of that
cause yet live." Christian noted the significance of monument dedications
and gatherings in terms of perpetuating Confederate memories. Their very
existence would remind future generations of the Confederate cause and
of those who had determined to suppress it. "Here," observed Christian
in 1898, "history will record a thrilling tale of outrage inflicted upon this
defenseless people by the mercenary hordes of the North, permitted and
encouraged by the remorseless cruelty and unquenchable ambition of some
of their leaders."[14]

The idea that Confederates fought for principles "they knew to be right"
rather than principles they "thought" right (implying that they could have
been wrong) pervades the commemorative literature of the era and shows
how the words of men such as Christian reflect a broader sentiment among
Confederate veterans. Proponents of spreading Confederate ideology
through written and other means took advantage of veterans' enthusiastic
support of the cause in the postwar years and argued for such a position. As
one Confederate veteran suggested in 1867, few would ever "question the
correctness of the principles we had laid down." Apparently, he was correct.

Few Rebel veterans questioned the notion that Confederates were right in fighting for independence. But for those who did, the unrepentant were quick to answer. John Herbert Claiborne, former surgeon with the Army of Northern Virginia, hospital administrator, and author of several books and articles on the Civil War, professed before a gathering of veterans early in the 1890s, "Away the maudlin confession that we fought for what we thought was right! We fought for what we *knew* was right." Claiborne argued, "We yielded, not convinced, but conquered." Claiborne, a prominent postwar politician who held multiple honorary degrees and served on numerous medical boards, wrote often of the war. Of particular interest was his effort to bolster the Confederate fight in print: a comprehensive collection of reminiscences in which Claiborne lambasted the northern fighting man.[15]

Former Confederates talked themselves hoarse telling and retelling the stories associated with the somewhat less vitriolic Lost Cause rhetoric. But they also merged resurrected Confederate principles with these stories to produce a commemorative culture that could rapidly shift from an innocuous to an aggressively reactive tone. John S. Beard of Pensacola, for example, agreed in typical form with many ex-Confederates, arguing "that the Southern armies really exhausted themselves gaining victories over the Northern armies. I say all of this is matter of such notorious history that it cannot be denied." The term "lost" however, rankled some who had followed their states out of the Union. Well into the twentieth century, former Confederates gathered in town squares, meeting halls, and other public places not only to "grasp the fraternal hand [and] revive our olden friendships," but to infuse Confederate principles into the reconciled Union. Only the radical few called for a renewed movement for independence. Political victories, including a reassertion of state rights after Reconstruction, meant that in a sense the Confederacy lived on. As Beard noted, we "reassert the justice of the cause which was never lost, only delayed for a time, that future wisdom and patriotism may lay deeper and stronger a willing union of the states that shall be perpetual."[16]

In an undated Memorial Day address, published as part of an edited collection in 1906, Alabaman John Levi Underwood fleshed out the "cause not lost" theme succinctly. Underwood was an ordained Presbyterian minister who had enlisted as a private in the 20th Alabama in 1861 and eventually became the regiment's chaplain. As a veteran, Underwood worked as an educator, a prominent church official connecting networks in Georgia, Alabama, and Texas, an attorney, and landholder. Somehow, he managed to find time to publish an exceedingly popular and widely distributed pamphlet honoring Confederate women. In his work, he focused on highlighting Confederate resonance in the postwar United States—noting that while the United States commanded a significant presence, reflections of the Confederacy constituted a vital component of the national culture. "People are prone to allude to all Lee fought for as a 'Lost Cause,'" he stated, yet "Lee has accomplished what he fought for." Underwood was arguing from the point of view of one who saw state rights as the principal Confederate ideal. In the early twentieth century, he clearly stood behind the United States, but rejoiced that echoes of the Confederacy remained. His words would appeal to those who hoped their efforts and great sacrifices had not been in vain. In a bizarre appeal to living Confederate veterans who viewed their cause as "lost," Underwood intimated that Confederates had (partially, at least) won in the long run, "Who would dare to-day to wipe out a State's individuality?" he asked, perhaps reflecting on a post–Reconstruction Era South, "and do we not find to-day, instead of a centralized power in Congress adjudicating things pertaining to the States, the States themselves settling these matters?"[17]

Bradley T. Johnson, an exceptionally vocal former Rebel, had made such claims at least since the 1870s. His speeches, frequently published and distributed in pamphlet form to veterans as commemorative literature, worked to neutralize despondent feelings among veterans who saw their cause slipping into a sort of romanticized hopeless fight. "I do not believe that we fought in any 'lost cause,'" he told the members of the Association of Confederate Soldiers and Sailors of Maryland in June 1874 to great applause, "I denounce the phrase as unworthy of our people and their position. Our cause was that of every lover of liberty, in all time, the world over, the right of a people to govern themselves, and it never has been, never can be 'lost.'" Later in the century, Johnson seemed to be gaining ground. He assured his followers that all joined, or would soon join, former Confederates in celebration of a cause above reproach. "There can never be two rights and two wrongs," he argued late in the 1890s, against those who would support the innocuous, national reconciliatory vision that some veterans staged in various parts of the country; "this is so of every question of morals and of conduct." But for anyone confused regarding the righteousness and soundness of the Confederate cause, he quickly pointed out, "The world is surely coming to the conclusion that the cause of the Confederacy was right." All "true men and women . . . will never believe that 'we thought we were right.' They will know that we were right, immortally right and that the conqueror was wrong, eternally wrong."[18]

Elaborating further, Robert E. Lee Jr. reminded the veterans gathered for a reunion in Richmond in 1907 of what they must certainly have accepted as fact. Lee's words carried a great deal of weight. As a living link between veterans and their former commander, Lee was a prominent individual. His 1904 publication, *Recollections and Letters of General Robert E. Lee,* was a favorite among those who had served under his father. As a renowned veteran who lived to see the United States rise in power unknown during or immediately following the war, Lee made sure to note the Confederate past had not perished as a result. "Let us not be content with the lukewarm and, if you please, molly-coddling expression that the Confederate soldier fought for what he believed to be right. If precedent is a guide, if argument has any convincing force, if approving consciences any solace, if subsequent approbation by those who once disagreed with him any justification, if duty magnificently performed any indication, then we can assert without fear of any successful contradiction that the Confederate soldier fought and died for what he knew to be right."[19]

Simply stating that their cause was "right" left former Confederates plenty of room for elaboration. Most turned to the controversial subject of state rights. Some implied it and others were explicit. Either way, during the reconciliation period, the topic could raise the ire of veterans from both sides of the Potomac. For Confederate veterans, the principle of state rights served as a guiding theme of Civil War remembrance. Functioning to associate so-called Rebels with the founding generation, state rights arguments stirred controversy because they necessarily pitted former Confederates against so-called tyrannical government and the alleged perpetrators of base lies. For the most part, Yankees had dismissed such arguments and accused Confederates of treason. Confederate veterans did not take such accusations well, and they therefore punctuated their commemorative speeches with defensive testaments to the virtues of state rights and their commitment to the original intent of the founding fathers. These speeches were not solely used to minimize other aspects of the Confederate cause, but were intended to underscore the misdoings of their northern country-men. For in their estimation, it was not the Confederates, but the Federals who had destroyed the Union.

Confederate orators thus turned their attentions to tyranny. Articulated immediately after the close of war and carried late into the reconciliation period, their words bore a striking resemblance to antebellum arguments for secession. In 1895, for instance, speaking before members of the Association of the Army of Northern Virginia, former general Clement A. Evans explained his version of the logic of secession. Evans, a Georgia attorney before the war, had organized a militia unit when he heard the news of Lincoln's election. By 1864, after commanding troops in a number of battles, he had risen in rank to brigadier general. After the war, he became both a powerful Methodist minister and influential editor who oversaw the publication of the twelve-volume *Confederate Military History*. He was very active in veterans' affairs. He helped organize the Confederate Survivors Association soon after the end of Reconstruction in 1878 and also served as a founder and the commander-in-chief of the Georgia UCV. Evans argued that reasonable southern statesmen "saw the hard hand of impatient fanaticism uplifted against their prosperity." He continued, "With unspeakable sadness they beheld centralization tightening its coils to crush out the Statehood of the States." Only then, was peaceable secession the "right way of relief."[20]

Six years later John Beard again reminded Florida veterans of the ideals common among many other Confederates. He spoke of the injustice of the northern states and their utter disregard of their constitutional obligations as perceived by white southerners. This, claimed Beard, forced the southern states to withdraw from a constitutional compact. In typical form, Beard argued on constitutional grounds. Calling attention to the evil goals prescribed by the Lincoln administration "for the unconstitutional, revolutionary and wicked purpose of coercing, conquering and subjugating the seceded states," Beard hoped to accent how the "false, hallow cry of 'save and preserve the Union' was raised." Bluntly asking his audience how the Union could be preserved "by destroying the Constitution," Beard revealed the crux of former Confederates' anxieties by illuminating northern efforts to affix unsavory terms to southern patriots. According to Beard, the southern states were not in rebellion and southern patriots were not traitors.[21]

Treason, particularly in a society bound by honor, was an undeniably inflammatory insult. When northerners leveled these accusations at heroic Confederates, especially when expressed by former Yankee soldiers, unrepentant Rebels fired back with vehemence. In Confederates' estimation, the act of treason involved the endeavored overthrow of a national government, something that the Confederacy did not attempt—thus these accusations did not apply. This argument persevered and remained a cornerstone for Confederate apologists after the close of the war. "Just history will say there was no treason in being a Confederate," suggested John Warwick Daniel in 1898. The epithet "traitor," he remarked, was "the frothy passion of wordy conflict" and not applicable to Confederate patriots. While Daniel alluded to northern accusations, others were specific. In typical form, former Confederate general P. A. McGlashan addressed a gathering of veterans in Savannah, Georgia, in 1902. "Northern histories would make the world believe that our motives were base and ignoble, that our defeat was a blessing to mankind, [and] that we were traitors to a kind and paternal government."[22]

This variety of resonant consternation was not merely the work of isolated agitators. Rather, their words were characteristic, suggesting that the Confederate veteran population had a great deal of grievances yet to express—and indeed a great deal of work to do when it came to crafting a reconciliatory commemorative culture on their terms. George Moorman, adjutant general and chief-of-staff of the UCV, connected the allegiance to union with an antipathy toward any false claims about the Confederate leaders and the Confederate war effort. At an annual UCV meeting in Richmond in 1898 he defended the pantheon of Confederate leaders—not incidentally considered in the same league with George Washington—from what he deemed unwarranted accusations of treason. "I cannot hold him wise who would wound the patriotism of any citizen of the Republic." Confederate veterans could so easily deny accusations of treason, express a commitment to the Confederacy, and embrace the postwar Republic at once precisely because they so vehemently connected their bid for independence with the original intentions of the founding generation. It was in this context that speeches were of such vital importance. For through speeches, prominent former Confederates could reassure their comrades that their fight had resonance in the present. The principles they had fought for between 1861 and 1865 could be brought to bear on the present political and social United States.[23]

With historical certainty, ex-Confederates challenged assertions that they had veered from the original intentions of the founders. Prominent veterans such as D. Gardner Tyler, Raleigh T. Daniel, and Fitzhugh Lee all scoffed at ideas that the Union victory had been a benefit for all sections of the country. Tyler was among the most vehement in this regard. Nephew of former United States president and member of the Confederate House of Representatives John Tyler, he remarked to a gathering of veterans at Charles City, Virginia, in 1900 that some believed that "it is better for us as a people and better for civilization; that we are now sharers in a greater destiny than would have been ours had the Confederacy become one among nations of the earth." Utterly disgusted with such sentiment, Tyler outlined a theme that resonated among many former Confederates. He chastised those who turned their backs on the Confederacy, claiming that they insidiously detracted from the glory of the contest and further, that they aided in destroying the "sublime principle of self-government for which Washington fought.[24]

Since 1865 former Confederates had claimed that the war was between two distinctive ideals: "The idea of local self-government and the idea of a Federal Union," suggested one disgruntled ex-Confederate, clearly aligning himself with the former. In so doing, they justified the actions of the past. But like so many others, this individual implied that a battle still raged between two wholly different visions of "nation." He came to terms with defeat on the battlefield by drumming up support for a Confederate war with words in the present. "To call it rebellion is to speak ignorantly; to call it treason is to add viciousness to stupidity." Moreover, when Evander M. Law defended "State sovereignty, the cardinal principle of the Confederate revolution, and the most majestic pillar in the temple of our constitutional Union," he made sure to point out that the sanctity of this specific principle "still lives to sustain and vitalize the grandest system of government which human wisdom has ever evolved, and must in some form always remain the grand conservator of American institutions."[25]

"This is what the colonies had won independence to secure."

Commemorative gatherings provided the foundation from which former Rebels could easily launch verbal attacks against their onetime enemies. Anyone who claimed that Confederates had violated the sanctity of the Constitution by seceding from the Union was more often than not answered with harsh words. Confederate veterans understood that Union victory had initiated the ascent of the United States into a world power on par with the great states of Europe. While this power represented a centralized state, one the Confederates had fought to avoid, many nevertheless benefited from United States prowess, internal improvements, and other things considered "new" in the postwar nation. This notwithstanding, ex-Rebels worked to ensure that within this context, their voices would be heard—particularly the voice endorsing self-government, a hallmark of the Confederate, and perceived national past. For instance, when it suited them to do so, ex-Rebels would condemn the imperial policies of the United States—just to make a point. "We see the government of the United States going to the far off Philippine Islands, and contending that it can take just as much of the Constitution as is necessary for its purposes," argued one individual. "This same destructive and revolutionary school has the effrontery to denounce Jefferson Davis as a traitor and the Southern people of '61 to '65 as rebels." Confederate veterans naturally underscored their interpretation of the Constitution and support of the old Union as the primary dynamic of their commemorative efforts. Offering his southern understanding of history, one veteran declared, "The Constitution was never denounced, but always upheld by the South, until it no longer gave protection against the 'Moral Anarchy,' 'the Fanatical, Political insanity' of the Northern self styled, 'Saints.'"[26]

At Confederate commemorative events such as Memorial Day celebrations, monument dedications, and veteran gatherings, many thought it a former Rebel's duty to defend the principles of the Constitution—what they had fought to preserve as Confederate Americans. "The true way to preserve it as inheritance," suggested a patriotic ex-Confederate, "is to perpetuate in it the principles for which the Confederate soldier fought—the principles of constitutional liberty and of local self government." Well suited to make observations linking the Confederate war effort to the Constitution, Washington and Lee University professor of Constitutional law John Randolph Tucker asserted, "The South strove to save the liberty of the people of each state, by preserving any interference with local rights by the Federal Government and securing the exclusive direction of them by its local government. "This," explained Tucker to a graduating class at South Carolina College, "is what the colonies had won independence to secure." Rallying around this profoundly significant theme, former Confederates were comfortable taking the ideological high road. Time and again, orators commemorating the Confederacy visited the Constitutional Convention of 1787 and reminded their audiences that the republican guarantees of personal liberties—owing to the "energy, the valor, the wisdom and the patriotism of Southern men"—were long established by 1861. The people of the North had violated sacrosanct principles by "forgoing virtues enshrined in the Constitution in the deplorable pursuit of mammon."[27]

So with constitutional principles supposedly on the side of the Confederacy, ex-Rebels saw northern "tyrannical" leaders as easy targets. In a particularly vicious oration, the president of the Hood's Texas Brigade Association, Colonel R. J. Harding, turned his hand toward political figures and pondered Lincoln's "kindness" toward the South. Speaking at the annual gathering in Corsicana, Texas, Harding stated, "You have been told often that Abe Lincoln was going to be good and kind to the South if he had not been assassinated." He further noted to his audience, "This is a big guess. There is no way of judging the future but by the past." Adding his thoughts supporting the claim that Lincoln and his generals were nothing short of tyrants, he enumerated attacks on civilians at Fredericksburg and in Georgia. In a speech that most certainly induced a hearty laugh from the Confederate audience, Harding added, "If Massachusetts, Pennsylvania, Kansas and the worst of the South-hating states will put Jefferson Davis' portrait in the halls of fame, we will then begin to consider putting A. Lincoln's in Mississippi's Hall of Fame, but the face must always be to the wall."[28]

It was quite clear that anti-Lincoln contempt seeped into all walks of life. James H. M'Neilly of Nashville, a reverend and well known among Tennessee veterans, was no exception. The respected orator and writer speculated in a 1917 *Confederate Veteran* article that the former executive had really not accomplished anything at all of note for the general population. As such he asserted, like many of his southern contemporaries, that Lincoln's government—and indeed the North in its entirety—was itself an agitator and perpetrator of civil war. "He set up a government acceptable to himself and his party," argued M'Neilly. "And when force tramples on guaranteed rights, that is not statesmanship, but it is only bald tyranny and bad faith; and no assertion of a purpose to preserve 'government of the people, by the people, and for the people' can make it anything else." M'Neilly was more noted for his earlier treatise attacking former Confederates who aligned with northern views after the war and especially northerners who overthrew the Constitution. Love of Union—the old Union—was not an issue. Love of perversions of constitutional liberty was another story.[29]

Because former Confederates reiterated that their fight for independence had been for the preservation of the original principles of the Constitution and that northerners deviated from the course set out by the founders, it stands to reason that the most extensive and resentful sentiments voiced against former enemies stemmed from what nearly all considered unwarranted accusations of treason. Most veterans accepted reunion as a fact—but found it difficult in many cases to mend fences with those who wrote a dubious history. Thus the perception among many former Confederates was that northerners thwarted southern attempts to reach across the bloody chasm, and it was this key idea that dovetailed well with the notion that northerners had always taken issue with the South and precipitated the war. Prejudice against former Confederates emanating from north of the Potomac moved one former Confederate to invoke the Old Testament. Choosing a passage from Genesis, James M. Mullen noted that "when they pour upon our heads the vials of their bitterness I am almost constrained to exclaim with old Jacob, 'Cursed be their anger, for it [is] fierce; and their wrath for it [is] cruel.'" Specifically addressing the words of Grand Army of the Republic men such as Union veteran and former governor of Ohio J. B. Foraker, Mullen condemned those who questioned southerners' loyalty as an "insult to our intelligence and good faith." John H. Reagan, who in the early twentieth century stood alone as the last surviving member of the Confederate cabinet, looked forward to the day "when the passions and prejudices of the war shall have died out." He nevertheless grimaced at the thought of the "sophistries, false statements and perversions of history employed by the victorious party." Such sentiment serves to further illustrate the anger expressed by veterans over the "base and false charges of treason and rebellion."[30]

And angry they were. Heated sentiments remained a prominent theme at Confederate commemorations from the Reconstruction era to well into the twentieth century. In 1878, at a commemoration honoring Confederate soldiers in Augusta, Georgia, Charles C. Jones made sure to remark, "[We] here protest that so far from being rebels against legitimate authority and traitors to their country, our Confederate Dead were lovers of liberty, combatants for constitutional rights, and, as exemplars of heroic virtue, benefactors of their race." Without question, Jones understood dedications of monuments to Confederate soldiers as a means to a future in which Confederate ties persisted unbroken. "Hither will manly forms repair to renew their allegiance, and here will unborn generations learn the truth of history." Anxieties shared by former Confederates did not fade as accusations from the North poured in. Primarily concerned with the future generations of the South, veterans such as W. W. Ballew added his apprehension to the chorus of voices in 1913. "To the World, you, Ex-Confederate Soldiers, have been denounced as rebels, traitors to your Country, criminals deserving an ignominious death." These were hardly benign words for a citizen who otherwise seemed comfortably reconciled as one of the most prominent citizens of Clark County, Arkansas. "The histories of our Country have been written by Northern, and prejudiced writers ... for more than seventy years, the slanderers of the South have posed as the only patriots, and lovers of the Union, and Constitutional Government."[31]

If reassurances at public gatherings were not enough, Confederate veterans were equally likely to put their sentiments in print. William L. Calhoun's words were typical concerning the Constitution. This veteran and historian of the 42nd Regiment, Georgia Volunteers, wrote in 1900 that the "North" had violated the terms of the Constitution and forced secession. The people of the South, he argued, fought "for the preservation of the Constitution, not as traitors, not to destroy, but to preserve the government—a principle which is not dead, but must live if the American government is to be maintained." Such emphasis on constitutional preservation opened the door to offer a contentious rebuttal across sectional borders. Former Rebels used the defense of the Constitution as a way to show their loyalty to definitive Confederate principles, and such references in Confederate commemorative literature often brought out the most hostile memories. In a candid reminiscence, Wayland Fuller Dunaway professed a love for the Union typical among many former Confederates but confessed, "The war waged by the federal government was a crime against the constitution, humanity, and God." Even incensed poets lent their skills to the effort:

> Weep on Virginia! Weep those lives given to the cause in vain—
> The Sons who live to wear once more the Union's galling chain;
> The homes whose light is quenched for aye—the graves without a stone—
> The folded flag—the broken sword—the hope forever flown.
> Yet raise thy head, fair land, thy dead died bravely for the right—
> The folded flag is stainless still—the broken sword is bright.
> No blot is on thy record found—no treason soils thy fame!
> Weep thou, thy dead—with cover'd head we mourn our England's shame.[32]

"Any charge of treason upon the South is simply puerile."

As argued in early commemorative literature such as *The Land We Love,* Confederate veterans authors were not likely to forget that they stood against what they deemed a perversion of power in a republican government. Initial commemorative activities claimed to "express the sentiments of an undoubted majority of [the white southern] people—the disapprobation of wrong and tyranny." These ideas echoed across the decades in precisely the same manner. Many of the contributors to the *Southern Historical Society Papers,* the commemorative literature arm of the Southern Historical Society, founded by Dabny Maury in 1868, suggested that some veterans considered the war a means to enforce the will of a particular section—actions that amounted to tyranny. Virginians especially, reflecting on their decision to secede from the Union, justified their actions on the merit of not taking part in the coercive aims of the North. One veteran argued, "To have remained in the Union and joined in the coercion of the seceding states would have been a repudiation of her principles and an act of tyranny and dishonor." Many considered "federal tyranny ... a cruelty which was only equaled by fiendish ingenuity."[33]

The vehemence published within the *Papers* addressed the concern among ex-Confederates that the world would remember their experiment in nationhood as an impediment to progress, a failed revolution, or simply, as treason. In 1886 the *Papers* published an 1874 speech by Georgian B. H. Hill. In this speech, he asked an Atlanta audience, "Were eight millions of people traitors? Were leaders who had only obeyed their states and served the people criminals worthy of death?" These were not mere rhetorical questions. These were vexing inquiries that authors grappled with in explicit detail. Hill, a prominent Georgia attorney who the *New York Times* had once called a "Union man down to the date of secession," refused to sit still for any accusations of treason. "Eight millions of people," Hill observed, "struggling as one man for liberty, were not traitors, only because power and treachery combined to conquer and enslave them." Hill objected to such claims diametrically. The very virtue of the United States government's *not* bringing so-called traitors to justice proved his case. But Hill did not rest his case on this one point alone. Admitting leniency, and noting that the federal government had overcome its "terrible dilemma," Hill nevertheless remained incensed over a "war of coercion…itself but a gigantic crime against humanity, and a wicked violation of their own form and principles of government."[34] Even former Confederate general Joseph Wheeler, who would eventually don a Federal uniform in the war against Spain, reminded the *Papers'* readers in 1894 of a coerced reunion, and that "A Union held together by the bayonet [is] nothing better than a military despotism." Remarking that southern states had asserted their "right of secession," he called on men of the North to make conciliation a reality.[35]

Late in the nineteenth century, the *Papers* revisited arguments dating back to the 1870s. The editors were particularly interested in contributions that admonished those who might hedge their support of the principles adopted by the Confederate government. Their numbers were not overwhelming, but nevertheless significant enough to warrant action. "[Confederates'] physical power was expended in the war, but their moral power still exists unimpaired," suggested Henry A. Wise in 1870. Wise, however, was careful to point out exceptions to this reverberating moral power. He excluded "those who call their consecrated cause 'a Lost Cause.'" According to Wise, those who said that *"the best they can do"* was to desert the faith of their cause and to beg for pardons was tantamount to confessing the charge of treason and acknowledging the highest felony know to human crime. In essence, these men "inscribed treason on the graves of heroic martyrs."[36]

Bold refutations of treason provided the framework for many addresses

and other writings published in the *Papers* over the decades. As much of
the national citizenry moved away from war issues as the years progressed,
Confederate veterans stood firm. Questions such as: "Were these men rebels
against constitutional government?" appeared often. It did not take long
for veterans to realize that honoring dead Confederates was not, by law,
treasonable activity. If that were indeed the case, said one, "then it would
be treason in us to honor their memory; to vindicate their principles." But
such denials did not stave off accusations of treason pouring continually
in from the North. Anxious former Rebels dug in and issued antagonistic
rebuttals. "Any charge of treason upon the South or its sons is simply puerile," wrote former Confederate secretary of state R. M. T. Hunter. "The man
who makes it is ridiculous, be he Conger or be he Blaine." Hunter asked a
troublesome question: "With what face could [the northern] states threaten
the punishment of treason to those who endeavored to defend their char-
tered rights?" It was this question that so agitated many former Confederates. So by the end of the century, when veterans' efforts to commemorate
the war were gathering steam across the South, former Rebels such as B. B.
Munford reminded his comrades, "While the erection of monuments to
commemorate the heroism of the Confederate soldier is a work worthy of
the highest commendation, there remains a more sacred and important
duty—vindicating his name from the charge of treason."[37]

But the *Southern Historical Society Papers* did not reach as many people
as its editorial staff and contributors had hoped. The publication functioned
as a repository—a collection of published and previously unpublished materials gathered together in a convenient form. Despite what seems like a
very appealing format for a voracious reading public, financial difficulty
and limited circulation, coupled with an exorbitant price, and the tendency
of the publications' authors to make long-winded, overly analytical arguments, meant that few ex-Confederates ever actually read the *Papers*. This
collection of newspaper articles, speeches, and other published materials
reflecting a wide cross-section of opinion in the former Confederacy may
have been more than the general reading public could handle. Instead,
many turned to the *Confederate Veteran*. There were many differences between the two publications—the *Veteran* was more easily accessible, the
contents were anecdotal and far more varied, and the publication was
relatively inexpensive. However, there were stark similarities between the

two. In terms of sentiment, contributors to both publications seemed to draw from the same well. Articles in the *Veteran* could even be described as commemorative entertainment, a description that could explain its vast popularity. But despite the magazine's colloquial literary/commemorative style, the *Veteran's* contributors were just as vehemently opposed to accusations of treason emanating from outside the South.[38]

Early in the *Veteran's* run of publication, veteran contributors noted that the preponderance of reunion activity worked to resuscitate the memory of the late war. After all, explained many veterans, their principal objective was to "consecrate the memory of the valorous soldiery we now monument." As one veteran put it, "In these times of reunions it is rather a difficult task for the old soldier to remain at his post of duty and not to be present and participate in the exercises which carry him back to those stirring scenes of war." But reunions and other gatherings as described in the *Veteran* were more than memorial meetings free from political discussion. The defense of Confederates' motives and purposes naturally came up at veterans' gatherings across the former Confederacy. "We shall look to these meetings to help us teach our children and the coming generations that the Confederate soldier was not guilty of treason, but fought from motives of patriotism, and that the South has a history of which she can justly feel proud."[39]

Topics such as the war's proper name, for example, clearly suggest that commemorations were not benign in the least. Even these seemingly trivial arguments worked to illustrate how former Confederates held fast to their determination to author the national commemorative ethos. "The Civil War is a misnomer," explained one former Confederate in 1903. "We were a band of Confederates fighting for our rights and firesides, and I think 'Confederate War' conveys the true meaning and is expressive."[40] Insisting that the war was not a rebellion, but rather a fight to preserve the ideals of the founders, many agreed with the *Veteran's* position on the war's name. "As to a name, I protest against 'Rebellion,'" argued another irritated ex-Confederate. "Yankee use has intensified its inherent hatefulness. I approve heartily your choice: 'The Confederate War;' so it *was in fact*." The more resentful acknowledged the deep divisions that remained in the country and blamed northerners for perpetuating them. "Is it not time, then, for people to cease talking about treason and rebellion, and to stop their insults in calling us rebels? If there were any rebels in that great contest, they were north of the Potomac and the Ohio—the men who trampled under foot the Constitution of our country and the liberties bequeathed us by our fathers." Former Confederates retaliated against those who would blame them for the war. John Henry Rogers, who after the war became a prominent lawyer and eventually served a term in Congress, wrote, "History, as written, if accepted as true, will consign the South to infamy... one of the most singular illustrations ever presented of the power of literature to conceal and pervert truth, to modify and falsify history, to transfer odium from the guilty to the innocent, is found in the fact that the reproach of disunion has been slipped from the shoulders of the North to those of the South."[41]

By 1916, contributors to the *Veteran* still questioned how people in the North could refer to the South as a "nest of treason filled with rebels and traitors," particularly since the seceding states had only carried out their rights of state sovereignty. Six years later, the *Veteran* printed a commemorative speech by the president of the University of Virginia, Edwin A. Alderman. This response to northern sentiment regarding the Confederate war effort concisely summed up the views of many of the *Veteran*'s contributors. "To call it rebellion is to speak ignorantly; to call it treason is to add viciousness to stupidity. It was a war of ideas, principles, political conceptions, and of loyalty to ancient ideals of English freedom." That same year, one contributor addressed the entirety of the North in an effort to defend the Confederate position that Lincoln had ignited the war. "It is exceedingly unfortunate that the Northern mind has conceived such a picture of Lincoln that any discussion of him whatever, unless couched in sycophantic terms, strikes them as profane and bordering on the sacrilegious." He attacked the "G.A.R. posts of the country" striking familiar chords. And it is doubtless true, strange as it may appear to the normal man, that, to their minds, any statement not in accord with the Lincoln apotheosis is really 'treason.'" In 1922, the few surviving Confederates agreed. Virginian Giles B. Cooke, like many other ex-Confederates, implied that the Lincoln government had denied southerners their rights and triggered the secession crisis and war. Cooke was not leaving the past behind him when he asked: "Are we Confederate veterans to be censured for resenting the false charge of being traitors because we fought to defend our homes and our constitutional rights?"[42]

Editors and contributors were determined to build the *Veteran*'s reconciliationist façade to their liking. The magazine admittedly featured numerous respectful pieces honoring regular Union veterans. After all, the overall tone of the magazine suggested that Confederates sought reconciliation with their former foes. But despite claims that "the Veteran is for making it known that Confederate veterans have a thoroughly fraternal regard for the men who fought us only to maintain the Union," some former Confederates suggested a diabolical plan on the part of "clever [northern] Republicans" to turn the written war reminiscences otherwise fostering reconciliation into the "vilest partisan pictures . . . exactly the opposite purpose for which they were designed and made."[43]

Such a commemorative style suggests unrepentant Rebels crafted their vision of commemorative culture in response to the Union version. They were tacitly reconciliationist, sometimes explicitly so. But nods to reconciliation notwithstanding, their commemorative forms were laden with confrontational language. Former Confederates' words were meant not to reestablish the Confederacy as they had once envisioned it: an independent nation. That prospect had been quashed in 1865, and the overwhelming majority of former Confederate soldiers had come to terms with that fact. But proving the rightness of their principles in direct contention with northern commemorations—those that also acknowledged reconciliatory efforts but equally reflected controversy—proved the paramount objective during the reconciliation period.

CHAPTER FOUR

THE ENDURING WORK OF THE REPUBLIC
COMMEMORATING FREEDOM IN THE ERA OF RECONCILIATION

> We are glad that the privilege was ours to make freedom a fact, our
> declaration of independence a truth, and slavery a thing of the past.
>
> —L. M. LANGE, Commander, Department of Minnesota, GAR

On July 1, 1889, New York veteran Charles A. Fuller linked succinctly the commemorative themes of union and emancipation. "Never forget," he noted before a gathering of veterans on the Gettysburg battlefield, "that we fought for Freedom and Union, and they for Slavery and Disunion; and that we stood for the right, and they for the wrong."[1] Union veterans such as Fuller and countless others considered their efforts to commemorate the war as "the concrete, crystallized expression of earnest men who hated human slavery, who fought for human rights."[2] Fuller's words mirrored those voiced at innumerable assemblies taking place all across the nation during this period. In his triumphalism and like many national celebrants recalling Union victory in the Civil War, Fuller connected the fight to preserve the Union with the sectional disruption over slavery. Moreover, he celebrated the institution's demise. The cursed institution of slavery stood at the very center of the conflict: a fact not lost on Union veterans.

During the 1880s and 1890s—and well into the twentieth century—Union commemorations resonated with tributes to emancipation. Fuller's speech was in every way ordinary. Prominent veterans such as Republican senator John J. Ingalls were likely to pepper their speeches with vehement assertions denoting slavery as the conflict's central factor. The Confederate States of America, claimed Ingalls, was "based upon the recognition of human slavery and the overthrow of human rights on this planet."[3] Union veterans' commemorative expressions in this way betrayed clear sectionalism during a period noted for its reconciliatory climate. Insisting that one section of the country had sought to undermine the national experiment while one had sought to sustain it, many remembered how a fight to preserve slavery had threatened the country's national integrity. In their efforts to commemorate the fight for union, veterans recalled the fight for freedom.[4]

White veterans belonging to organized groups in many ways echoed the attitudes of their black counterparts. The Grand Army of the Republic was the largest and most powerful fraternal and charitable organization of the nineteenth century—not incidentally, the veterans' group was integrated. Black GAR posts naturally promoted the memory of the fight to destroy slavery. The GAR, especially (and surprisingly) in the South, was also integrated at the post level—where black and white veterans stood in ranks side by side and likewise included emancipation in their commemorative efforts. While there were numerous integrated posts throughout the nation, the overwhelming number of GAR posts and other veterans' organizations were comprised entirely of white veterans. Still, white-only veterans' posts did not need to have black people around to advance memories of the emancipationist cause. Regardless of class makeup or geographic location, white veterans' organizations seemed in agreement on the endorsement of this very significant aspect of the Union war.[5]

"Their valor and their cause cannot be separated."

In 1865, "moralizing self-righteousness" pervaded the minds of victorious Unionists based in part on firsthand recollections of slavery in practice. During the war, many seeing slavery up close found it appalling. Literate soldiers, many of whom came of age in the era of Harriet Beecher Stowe's *Uncle Tom's Cabin,* could only have imagined the cruelty of the institution before 1861. Experiencing the degradation of a race of people face-to-face greatly affected a significant number who recorded their sentiments in diaries and letters home. One soldier wrote his sister shortly after he heard of the Emancipation Proclamation: "The curses of slavery has become knowledge and instead of thinking les of a negroe I have learned to think them better than many wight meen." Yet another, a soldier with the 2nd

Massachusetts Infantry, acknowledged that the proclamation "was the beginning of a great reform and the first blow struck at the real, original cause
of the war." Soldiers such as Thomas Wise Durham, a veteran of Wallace's
Zouaves, even suggested exhibiting a "young negro" who had escaped to
Union lines "to our Copperheads in the North so they could see and have
some conception of the curse of slavery."[6]

In the wake of war, former soldiers would thus celebrate the demise
of slavery alongside the preservation of the Union as a cause worthy of
their efforts. As time passed, veterans galvanized behind their efforts to
destroy slavery and elevated it to near equal importance with union. By the
twentieth century, most veterans' public talks and publications resonated
with tributes to emancipation. During the war, union was the paramount
objective—and the destruction of slavery aided in that cause. The voices of
abolitionists, who sought to pursue freedom from a moral standpoint at the
war's onset, were relatively few in comparison to those who took a practical
approach to emancipation as necessitated by the war. While the cause of
emancipation first began to make inroads into commemorative efforts in
1865, Union commemorations immediately following the war sometimes
(but not always) reflected these attitudes. But as time distanced Union
veterans from the war and their sense of self-righteousness grew, veterans
would retrospectively contemplate the war years with an added emphasis
on freedom and personal virtue. They had saved the United States—and
had done so as liberators.[7]

Union veterans were not confused when it came to slavery and the cause
of the war. In time, moral attitudes concerning the destruction of the root
of secession folded neatly into their grasp of the issues that had sparked
armed conflict. Former officers such as Wisconsin's Henry Harnden resolutely maintained Confederate culpability and Union righteousness when
he asked late in the 1890s, "Did not the sin of slavery bring this nation to
the verge of ruin, and did not the righteous act of Abraham Lincoln, in
emancipating the slaves, exalt it?" Some were quick to point out the align-
ment against the institution during the war and the connections many made
with slavery and secession. A good example of a Union veteran recalling
the fight for union and freedom is a GAR post meeting minute book entry
for September 14, 1923—very late in the reconciliation period. The author

describes how "Comrade Unkrick," a German immigrant, "entertained the Post with reminiscences of his arrival in the U.S.—the desire of the family to avoid that portion affected by slavery & his final enlistment with the 'Lincoln Soldiers' to help destroy that evil and save the Union."[8]

Connections such as these were typical. In fact, Union veterans such as George E. Sutherland would always insist, "Had it not been for Negro slavery, we should have had no rebellion to put down."[9] This sentiment partially formed the foundation of the Union commemorative culture. Veterans dismissed the "right" of a state to secede from the Union as "flimsy dogma." Assertions of this right only worked as a pretense by which leaders in the slave states sought to build an empire of the "cornerstone" of slavery. Veterans would point out that this was precisely the language used by the Confederate vice president Alexander Stephens. His March 1861 "Cornerstone Speech" was irrefutable evidence of the southern slaveholder's intentions.[10]

So Union veterans condemned the Confederate cause and its cornerstone of slavery with vicious acrimony. Respectively comparing the Union and Confederate causes with "paradise and hell," they attacked former Confederates "in whose hearts smolder the fires of secession."[11] As late as 1930, the few remaining federal soldiers were wont to censure their former adversaries. In an anonymous letter addressed to the "National, Department and local Officers and Members of Patriotic Organizations, Auxiliaries of the Grand Army of the Republic," one individual, claiming to have fought with the 31st Ohio Infantry, reminded his comrades of Confederate evils. "The plunder for which Confederates fought was slavery, for the power to earn their bread by the sweat of other men's faces, as Lincoln put it. Their valor and their cause cannot be separated."[12]

Veterans' activities of this type underscore an important obstacle for those leaning toward reconciliation. Do GAR events and individuals honoring emancipation stand out as aberrations tidily delineating the salient differences between reconciled Americans and bloody-shirt Yankees? Veterans' sentiments illustrated not deviations from but clear representations of a prevalent theme in northern reconciled commemorations. Individuals such as former Union general and congressman Benjamin F. Butler promoted "letting bygones be bygones" and insisted he was not acting "for the purpose of reviving old controversies." Nevertheless, he pointed out much to the consternation of his former enemies, "Slavery was repugnant to the moral feelings of a great many citizens." Butler, with all his reconciliationist inclinations, reduced the "causes and events which led to the War of the Rebellion [to a] single phrase—*the perpetuation of slavery.*" Many veterans, like Butler, rejoiced in the reunification of formerly warring sections into one undivided nation. But while willing to offer the hand of brotherhood to former opponents after the great conflagration, they never forgot that "such a war could not have been provoked except for the passions excited in the defense of slavery."[13]

Many shared these views. Well into the twentieth century, veterans were steadfastly determined to make sure the cause of freedom was deeply embedded into the overall drive to commemorate Union victory—despite whatever hullabaloo such efforts stirred. In 1915, just across the Potomac from Washington, D.C., at Arlington, Virginia, the former home of Robert E. Lee became a focal point for controversy. Prominently displayed in the Arlington mansion, a collection of printed copies of Union orations sparked the indignation of the United Daughters of the Confederacy (UDC). Endorsed by both the Sons of Confederate Veterans and the UCV, the UDC's protests focused on former commander of the 11th Illinois Cavalry Robert G. Ingersoll's Memorial Day oration:

> The past rushes before us—we see four millions of human beings governed by the lash, we see them bound hand and foot, we hear the strokes of cruel whips, we see the hounds tracking women through tangled swamps. We hear babes sold from the breasts of mothers. Cruelly unspeakable! Outrage infinite!
>
> The past rushes before us—we hear the roar and shriek of bursting shell. The broken fetters fall. There, heroes die. We look—instead of slaves we see men. The wand of progress touches the auction block, the slave pen, and the whipping post... and where all was want and crime we see the faces of the free.

The author of a report on the display in the Grand Army newspaper, *The National Tribune,* pointed out that most orations on display at Arlington could describe "one war as well as another, [yet] these paragraphs are the ones that make the Daughters of the Confederacy hate us."[14]

"It was not a battle of North against South, but of right against wrong."

Union veterans celebrated emancipation and the moral victory over slavery at innumerable monument dedications and reunions, through their published works, at post meetings, and at other gatherings. Former soldiers involved in monument dedications and other forms of war commemorations unquestionably shared the racist assumptions common among white Americans during the late nineteenth and early twentieth centuries. However, the tendency to overlook racial inequities was not inconsistent with veterans' frequent assertions insisting slavery had provoked sectional conflict and weakened the Union. Veterans such as Thomas M. Woodruff would share the opinions of many others. Woodruff was fond of describing the cobblestones of antebellum Washington City as a repository of "some of slavedom's nastiest slime... typical of the dark cloud that had settled over the Southern States, that just needed the Emancipation Proclamation to clear away and let in the whole sunlight of freedom." He never mentioned racial equality.[15]

Nor did former governor of Ohio and Union army veteran Captain J. B. Foraker: memorializing the illustrious career of William Tecumseh Sherman, Foraker summed up the blessings of emancipation for the Fred. C. Jones Post, GAR, in February 1891. For Foraker, who, not incidentally, incited a vehement response in the southern states whenever he issued statements such as these, noted that those who had suffered at Sherman's hand were now rejoicing. "The people of the Southern States," he claimed, "will thank all who aided to save them from slavery, disunion and political death." Perhaps exceedingly optimistic, his message is significant nonetheless. Foraker articulated neither demands for racial equality nor empathy for the plight of former slaves. Still, similar to many orators during this period, he explicitly linked slavery to disunion and emancipation to the Union cause.[16]

Regardless of veterans' presumably racist proclivities, the dominant theme of many commemorative speeches and monument dedication addresses illustrates the virtues of union and emancipation together. Contemporary testimony ranging from the celebrations of white only Blue-Gray reunions to open hostility toward emancipation suggests a southern tenor due to some implicit and explicit dismissal of the cause of freedom. However, these events and sentiments were hardly characteristic of the broader drive to commemorate Union victory. Further, such evidence provides only a glimpse of Union war commemoration undertaken throughout the reconciliation era. Veterans and other dignitaries honored rank-and-file war heroes not only as saviors of the Union but also as liberators—eliminating the stain of slavery from the national fabric.[17]

Perhaps the most popular and tangible form of commemorative activity was the monument dedication. For veterans, monuments functioned in two ways. First, the monument itself provided a lasting reminder of the sacrifices made by the Civil War generation. Most monument inscriptions mention only union, suggesting that the commemoration of emancipation never eclipsed or even came close to equaling the celebration of the fight to preserve the nation. The physical monument most often offers nothing on emancipation. But the second significant function of monument dedications offers evidence that the emancipationist cause came close to equaling celebrations of union in many cases. Monument dedication ceremonies offered Union veterans the perfect platform from which they could articulate what they deemed worthy of their fight. Beginning at some of the earliest monument dedications in the 1860s and 1870s, veterans commemorated union and freedom together—a theme that would reverberate for many years to come. At a dedication ceremony to Union soldiers in North Weymouth, Massachusetts, on Independence Day, 1868, Bay State veteran George B. Loring helped set the tone for the ensuing decades by describing how soldiers of the Union fought against "slavery and treason alike." In their success, they had delivered to the people of the republic a "nationality with human equality as its cornerstone." Other veterans in the early commemorative period agreed. They spoke often at monument dedications across the country reiterating their strong feelings concerning treason and the culpability of southern leadership. Opposition to slavery and the celebration of the institution's demise appeared with equal frequency. Observed one Rhode Islander, "We did not fight you in anger or from selfishness, but in pure love of Union and Freedom. It was not battle of North against South, but of right against wrong."[18]

By the late 1870s, such commemorative activity was commonplace in public squares and on courthouse lawns across the North. In fact, by this time, the theme of emancipation had already occupied a prominent place in a Union commemorative script. Alongside union, and sometimes over-shadowing other important aspects of United States victory (such as the significance of law and order in a democratic republic), veterans recalled the demise of slavery as among the most important when enumerating the many virtues of their triumph of arms. In 1879, a gathering of Union veterans assembled in Manchester, New Hampshire, to dedicate an elaborate monument to the heroes of the Union. The unveiling of the towering granite shaft, surrounded by bronze figures representing each of the branches of the military and topped with Liberty, certainly captured the momentous nature of the occasion. Preservation of union and the destruction of slavery received the highest honors in the ceremony. "The war is over, and peace has come," said Union veteran Daniel Clark. "Rebellion has been crushed, and slavery, which incited and envenomed the contest, has perished in the struggle." Acknowledging the finality of their victory over the institution, another veteran, J. W. Patterson, added: "The restoration of slavery to any part of our blood-stained domain, is as impossible as to unfix the decrees of fate."[19]

The rhetorical power of veterans' early statements ensured that the 1880s and 1890s, as well as the first decades of the twentieth century, resounded with testaments to the emancipationist cause. Here, during the height of the reconciliation period, when much of the United States citizenry was shifting their attentions away from Civil War era issues, veterans' memories of slavery and the fight for emancipation were on near equal footing with the cause of union. When Union veteran Seth Low addressed his comrades at the dedication of the 84th New York Volunteer Infantry Regiment's monument dedication in October 1887, he spoke for many: "Whatever other issues of constitutional interpretation were involved, they all hinged upon slavery. The preservation of the Union was the rallying cry. Without the abolition of slavery the preservation of Union was a dream."[20]

Again and again, men rallied to the banner of emancipation at monument dedications and provided words confirming that those in attendance would never forget their struggle to eradicate the institution. "If slavery were made legal to-morrow," stated one Massachusetts veteran in 1889, "no one would take advantage of it." Indeed, veterans knew that they had destroyed for all time a cursed institution that had once dogged the nation and potentially forecast its ruin. When a group of Indiana veterans dedicated their state monument at Andersonville, they made it clear that their comrades buried there had not died in vain. "The cause for which they died is enthroned," stated one former soldier; "slavery is dead. Freedom lives. The constellation of Union remains in the sky, its splendor ever growing." Those memorializing individuals with monuments were also likely to use the occasion to commemorate the fight against slavery. The monument erected to the memory of Matthew Thornton serves as a perfect example. While heaping accolades on Thornton, a founding father and signer of the Declaration of Independence, one New Hampshire veteran recalled men of a later age "whose dauntless courage and splendid powers delivered terror to a brutal system of slavery, and helped lead the way to emancipation and freedom."[21]

But while Union veterans dedicated monuments by the thousand in towns, cities, and other sites of memory across the nation, the most conspicuous monument dedications took place on Civil War battlefields. Perhaps unveiling a monument to an individual, regiment, or state on the field where the contest played out touched veterans' hearts with added fire. The veterans clearly thought so. Battlefield dedications were often delivered with references to specific ground and the bloodiest part of the battle—often either on or within sight of the ground of the monument dedication ceremony. Of all the battlefields, Gettysburg is among the most important in this respect. With over nine hundred individual monuments dedicated by the first decades of the twentieth century, the battlefield clearly stood apart from others in importance.[22] Many Union veterans retrospectively recognized Gettysburg as the war's turning point. Although the battle of Antietam more accurately marked the point in the war when the prospect of emancipation became a reality, for many, the battle of Gettysburg denoted the beginning of slavery's irreversible end.[23]

Two powerful memories suggested this idea to northern veterans. First, veterans from the Union widely acknowledged Gettysburg as the high tide of Lee's army. Though this had yet to be determined in July 1863, many Union veterans retrospectively recognized Gettysburg as the war's turning point. While this was a problematic assessment couched in terms of a "road to Appomattox" view of the war from the summer of 1863 on, veterans nevertheless remembered the three-day fight in southern Pennsylvania as the pinnacle of Lee's fortunes and the beginning of a downward trajectory toward Rebel defeat. In 1889, Pennsylvania cavalryman John W. Phillips referred to the battlefield as "this historic field [that] marks the high-tide of the great rebellion." Years later, veteran Robert Laird Stewart, also a Pennsylvanian, dedicated two entire chapters of his regiment's history to the "Turning of the Tide at Gettysburg" and the "High Water Mark on Cemetery Hill."[24] But beyond simply recalling the military contexts of the historic battle, veterans attending Grand Army of the Republic and other encampments at Gettysburg frequently revisited the battle's deeper meaning.

Illustrating the link between treason and a war to perpetuate slavery, veterans used the "high tide" leitmotif to emphasize the very spot where slavery met its end. GAR comrade Cole of New Jersey proclaimed in 1915, "I speak with all my heart when I say that you and your confreres, when you swept back the tide of rebellion and disunion—when you kindled the light again the fires of liberty that had almost been extinguished, and you swept the rebel horde back on the field of Gettysburg and buried for all time rebellion, treason, slavery, and the degradation of human labor." Years earlier, Maine veteran and former brigadier general William Hobson had voiced similar sentiments. After a detailed address on the origins of American slavery and constitutional government, Hobson reminded his audience that "the thunders of the artillery at Gettysburg proclaimed that none but free men should live in a free country, and that they all should have equal rights and power under the laws."[25]

Second, recollections of Lincoln's Gettysburg Address changing the character of the war as a "new birth of freedom" contributed to the drive to commemorate union and emancipation together. In the North, this site took on near-mythical proportions. Civilians and military veterans alike made pilgrimages to the very spot where Lincoln defined the war. Veterans thus cast the battlefield as the ideal place to celebrate the twin causes—if not always with physical representations, at least with their words. So said Pennsylvania veteran A. J. Sellers in 1888 when he delivered an oration before his comrades of the 90th Infantry Regiment on the Gettysburg battlefield. Sellers was certain to note that Lincoln's words in 1863 lifted a war to preserve the Union to a higher plane. Lincoln's "immortal words," as Sellers described them, proved the undoing of an age-old national dilemma: the problematic nature of slavery in a free republic. Such "far reaching consequences," he suggested, placed Gettysburg "among the world's greatest battles." Sellers also pointed out that "as the years roll by interest [in Gettysburg] increases."[26]

Gettysburg, "this 'Calvary of American Freedom,'" as Pennsylvania veteran John A. Danks called it in 1889, did indeed maintain an important place in the memory of the fight for freedom and union. In terms of a national commemorative culture, for Union veterans searching for a place to both advance a reconciliatory message and underscore the various ways in which their cause proved noble, Gettysburg provided the ideal commemorative spot. Shortly after the turn of the century, New York veteran Cornelius R. Parsons reminded the veterans of the Empire State's 108th Regiment that he needed not discuss the soldiers' "brave deeds or achievements" that played out on the field. Rather, "with no enmity for the foe lingering in our breasts," the battle's twin meanings in memory assumed the crux of Parsons's speech. "I would not have any of those," stated Parsons, "who have never before visited this sacred field forget that here was fought one of the greatest battles ever known, and here was won for the cause of Liberty and Union, for the cause of Freedom and Justice, a most substantial victory."[27]

In relative terms, veterans often described the commemorative significance of union and emancipation equally. In the 1880s, a pair of monument dedications commemorating the fighting tenacity of New Jersey units showed considerable dedication to both causes. In a simple, straightforward manner, the men of the 8th and 13th New Jersey Infantries sought to teach future generations of the importance of the twin themes and of those "who dared to die for the hopes of man and the redemption of a race from slavery." While one veteran mentioned that these were "silent sentinels," implying that they would not have much to show to visitors yet to come, the crux of both dedication ceremonies cemented the ideals of union and freedom together, acknowledging tacitly that the next generations would understand: "The result of the battle decided that the Republic would be saved. That this was to be a land of freemen. That the shackles of the slaves should be sold for iron. That the auction block should be burned. That all free men should breathe the fresh air of heaven direct, and not by inhalation from a master."[28]

Others added the spirit of progress to the mix. Thoughtful observers recognized changes taking place in the world around them stemming from the antebellum period. Free labor ideology echoed in a nostalgic way joining

the forces of commemoration with the flow of history. In the North, reminiscences of southern individuals working against the tenets of free labor
reminded Union veterans that they were on the right side of history and
that the demise of slavery was crucial to the progress of mankind. Asa B.
Isham, a former officer in the 7th Michigan Cavalry, former prisoner of war,
and MOLLUS companion suggested that "in the Confederacy, founded upon
servile labor, the leaders held all labor as degrading, and the worker as but
little superior to a brute."[29] Veterans connected a war fought for emancipation—and the death and destruction that accompanied it—to the promises
of free labor and all its accompanying virtues. Speaking before the veterans
of the 76th New York Infantry Regiment, again on the field at Gettysburg,
Union veteran Benjamin F. Taylor attested, "There is not a slave in all the
broad domain.... Already are the harvests of liberty being gathered from
the fields of carnage."[30]

The frequency of commemorative activity at Gettysburg early in the
reconciliation period illustrates how the battlefield held a prominent place
in the memories of Union veterans. Speeches inextricably linking union
and emancipation there further show the significance of both commemorative themes. General N. M. Crane, speaking before a gathering of New York
veterans at Gettysburg in 1888, declared that by "your deeds and suffering
this grand and glorious Nation was preserved, and the curse of slavery was
forever wiped out from this continent, and millions of human beings forever made free." Earlier that year, T. L. Barhydt also used Gettysburg to make
similar observations suggesting that the preservation of a "great Republic"
ensured that a "new confederacy" where cotton would have been king and
the traffic in human beings of no less prominence" would never be realized.
Such words and sentiment were typical across the northern commemorative
landscape and throughout the decades following the Civil War. They were
unchanged in tone and language from the dedication of the first monuments in the national cemetery to those of the early twentieth century.[31]

But these words should in no way suggest that Union veterans were
steadfastly opposed to the idea of national reconciliation. Union veterans
frequently used Gettysburg to illustrate bonds of fraternity, even though
they did so while demonstrating the righteousness of their cause. Their
intentions were to promote reconciliation on strictly northern terms. "My
brothers," said the Reverend James H. Potts before the same gathering of

Michiganders, "I am not here to arouse a spirit of rancor. . . . I honor our Southern brethren." Yet Potts nevertheless followed familiar patterns reminding his audience of the evils of the southern cause. He asked, "What were the causes leading [to the war], and what the motives which inspired it? I can find no answer to them than this—the cause of that great rebellion was the growing power of slavery." Finally, adding his personal moral judgment along with a humorous quip, he offered a few telling words. "Say what you will of the glory of the 'lost cause,' tell what you may of the unselfish devotion and courage and pluck of the Southern soldiery, still it is true that the rebellion never had a motive, and never had an inspiration higher or nobler than it drew from secession and slavery, and their logical fruits and concomitant. I love them to-day—that is, some of them, those who thank God that they got whipped."[32]

Such reconciled veterans would not diminish sentiments illustrating a conflict between two cultures that had grown apart leading to the conflict over slavery. At the dedication of the monument to the 24th Michigan Infantry at Gettysburg, for example, Luther Stephen Towbridge, formerly of the 10th Michigan Cavalry, noted that at Gettysburg two hostile ideas met in deadly strife. With visions as clearly delineated as any, one drew their sword to "murder the State" and establish a vast empire of slavery. The other struggled for human liberty.

Towbridge argued that the battle of Gettysburg marked the significance of the Union cause in terms of human progress—here he touched on a central commemorative theme and fell in line with many of his comrades. "Never before in the history of the world was any cause tested on the field of battle in which humanity had so much at stake," he suggested, and he closed by striking a further chord linking the demise of slavery to the future of mankind. "For here, on this field, not only the redemption of a race from slavery, but the possibility of self-government by a free and intelligent people hung trembling in the balance."[33]

"It is worth all the cost. Slavery has been destroyed."

While Union veterans used monument dedications as a vital component of their overall commemorative drive, in an immediate sense messages issued at such dedications reached relatively few people. Further, veterans etched hardly anything on the actual monuments summing up the key commemorative points regarding the fight to end slavery with words such as "Freedom" or "Emancipation." Only those in attendance heard firsthand the subtleties and details of veterans' speeches on this subject. Newspapers helped. Many of the nation's major news sources sent correspondents to some of the bigger events. In September 1877, on the twenty-fifth anniversary of the battle of Antietam, the *New York Times* covered the proceedings of a monument dedication to Union soldiers in Boston. Usually, speeches were either reprinted verbatim or the correspondent highlighted major commemorative points. In this case, as with many others, the *Times* reported on the prevalence of the celebration of emancipation. "Now that the system of slavery is destroyed," reported the journalist, "[no one] would raise a hand or lift a finger to replace it. The cause for which they have suffered so much will still be dear to those who have fought for it."[34] Local press in towns hosting smaller events generally covered any commemorative festivities, and larger papers picked these stories up from time to time. It was not unusual for subscribers of the *New York Times* or *Washington Post* to read—sometime after the fact—of a particular event held in a small, far-removed community.

In July 1869, for instance, the *Times* covered the speeches of General George Gordon Meade and Senator O. P. Morton at the dedication of the soldiers' monument at Gettysburg. Here, Morton suggested, "The rebellion was madness. It was the insanity of States, the delirium of millions, brought on by the pernicious influence of human slavery."[35] *Times* journalists especially praised veterans' efforts to both save the Union and destroy slavery by emphasizing key battles. The Union victory at Antietam in September 1862 figured most prominently as the precursor to Lincoln's Emancipation Proclamation. "The battle freed the slaves," described one report, and "the stake for which your battle was fought was the Republic itself. The reward you received was liberty for 3,000,000 slaves."[36] Offering an additional argument promoting economic and cultural expansion, vital components of America's emergence on the world stage in the latter part of the nineteenth and early part of the twentieth century, journalists saluted former United States soldiers and sailors for bringing about the death of an institution regarded by many as directly antithetical to the extension of liberty. Asked one such member of the press, "What fields of gold or wide expanse of land have done mankind one thousandth of the real good of the Proclamation of Emancipation?"[37]

Lesser-known papers worked in similar fashion. The *Brooklyn Eagle,* a pro-Union veteran paper dedicated to preserving the memory of the Union cause, serves as an example of the press at work perpetuating all components of Union memory. Editorials recounting veteran events and private GAR post activities offer additional insights illustrating how the death of slavery and the preservation of the Union were celebrated together. Reflecting the opinion of many articles of the same nature, one editorial of a banquet honoring U.S. Grant's birthday, where Union general Horace Porter declared "the last gun [of the Civil War] sounded the death knell of rebellion *and* put an end to slavery," exemplified how both Union causes flowed naturally together. The article provided a lesson, not only for the people of the United States but also for "all the freed peoples of the future."[38]

In addition to the mainstream press, the distribution of pamphlets to various meeting places, libraries, public buildings, and schools allowed veterans to transmit their messages to a wider audience. This integral component of the broader commemorative press, usually underscoring the significance of the cause of freedom, allowed the general public access to the speeches of GAR veterans such as Nelson Miles, who pointed out to his comrades amidst enthusiastic applause that "you left your homes [to] sustain Abraham Lincoln and the Government; you held the Nation together; you destroyed the very cause of that war; you swept for all time the accursed institution of slavery."[39] Published journals of Grand Army National Encampments further contributed to this form of the commemorative press and illustrated commemoration of both union and emancipation. The Department of the Potomac, GAR, held celebratory banquets at each yearly encampment where speakers took turns paying homage to their departmental commanders. While toasts to such men as GAR commander in chief Samuel R. Van Sant generally lauded the virtues of heroism and patriotism, many speeches also linked Lincoln, his soldiers, the preservation of union, and "the granting of freedom to an enslaved race."[40]

Speeches included within published accounts of Grand Army proceedings confirm that the topics of slavery and emancipation never strayed far from veterans' minds. The words offered at memorial services for veterans seemed to Grand Army comrades suitable vehicles to voice their approval of the Union cause to end slavery—and also appropriate words for publication. For the deceased, surviving comrades secured honor and import by describing how their brothers had fought for the progress of mankind. The narrative form worked effectively to situate the honored dead in this context. For instance, at a Decoration Day ceremony in 1889, veteran William E. Chandler acknowledged before New Hampshire's John G. Foster Post, GAR, that slave owners had once dominated the nation with an "inexorable power." Eventually, Chandler argued, "the hatred of slavery, based upon its inhuman and unchristian character, grew stronger in the North; and the great slavery conflict ensued." Others simply stated the particulars without lengthy elaborations. The sentiments, however, were precisely the same. Early in the twentieth century, John S. Maxwell, commander of the Department of New York, GAR, found it fitting to praise the "brave men who fought their battles on land and sea," who had "settled the question once for all that this fair land of ours shall ever be a land of free men and free women in fact, as well as in name."[41]

Pamphleteers issued instructional booklets and "souvenirs" similarly stressing the cause of freedom. Leaders of the GAR, as well as those of other organizations, distributed these booklets widely among the veteran ranks: they were available at post meeting halls and handed out at reunions and other gatherings. In some cases, veteran commanders issued notes requiring members to read this literature. One pamphlet outlining the appropriate dialogue for Memorial Day services included these mandatory spoken words: "To us, this is the memorial day of stalwart bravery, of patriotic heroism, of national faith. It is the freedom day of a race emancipated from bondage, and of a nation redeemed from iniquity."[42] Grand Army of the Republic members such as Nelson Monroe wrote of the slave-power conspiracy. His 1893 "souvenir," *The Grand Army Button,* suggested that "Southern leaders, accustomed to control Congress by their demands and threats," were chiefly to blame for the conflict. They "sought to make slave territory all of the region. They claimed also the right of reopening the slave trade." Monroe's treatise placing blame squarely on southern shoulders had an additional component that mirrored antebellum abolitionist sentiment. His "abhorrence for slavery and the poor bondmen flying from its torments, its indignities, and its vicious indulgence" began an intriguing narrative that concluded with a salient moral lesson justifying the staggering cost of the war. "Thus ended the rebellion. It had cost more than half a million of lives, and in the debts of the two sections and the destruction of property and values not less than eight thousand millions of money; but fearful as its expense had been, it is worth all the cost. Slavery has been destroyed."[43]

Published pamphlets worked in a variety of ways. But the emphasis on the fight for emancipation remained an important element regardless of the author's stated objective. In some instances authors mocked the efforts underway in the South to commemorate the Confederacy by illustrating the absurdity of honoring a "nation" committed to slavery. First of all, most denied the Confederacy national status. Many considered tributes to the heroes of the Confederacy unfolding at monument dedications nothing more than "follies to the conquered foes." Some even went as far as to predict a time when even southerners would show contempt for the efforts of the former citizens of the Confederate States to keep slavery perpetually intact. "Before the middle of the twentieth century," one GAR comrade gleefully predicted before a gathering of Minnesota veterans: "Two hundred millions of happy Americans will look back with horror and scorn upon the incredible baseness of a rebellion in the interest of human slavery. The grandsons of the Confederates will go forth in storm and darkness to tear down the marble shafts which are now rising in the South, and grind to tongueless dust the momentoes of confessed and pardoned crime."[44] This comrade may have missed his mark, but his hopes well illustrate one strand of an extensive refutation of the Confederate cause so intricately bound with slavery.

The Military Order of The Loyal Legion of the United States likewise functioned to broadcast veterans' commemorative messages. Each state Commandery collected MOLLUS companions' addresses to be later published in multiple volumes and distributed to libraries across the country and by subscription. Many of the pieces within these volumes concerned military sketches, anecdotes, and other war stories. But the stories were often laced with ideological, political, and social subjects. Of these concerns, slavery and emancipation assumed a prominent place. Contributors to the voluminous MOLLUS "War Papers" assumed what other veterans did when it came to being in step with historical currents. The factor of inevitability— the inexorable march of progress—fashioned the commemorative foundation for many of the War Papers' authors. In typical form, an address given in February 1895 by former brigadier general Bishop Samuel Fallows at a MOLLUS "memorial meeting" in Wisconsin underscored the connections between Lincoln's Emancipation Proclamation and the "unending work of the Republic." "[Lincoln] knew after the first shot against Sumter that freedom and union would ultimately have the grip of life. With the Union, slavery had ultimately nothing to hope."[45]

Such sentiment was as characteristic as it was commonplace. Coupled with the notion of inevitability, words spoken at MOLLUS banquets, reunions, and other gatherings also conjured images of an evil Confederacy, a wicked institution, and a cause led by avarice intent on perpetuating slavery. At a banquet honoring Union general Phillip H. Sheridan in 1883, MOLLUS companion W. Huntington Jackson highlighted what he and many of his fellow veterans saw as the crucial point: the Confederacy's leaders were "solely influenced by selfish ambition and a determination to perpetuate the curse of slavery." At the same event, former general John L. Beveridge spoke of a South "with a soul worshipping the god of slavery, with a heart filled with bitterness and hate, and with a feeling of superiority." Another referred to the "irrepressible conflict between slavery and liberty" that typified many speeches of the period.[46]

Overall, MOLLUS companions were just as intent on commemorating their fight against slavery as the GAR and other veterans' groups. At an annual meeting of the commanders in chief in Philadelphia in 1913, Commander in Chief Arnold Rand articulated the fundamental theme embedded within Union commemorative culture. Rand's words celebrating emancipation reflected those of other MOLLUS companions from the previous decades. Prominent individuals such as Rutherford B. Hayes, former Union general and nineteenth president of the United States, enthusiastically joined in the chorus of voices noting how the "greatest war in all history" had "established the Union and abolished slavery." In ways fundamental to commemorative activity in the North, companions interpreted the war as a fight to preserve the Union and rid the nation of slavery once and for all. In this manner the Unionist and emancipationist memories were inextricably bound. One complemented the other, often to the point where "cause" referred not to a singular, but to the twin themes so significant in commemorations. Speaking of Lincoln in 1907 and illustrating that by the twentieth century the memories of the Union's two causes had blended seamlessly together, one veteran reminded his audience, "Lincoln embodied to the mind of the people two great issues that were really only one—the preservation of the American Union and the abolition of slavery. At the root of both there lay a moral principle, and both appealed with overwhelming force to sentiment."[47]

"Slavery made callous the heart of the keepers of their prisons."

It was precisely the abundance of the written narrative—the exciting, riveting, and often painful war stories—that added so much weight to freedom's cause. Veterans celebrated freedom in an extensive body of regimental histories, autobiographies, and other collections of war stories and anecdotes to punctuate their countless written stories of heroism, fortitude, and suffering. They likewise used it to paint negative, sometimes demonic portraits of their former enemy. In regard to the secession crisis and war causation, some veterans dedicated lengthy passages or entire chapters to the discussion of slavery. Albert Gallitin Riddle, a wartime congressional representative from Ohio who had once written copiously in favor of arming former slaves, weighed in with elaborate detail on the dominance of emancipation as part of the Union war effort in one of his most popular postwar commemorative works. His *Recollection of War Times,* published in 1895, explained in great detail the cause of war in a chapter aptly named "Slavery Again." He further noted that waging a war against the "rebel master" had made the Union allies of the slave. Most, however, put it simply and directly. "The great embarrassment of the fathers of this country," noted Union veteran Le Grand B. Cannon, again in 1895, "was in the effort to establish and maintain a system of government under two widely different forms of civilization, the one based on freedom and the other slavery." For Cannon, a distinguished and wealthy New York banker and author, who had once been instrumental in raising the Empire State's first black regiment, the "aggravation" between these antithetical civilizations naturally led to war. By the end of the century, a near-unified commemorative script developed in the North, with many proponents agreeing that "sufferings, perils [and] death helped to preserve the national union and to free a race from chattel slavery."[48]

Prominent veteran speakers, authors, and especially regimental historians shared general agreement on the slavery and emancipation issues. A random sampling of several regimental histories, published between the end of the war to the early twentieth century and from various loyal states, reveals an unmistakable consistency over time and across place. Recalling four years of struggle, veterans of one New York unit proclaimed in the same fashion as countless other Union veterans, "The war [would] go on until the South should be hopelessly crippled, and would of necessity, yield all claim to slavery." Further, victorious Pennsylvania veterans rejoiced in a "holy trinity of results: the saving of the Nation's life, the extinction of the blot of slavery from the National escutcheon, and the establishment of the principle of the equality of all." Other veterans agreed. "O! Hateful pro-slavery rebellion!" trumpeted one Illinois volunteer in 1865 when he recalled the recent death of a comrade. "Such are the victims immolated on thy polluted shrine." By the end of the century, Union veterans had not hedged their sentiments regarding the institution. Many described the "damnable features of slavery" and frequently summarized the war as a struggle between freedom and slavery. Even when admitting that Rebels had been formidable soldiers, Union men connected the Confederate cause to the South's peculiar institution. "These old planters were kings in a way," argued a Connecticut veteran; "no wonder they fought well for their institution of slavery."[49]

The regimentals generally suggest that veterans had more on their minds than battle exploits and virtuous deeds. While a handful of authors disregarded the salient political, social, and ideological questions of the time in favor of solely military topics, most touched on subjects that were controversial nationally while generally accepted among northern veterans. The postwar commemorative culture had a curious effect on some authors, suggesting that they overestimated the positive reaction to certain elements of the Union war effort. A number recalled the day that soldiers of the Union army first learned of the Emancipation Proclamation as a day of great joy, disregarding the negative responses from a significant portion of the army and northern population in fall 1862 and winter 1863. In terms of a commemorative ethos, perhaps this part of emancipation history mattered little. Veterans certainly galvanized behind the proclamation later in life. In

1888, New Yorker Charles Bryant Fairchild called to mind the first of January 1863 as the moment when the army was "thrilled by the advent of the 'EMANCIPATION PROCLAMATION.'" Nearly twenty years later, Pennsylvanian Robert McCay Green remembered vividly his thoughts of September 1862. "A decree has gone forth declaring the emancipation of the slave, and hence the removal of the cause of the war." These men were not alone in their recollections. "Here came word of the Emancipation Proclamation," noted New York veteran Ezra de Freest Simons in 1912, recalling an encampment a few days after the battle of Antietam. "[It] thrilled the minds of the thoughtful with new hope and to intenser purpose—Providence would break the chains of the bondman."[50]

Northern commemorative forms of all types took on a similar cast. The list of examples is exhaustive, but a few notable works include personal reminiscences by John Pope, Carl Schurz, and John McAllister Schofield and narratives by Theodore Ayrault Dodge, John A. Logan, and Abner Doubleday.[51] Their consistent claims that slavery was the cause of the late civil strife and that emancipation was a worthy cause support the conclusions in perhaps the most widely read Civil War narrative published in the nineteenth century: Ulysses S. Grant's *Personal Memoirs of U.S. Grant*. Grant was revered by Union veterans and respected by many ex-Confederates for his magnanimity at Appomattox. His efforts to ease bitter sentiments in the former Confederacy, as proposed in his impressive account of the war, won him further admiration from reconciliationists. "I feel that we are on the verge of a new era," he wrote shortly before his death, "where there is to be great harmony between the Federal and Confederate. I cannot stay to be a living witness to the correctness of this prophecy; but I feel within me that it is to be so."[52] But coupled with Grant's reconciliationist bent was a steadfast devotion to the Union cause of freedom. Soon after the war, Grant acknowledged in a rousing speech honoring General Daniel Butterfield that Confederates had sowed the "germ of treason, in the vain attempt to overthrow this Government, that slavery, despotism, and sin might thrive upon its ruin." He later affirmed, "The cause of the Great War of the Rebellion against the United States will have to be attributed to slavery" and reminded Americans that the Confederate cause was "one of the worst for which a people ever fought, and one for which there was the least excuse."[53]

Grant's estimation that it was "well that we had the war when we did" underscored the institution of slavery as a hindrance to rapid expansion of trade and infrastructure that formed much of the Republican Party's "free soil" platform.[54] The editors of the *National Tribune,* the Grand Army of the Republic's principal publication, claimed, "There is no great organization of men in the country which is so thoroughly non-partisan as the G.A.R."[55] Nevertheless, in both subtle and overt ways, the organization generally endorsed the Republican Party. Comrades of the GAR often voiced ideological sentiments closely linked to Republican Party politics.[56] Republicans had devised benefits to Union soldiers in the forms of pensions and homesteads for western pioneers that were included in broader economic and expansionist policies such as land grants to railroads and tariff benefits to industrialists. The moral victory over a slavocracy only enhanced the push for these partisan political ends. Victory had stemmed a tide of stagnation intricately linked to the slave labor system and thrown open the doors for progress on Republican Party (or as defined by GAR veterans, Union) terms.[57] Prominent Republican John Hay—diplomat, assistant secretary of state, and President Lincoln's former executive secretary—touted such principles early in the twentieth century. He regarded the Republican Party and its supporters as virtuous in their moral victory over slavery. His collection of speeches reminded those willing to look beyond the "forgetfulness" of Blue-Gray reunions that since the [Republican] soldier "checked the aggression of slavery, the humblest old Republican in America [had] the right to be proud that in the days of his youth in the presence of the momentous questions he judged right; and if he is sleeping in his honored grave his children may justly be glad of his decision."[58]

Veterans' public sentiments in the form of published speeches, memoirs, and narratives sounded much like the private opinions voiced at GAR meetings away from the public eye. But most Americans would never hear (or read) the words spoken behind the closed doors of private GAR post meetings. For this reason, meeting minutes alone provide little in regard to understanding broader public memory or veterans' message to (and influence on) the public at large. However, veterans' private discourse with their comrades compared to what they intended for the public reveals many similarities. This striking comparison suggests that veterans were not creating dissimilar public and private messages, at least in terms of slavery and emancipation. Their public messages concerning this delicate and controversial issue were genuinely shared among many former Union soldiers.

But: "Beside these grand results," mentioned one Massachusetts veteran late in the nineteenth century when discussing the preservation of the Union, "others—freedom to all men and the elevation of the oppressed, and the destruction of the great barbarity of the age, slavery, the fruitful cause of all our national troubles—are among the blessings which flow from our successes." Many agreed. In 1884, veterans of the Phil Sheridan Post 10 in Oshkosh, Wisconsin, memorialized their fallen comrades by voicing "a kindly feeling for those who gave their lives in defense of our country and who are willing to do what lies in their power towards keeping in remembrance the honored dead—who helped to make this land of ours free." In 1891, members of Ohio's Fred C. Jones Post 401 in Cincinnati noted that the nation had once been "stranded on the rock of human slavery, a curse that could only be obliterated from our fair republic but the "sacrifice of blood." And in January 1905, the celebration of slavery's demise moved one New Yorker to voice his sentiments in verse:

> In God's name let us march to the mutinous South
> I shall fall, as will many of you
> But halt not till slavery's rebellion shall cease—
> Till the Father of Waters shall flow
> Unviewed by a slave from Itasca Lake
> To the far Gulf of Mexico.[59]

Early in the twentieth century, the recording officer of the Charles Graves Post, Department of Wisconsin, GAR, voiced his approval of the fighting spirit of state commander Henry Hamden. In a lightly punctuated, yet moving tribute shortly following Hamden's death, the Wisconsin veteran eulogized: "We have lost a brother Comrade A man of courage A Champion and a Leader He battled for a Nations life for the rights of slaves, the dignity of labor and the liberty of all. What more can we ask man Let him rest in peace."[60] As late as the 1920s, Union veterans, their ranks inexorably thinning, gathered in reunion to recall their wartime adventures. In some ways they fought the war over again—if not with musket volleys, with words. Although time had passed, wartime issues remained as salient late in the veterans' lives as they had in the 1860s. Suppression of treason had been their guiding cause in 1861; they now added additional emphasis to the cause of freedom. "We all consider it a great pleasure to meet as often as possible to live over again those stirring times from 1861 to 65, and keep ever alive the memories of those days, when we left home and loved ones, to fight and die, if need be, to preserve the Union and make our Nation free."[61]

Former Union colonel and GAR comrade Stuart Taylor once asked the crowd attending an 1887 Memorial Day gathering at Grant's Tomb in New York City, "Was the appeal to war unproductive, oh! soldiers?" Not surprisingly, Taylor expressed his utter satisfaction with the war's results: "We had solved the great problem which had been too hard for civic wisdom. With a territory unmutilated, our Constitution uncorrupted, a united people crowned with added glory the immortal truths of the Declaration of Independence of a race. Liberty stood erect without a frown."[62] At the same event, poet Red Emerson Brooks offered his opinion with verse noteworthy for its reconciliatory title, *All hail to the North! And all hail to the South!*

> An army sprang up as the storm comes at sea;
> O'er the peace-ladened air, when the winds are set free!
> Gath'ring fury anon,
> This fierce cyclone moved on—
> Till down went the foes of this heaven-cherished Nation!
> And Slavery lay buried 'neath wild desolation.[63]

Generally agreeing that slavery had equaled degradation for all Americans, black and white, Union veterans used commemoration to underscore how slavery weakened the moral fiber of the slave owners. First, the institution made southerners coldhearted men, as evidenced by the harsh treatment of Union prisoners of war. "Slavery," suggested one Pennsylvania veteran, "made callous the heart of the keepers of their prisons." Another veteran simply stated that "this [was] a war to free the master as well as the slave. It [was] a war to break the shackles of ignorance, prejudice, malice and hate that fetter the souls of our misguided brethren who shot to death your comrades in the name of the 'commercialism' in human slavery. It [was] not a war to save the Union alone, it [was] a war to make the Union worth saving."[64]

CHAPTER FIVE

CALUMNY MASQUERADING AS HISTORY
REBELS' RESPONSE TO THE EMANCIPATIONIST CAUSE

> The crusade not only destroyed slavery, but entailed upon the South a social
> condition for which the crusaders suggest no relief, and a condition which
> seems to be without the hope of peaceful solution.
>
> —JOHN RANDOLPH TUCKER, wartime attorney general for the state of Virginia

Confronting the issue of slavery within the context of a national commemorative ethos was an unsettling problem for former Confederates. Most set
out to paint a noble picture of the Confederate States of America despite the
existence of slavery within its borders. With sweeping strokes, they lauded
heroes, despised villains, both internal and external, and insisted that the
slavery issue had meant little to Confederate independence. In so doing,
former Confederates were fabulously successful at convincing other white
southerners and their sons and daughters that slavery was incidental to
their cause. Many remarked that the institution was a dying system in 1860,
stating that even without war, slavery would not have lasted much longer
in the southern states. But their efforts fell largely on deaf ears outside the
South. Try as they might, they could not separate their cause from the vexing reality that slavery, from the perspective of their northern counterparts,
was intricately connected to the Confederacy.

In the battle to control the memory of the war, general agreement among
the veterans instrumental in creating the Confederate commemorative culture materialized in the form of rebuttals defending the Rebel cause. Slavery was among the most prominent of topics, and heated arguments over
the institution weakened any glimmer of an uncontested reconciliation.
The veterans' words offer substantial evidence regarding the recognition of
slavery as an important factor in national Civil War memory. Their reactive,

sometimes defensive, but often antagonistic positions and lengthy discussions of the insignificance of slavery in opposition to arguments to the contrary suggest a sectional contention over the fundamental significance of slavery to the war and the profound connections between the institution, secession, and the establishment of the Confederate States of America. Former Confederates, perhaps unwittingly, thus articulated double-edged implications. They argued that slavery was not a contributing factor to secession and war but acknowledged that Union veterans disagreed. As a result, slavery and emancipation became, whether ex-Rebels liked it or not, a central component of the effort to commemorate the Confederate cause.

Despite Confederate veterans' attempts to distance their cause from their peculiar institution, they nevertheless engaged the postwar slavery/emancipation discussion and used it as a sounding board to emphasize various commemorative themes. Their commemorations exposed the perceived malevolent designs of their former enemies and provided justification for former Confederates venting sectional hostilities. Few sat still and allowed Union veterans to dictate the terms of reconciliation. While rebutting the Union emancipationist cause, former Confederates seized opportunities to attack. Commemorative themes initiated the slavery topic as a means to segue into the "real" reason for the war, blaming northerners for suppression of rights, jealousy, vindictiveness, abuses of power, and other wicked deeds. The many who recognized slavery as at least the "occasion" of the war or the few who outright acknowledged slavery as a causal factor offered similar critiques of their Yankee foe. They exposed northerners as fanatics determined to use emancipation as a tool to punish the South. All of these themes, sometimes existing alone and sometimes in combination, did more than simply vindicate the southern cause. They illustrated a problematical road to reconciliation and a contested commemorative culture.

Driving a wedge between sections, former Confederates used memories of slavery to their advantage. Veterans maintained as the cornerstone of their commemorative efforts the fundamental assertion that northerners had burdened the nation with and profited from the institution. But as many ex-Rebels deduced, because slavery was short-lived in the northern states, antebellum northerners turned their attentions to sectional agitation over the institution. This line of reasoning supported arguments that sweepingly referred to nearly all northerners as emancipationists. Confederates could go as far as to depict Yankee crusaders ruthlessly invading slave-holding states forcing abolition at the point of a bayonet—in effect realizing the ambitions of the fanatical John Brown, the man many considered "The would be Catiline of the South, the demigod of the abolitionists."[1] Late in the reconciliation period former Confederates would persistently equate the North with the fanaticism of John Brown and other abolitionists, suggesting retrospectively that most in the North had been aligned against the southern institution. John H. Reagan reported at an encampment of Confederate veterans, immediately following a reconciliationist speech by UCV commander John Brown Gordon, that when John Brown was convicted and hanged by the authorities of the state of Virginia for "levying war on the state in an effort to bring about a horrid war between the negroes and whites" many of the northern churches were draped in mourning and northern people "applauded his efforts and eulogized this felon as a hero."[2]

As former Confederates crafted their version of history, they generally did so as antagonists. They were out of step with a significant number—perhaps millions—in the North who had lived through the turmoil of war and commemorated their fight as a clash over slavery. First, writings and speeches illustrate that while they attempted to dominate the memory of the war, theirs were contested efforts—efforts that ultimately revealed the sectional character of reconciliatory trends. Second, the fact that former Confederates reacted aggressively when discussing slavery reveals that Americans were in fact contesting any reconciliatory commemorative culture founded on southern terms. Granted, a few former Confederates diverged on the relationship between slavery and the war and agreed with their northern counterparts. Individuals such as the famed "Gray Ghost" John Singleton Mosby matter-of-factly pointed out in his personal correspondence, "If it was right to own slaves as property it was right to fight for it." Mosby maintained, "The south went to war on account of slavery." But these men were clearly exceptional and in terms of how former Confederates shaped the memory of the war, greatly outnumbered by their contemporaries. Most commemorating former Rebels fell in Confederate line, vehemently defended their position that slavery was only an occasion, rather than the cause of the war, and finally insisted that Federals had used emancipation to weaken the Confederate fighting strength.[3]

In so doing, ex-Rebels faced a Herculean task. In many ways, Federals had the upper hand. After all, commemorating Union veterans rarely missed a chance to remind a reunited nation that soldiers of the United States had saved the Union and destroyed slavery. Not only had they preserved the idea of a democratic republic, but they had also hastened the termination of an institution reviled by much of the rest of the world. History, in a progressive sense, favored the Union—a point that many in the world recognized and embraced. Few things irritated former Confederates more. So they took commemorating Union veterans to task for suggesting that Confederates supported a disruptive, treasonous cause, bent on maintaining a backward slave system. Their words resounded throughout the Confederate commemorative press and created a lasting culture.

"Were you thinking of your slaves when you carried all in the balance?"

Whether writing general narratives or testifying on the strengths of Confederate ideas, former Confederates almost unanimously framed the war as a battle in defense of home and hearth. Widely accepted in the South and sometimes acknowledged in the North, this emphasized bravery and fortitude against long odds and could support the reconciliation premise precisely because so many left slavery out of this part of Confederate history. Indeed, former Rebels often told their noble story without directly confronting wartime issues. In a national context, many Union veterans could agree that Confederates had exhibited superlative bravery and had indeed fought a defensive war against invasion, just as Union soldiers had done in Pennsylvania, Maryland, and Kentucky. However, popularity notwithstanding, Rebel war stories about defending their homes against invasion offer no ironclad proof that Americans in general dismissed the slavery and emancipation issues during the postwar years—it only suggests that many Americans recognized that Confederates had demonstrated bravery in defense of their homes.

But the defense of home theme could readily supplant outsider allegations about the preservation of slavery. Even if ex-Confederates were not pushed on the slavery issue, ordinary veterans and prominent former soldiers—men of diverse origins and opinions—differed little in their approach to this topic. Well-known veterans such as Virginia politician and Richmond Howitzers member James Taylor Ellyson numbered among the many who shared this idea. Ellyson's words carried with them a great deal of import. After the war he had served Virginia as a state senator and as the mayor of Richmond. He would eventually rise to the office of lieutenant governor in the early twentieth century. In 1895, he suggested in a speech reprinted in the *Southern Historical Society Papers* that no one would believe that "the men who drew their swords in defense of [their mother's] hearth-stones are worthy of reproach."[4] His words were like Gospel to former Confederates and his sentiment would echo with others' contributions reflecting on the southern cause. Ellyson's reasoning stemmed from treatments written immediately after the war, many of which contemplated the deaths of southern soldiers. Articles appearing in such publications as *The Land We Love* in 1867 suggested that a noble death in "defense of home is equal to a life-time of glory."[5] Such testimony continued to reverberate as more and more former Confederates joined in the commemorative effort later in the nineteenth century with the growth of the UCV and their official publication, *The Confederate Veteran*. As wartime reminiscences and published regimental histories grew in number, a diverse group of former Confederates mirrored the "defense of home" theme in their writings. Simply put, offered one unnamed Confederate veteran in 1922, "The Confederate soldier fought and suffered for defense of home without hope of reward." From 1865 to the twentieth century, this theme remained prominent and virtually unchanged in commemorative writing.[6]

Their contention was clear, straightforward, uncomplicated, and unencumbered by long-winded ideological arguments. In June 1893, former Confederate Robert Stiles summarized veterans' sentiments regarding the defense of home in a brief eulogy to those University of Virginia students who perished under arms: "There is a naked simplicity and sincerity of right in the man who defends his hearth-stone, which does not belong to him who invades it," he pronounced in ways that sounded much like a sermon. Stiles deemed the defense of home argument "God-implanted" and an irrepressible right that called nearly half of the University's students to war in 1861, many of whom did not return. Three years earlier, veteran W. Gordon McCabe, a former soldier who had withdrawn from the University of Virginia when war erupted, had expressed views very similar to Stiles's

"naked simplicity and sincerity of right" when he spoke to a gathering
of former Confederates. Instructing his comrades to teach "our children
and children's children of the courage and devotion of [Confederate] heroes," McCabe taught that southern patriots had "freely shed their blood
for hearth, home, and country."[7]

Were such authors deliberately attempting to excise the problematic
slavery issue from Confederate commemorations? Perhaps. One cannot
readily or always clearly recognize their intentions regarding this issue but
merely take note that slavery was absent from their commemorative narratives. Because slavery cast such a negative shadow over the memory of the
war in a national context, one can safely assume that most Confederates,
given the choice, would rather have ignored slavery when commemorating
their cause. But those commemorating the Confederacy added multiple
layers in addition to the theme of defense against invasion and developed
a commemorative culture steeped in divisive sectional argumentation. They
disputed those in the North who insisted the war had been carried out by
Confederates to protect slavery—as a clearly defined group they balked at
this notion and defended a war to protect constitutional ideals. Yet disagreement with their former enemies necessarily meant that ex-Rebels had
to contend with the volatile slavery subject. Ignoring the issue was rarely
an option. The onus of commemorating the Confederate cause with this
very obvious blemish proved vexing for many—and thus they redirected
culpability northward.

Former Confederates could not simply disregard slavery, although many
would have gladly done so. Often, the theme of fighting for home and
hearth served as a direct response to the contention that Confederates had
enlisted to preserve slavery as an institution. Thus they coupled one commemorative theme with clear refutations of outside attacks, building on a
prominent Confederate commemorative motif. In reactive style, Benjamin
Washington Jones, a young, self-educated farmer from Pearson's Swamp,
Virginia, recollected early in the twentieth century his reasons for enlist-
ing in the Surry Light Artillery: "I marched and camped, and labored and
suffered, in the effort to turn aside the tidal wave of a ruthless invasion
that was sweeping over our land from the Potomac to the Rio Grande,
and leaving behind it scarred and desolated homes, and destitution and
misery." But Jones, who so adamantly saw the war as a fight over personal

rights and property, recognized the lack of consensus in terms of how all Americans remembered the war—like so many who shared in his postwar sensibilities. Acknowledging an entirely differing view of the meaning of the war, Jones betrayed a number of lingering sectional issues. "These were the principles for which we contended. It were these incentives, and not the narrow question of perpetuating negro slavery, that animated the heart of the private soldier of the South."[8]

Jones's reflective message resounded throughout commemorative literature dealing with the war's origins. In 1889, J. Schiebert, a former observer from the Prussian Army who had seen action with the Confederacy, noted that the slavery issue only became "inscribed on the banners of the war" when it "was seen [that it could be] enlisted on the side of the North." He had a point; most in the Union army had enlisted to preserve the Union. Schiebert neglected the facts however, that the slavery issue had incited war and that many Union soldiers accepted the destruction of the institution as both a necessary war measure and a moral good. These two troubling (from a southern perspective) particulars were lost on most former Confederates. Seven years earlier, South Carolina veteran Edward McGrady stated to a gathering of his Palmetto State comrades, "From the origin of our government, the war was inevitable, had slavery never existed." While the reasoning behind secession seemed to be lost on McGrady, his insistence that the actual fighting rested on other motives is noteworthy. By the late 1890s, most, in line with the *Confederate Veteran* historical committee, were content with reporting that "the true cause of the war was the dignified withdrawal from the United States to avoid continued breeches of domestic tranquility." It was not, as northern authors claimed, to prevent "the high moral purpose to destroy slavery."[9]

Others were compelled to deal with the slavery issue, if only to write it off to political folly. Confederate veterans reflected on the politics of the 1850s and attributed much of the sectional discord to northerners—particularly the antislavery/free labor faction. These people, lumped together as abolitionists, forced the slavery issue on the national Democratic Party, leading eventually to its disintegration and an open door for black Republican abolitionists to seize the executive branch of government. Isaac Gordon Bradwell, who was an eighteen-year-old student when he enlisted to serve with the 31st Georgia Infantry Regiment and who, like Benjamin

Jones, resolved to fight when "Lincoln sent his armies across the Potomac to kill the citizens of Virginia and burn their homes," implied much more regarding the slavery issue. Abolitionists, suggested Bradwell in 1923, were enemies of the South and forced irrevocable splits in the Democratic Party, "while we floated down stream to our inevitable destruction." Although he did so obliquely, Bradwell described a series of events originating with the sectional disruption over slavery. Defense of home became necessary only after Lincoln, who Bradwell described incorrectly as an avowed abolitionist, thought it necessary to invade and destroy the South and its institutions.[10]

Even if some, like Bradwell, could admit that slavery pushed the sections farther apart, few would admit that they fought to preserve the institution. Rather, the overwhelming majority of former Confederates who mentioned slavery adamantly denied this troubling "slavery as the cause" accusation emanating from so many northern sources. But they engaged in debate with their former enemies nonetheless. "It is charged that slavery was the corner stone of the Southern Confederacy," reported a cross former Confederate in 1905; "what are we to say about the Constitution?" Like those of many of his comrades, this former soldier's words revealed a persistent resentment over the subject: "We are told that slavery was the cause of the war and that the citizen-soldiers of the South sprang to arms in defense of slavery." Adding further exclamatory remarks, he added, "Calumny, masquerading as history, has told the world that that battle flag of yours was the emblem of slave power, and that you fought not for liberty but for the right to hold your fellow man in bondage." Apart from his surprising, albeit suspicious, spirit of kindness toward his black "countrymen," this Rebel's remarks were altogether ordinary. "Tell me, were you thinking of your slaves when you carried all in the balance, your lives, your fortunes, your sacred homes?"[11]

Sidestepping or simply denying that Confederates fought to preserve a social system was only a segment of the overall Confederate commemorative culture. Confederate veterans sensed outside judgment reminiscent of the days when *Uncle Tom's Cabin* helped galvanize the North against southern slaveholders—a postwar moral judgment depicting the evils of slavery and by implication the Confederate cause. This inspired more heated and argumentative rebuttals directly addressing northern veterans' commemorative efforts. Former Confederates feared that future generations would look negatively upon their war for independence, especially since world opinion seemed to be aligning in favor of progress and basic human rights, and northerners were making great headway in painting a picture of a backward, arrested, and inhumane old South and Confederate society. Rebel veterans thus scrambled to correct any Yankee misconceptions. The resulting commemorative writings were part of a concerted effort to destroy northern credibility. Prominent Louisville, Kentucky, native Manly B. Curry felt it necessary to explain that something malicious was taking place in regard to how northerners viewed slavery. "Our opponents," stated Curry, "have published tons of literature giving the dark side of slavery. We have little telling of its bright side." Modern readers may find such statements perverse, but contemporaries were likely to cast slavery as a positive good, indicating how slavery introduced Christianity, morals, and a work ethic to black people.[12] Curry's principal objective was to admonish his fellow southerners, advising them not to build monuments to heroes but to counteract the "influence and misrepresentation" of modern reflection of *Uncle Tom's Cabin* and other works so as not to style those heroes as objects of contempt. Apparently, Yankee authors had already inflicted a great deal of damage on the American youth. "For the past eight years I have been living in St. Paul, Minn. I have talked with children there on the subject of slavery, and the poison is doing its work, and doing it effectually." Curry enlisted all who would listen to help reverse this alarming trend, observing "Even this day a man who owned slaves is looked upon as little, if any better, than a slave trader, a pirate, or a brigand, who held prisoners for a ransom." The great names of our ancestors, Curry feared, were destined to be the "theme of jests and the subject for taunts."[13]

Although a great number of northerners looked favorably on a romanticized notion of the "faithful slave," popularized by southern literature depicting a bygone age, former Confederates perceived, rightfully so, that a broad cross-section of Union veterans cast a negative light on their way of life. Faced with persistent challenges, ex-Rebels attempted to head off the sentiment resonating loudly throughout much of the rest of the nation. They compared northern accusations in the late nineteenth and early twentieth centuries to antebellum reactions to Harriet Beecher Stowe's novel. This worked effectively as ammunition to illustrate a northern pattern when it came to misleading the nation about slavery and the war. Concerns over contemporary resonance of an *Uncle Tom's Cabin* sentiment were part of a general feeling that all in the North had aligned against them. The trouble was, Confederate veterans feared that northerners were making, or could potentially make, interpretive inroads south of the Mason-Dixon and effectively change history. While reactions to commemorations lauding the demise of slavery varied in intensity, many would agree that sectionalism remained alive—at least in terms of exactly how soldiers remembered the war.[14]

The ongoing battle against the use of northern textbooks in southern schools serves as the clearest example of overt postwar hostility toward Yankees regarding slavery, emancipation, and the meaning of the war. Those with a vested interest in keeping a Confederate history alive for southern schoolchildren generated a great deal of antagonistic opinion during the decades leading up to the twentieth century. The indefatigable work of women's organizations such as the United Daughters of the Confederacy ensured that textbooks would not go unexamined. Their principal motive was to counter a dubious history which taught Southern children that their Confederate fathers were guilty of any number of crimes. In so doing, the UDC committed itself to a highly politicized agenda in the face of outside agitation—their primary mission being to eradicate unsuitable textbooks from southern classrooms.[15]

Without question, women's groups' unrelenting campaign against northern interpretations of the war fostered and even accelerated resentment among the white southern population, a point that veterans were quick to illustrate. Yet, to emphasize the women's crusade against northern textbooks would be to obscure the degree to which men's activities colored the reconciliation façade. Confederate veterans were equally appalled at the attempts made from outside the South to establish Civil War history from a Yankee perspective. Vicious attacks against specific northern authors in such publications as *Confederate Veteran* seemed to negate the publisher's apolitical claims. "If a roll call were taken of the children in the South to-day," suggested one veteran, "they would in large numbers be found to be abolitionists, intense and fanatical, and in full sympathy with the Northern side." This assumption stemmed from evidence denoting that from childhood they had been taught by teachers who believe this and had been "fed on such children's books as 'The Elsie Books,' Louisa Alcott's stories, and kindred ones, besides being allowed to see moving-picture shows of 'Uncle Tom's Cabin,' Sheridan's ride, contest between Merrimac and Monitor, and the like."[16]

Confederate veterans named names and enumerated in excruciating detail the Yankee offenses against postwar southern schoolchildren. By the turn of the century, former Rebels noted glowing northern affirmations of the emancipationist cause as their principal grievance. Veterans lashed out especially at northern author John Fiske, a Connecticut-born intellectual who spent the war years studying at Harvard University. Fiske, whose writings included philosophical interpretations of the works of Charles Darwin, also wrote numerous histories. Among these were a study concerning the Mississippi Valley during the war and a general survey of United States history for schools published in 1895. The latter drew the most fire from former Confederates. "With elegance of diction and wealth of knowledge sufficient to blind and interest a multitude of readers," reported the *Veteran,* "he devotes himself to this object. He is an advocate seeking to procure pardon for the wrongdoings of his own section by persuading the world of the guilt of ours." Attacking Fiske's words as "unsavory" and "slanderous sentences," particularly in regard to his claims that Virginians were slave breeders who fought solely to protect their institution, this former Confederate fired missives north to expose unwarranted sectional attacks.[17]

Contributors to commemorative magazines such as *Confederate Veteran* also harshly condemned general histories written with a northern bias. In 1884, Confederate veteran William Allan, a "distinguished Master of Arts at the University of Virginia," former staff officer under both Stonewall Jackson and Jubal Early, and former confidant of Robert E. Lee, offered his opinion on M. E. Thalheimer's *Eclectic History of the United States.* "This is one of those worthless histories which we suppose will be written and printed so long as money can be made by doing so.... Many devices have been resorted to in order to increase its salableness, some good, but more of them bad." Apparently, the only good things about this book that Allan could find were its "good paper and clear type." Otherwise, he attacked with ferocity, arguing that its analysis of the slavery issue was both "unfair and disingenuous."[18] Fortunately for southerners thirsting for an "unbiased" history, the *Veteran* gladly provided an acceptable reading list. Yet again, an underlying sectionalism informed the *Veteran's* position. Books such J. L. M. Curry's *Southern States and Constitution* and George Lundt's *The Origin of the Late War,* among others, were suitable for "our people."[19]

In the early decades of the twentieth century, UCV veterans looked northward and found abolitionist sentiment still alive and well. The principles found within the pages of such publications as William Lloyd Garrison's *The Liberator* seemed, to incensed former Confederates, to be informing the writings of Yankee authors. In 1912, the UCV endorsed Hilary A. Herbert's *Abolition Crusade and Its Consequences*. The author, a Confederate veteran who served as a congressman from Alabama and Grover Cleveland's secretary of the navy, divided his book into four parts, surveying American history as fundamentally sectional. "Sectional agitation brought about secession," claimed Herbert, and after the war, southerners finally reclaimed self-government despite "the sectional movement started by the Abolitionists." Herbert admitted in his study that slavery functioned as the primary sectional issue both before and during the war, and that the aims of abolitionists dominated the political landscape in the postwar years. "In my opinion," stated Herbert, "the best way to study history is topically, especially if the periods are dominated by one single movement [abolition]." "My idea was to give in a connected way the underlying reason which, on the one side, brought about secession, and on the other brought about a war of coercion." This was a curious book for the UCV to endorse, simply because slavery figured so importantly. Yet they endorsed it nevertheless, perhaps because the volume essentially indicted outside agitators—thus absolving southerners of blame for the war. One reviewer proposed that this work, steeped in sectionalism, "be adopted as a school textbook, so that thereby our children may learn the history of their country aright." Although clearly it was a book biased from a southern perspective, reviewers claimed that it contained a "compass truth of history, written by an impartial pen."[20]

While northern works of history made easy targets, ex-Rebels also set their sights on the other commemorative forms resonating in the North. These attacks likewise gained steam in the late nineteenth and early twentieth centuries and functioned as a significant component of Confederate commemorative literature. Former Rebels drew on any number of themes concerning the slavery issue, including causation and abolition. Like other commemorative authors, most assumed a defensive posture when discussing the Confederate cause but were just as likely to attack those whom they saw as perpetrating vicious lies. Ex-Confederates' personal reminiscences were well suited for attacks along these lines. In varying degrees of emphasis, most Rebel contributors to this strand of commemorative culture agreed that Yankees were rewriting history in their favor. Although time separated the veterans from the events of war and may have clouded the memories of some, the meaning of the war from their perspective remained fresh and vibrant. If anything, preserving a memory of a noble war demanded that former Confederates lash out at their onetime enemies—contentions, in this regard remained as robust as ever.

"Did you ever see a Confederate soldier who was fighting for slavery?"

This recurring tendency to assess the reliability of northern commemorations appears to have been one primary motive for authors of Confederate reminiscence and regimental histories. Again underscoring one or more slavery-related topics, authors of personal recollections were wont to highlight discord in otherwise reconciliatory works. Most were highly suspicious of their Yankee counterparts' assertions. "With the greatest regard for truthfulness," stated Marylander George Wilson Booth long after the war, "I can say that never for one moment did the question of slavery or the perpetuation of that institution enter into the decision of my course." Booth, a Baltimore native who enlisted in Confederate service at the age of sixteen, seemed determined to interject into his otherwise benign narrative a point of contention. Implying that there was more than one interpretation of the slavery issue, he clearly aligned himself on the Confederate side. Yet Booth did not simply dismiss the point of slavery and move on; he used the issue to accent a Confederate perspective: "What caused the war?" Booth was ultimately elusive on this point but he alluded to the "vindictiveness of the northern politician and his hatred of our southern brethren." While not explicitly responding to any particular northerner, this manner of war reminiscence was a response to the "perverted Yankee histories" of the war nonetheless.[21]

"Not to gain military glory did [Confederates] fight," argued Waylon Fuller Dunaway, "although this meed must be awarded them. Nor was the perpetuation of African slavery the object for which they took up arms." Dunaway, a veteran of the 47th Virginia Infantry, an attorney who was

disbarred for failing to take the loyalty oath, and a Lancaster County minister, added his voice to the many who pointed out that most Confederate
soldiers owned no slaves. Here he picked up on a common argument that
former Rebels repeated for as long as they lived, despite the clearly flawed
logic: most Confederates were not slaveholders, therefore they could not
have been fighting to preserve the institution. But his real aim seemed more
to recall the sectionalism defining the United States at the time of the secession crisis. "They simply resisted subjugation by a hostile government;
whose right to rule them they denied." Using the slavery issue as a rhetorical device to revisit wartime sectionalism in early in the twentieth century,
Dunaway's words suggest this vital issue still weighed heavily on his mind.[22]

Again defying logic, many former Confederates shared the idea that all
Yankeedom sided with the tenets of abolitionism and reinforced notions
of antebellum sectionalism early in the twentieth century. For William E.
Bevens, veteran of the 1st Arkansas Infantry Regiment, recollections of
the war resounded with sectionalism related to slavery. "The Yankees," he
argued, "were burning with sympathy for the poor, oppressed negro, and
negroes were permitted to do pretty much as they pleased."[23] Like Bevens,
others supported the antebellum Union, but recognized the divisions over
the institution and sought to record them for future generations. Other old
Unionists could agree with former Confederate surgeon Ferdinand Eugene
Daniel, whose main contribution along these lines directly illustrated sectional contention. "The love of Union was strong, and the opposition to
slavery, the result of fifty years' quarrel over it, had attained almost the
aspect of a religious crusade. [The] abolitionist party in the North, practi-
cally said: Constitution be hanged! The evil of slavery must go."[24] Daniel
conceded that slavery had played a pivotal role in the secession crisis and
ultimately to the war for Confederate independence—something worthy
of remembrance decades later.

But Daniel was not merely acquiescing to the Yankee idea that the war
was over slavery; he was turning the accusatory table—a key element of
the Confederate commemorative script. These commemorations sounded
more akin to polemics than simple defenses of a way of life, even if former
Rebels had to admit that slavery was somehow involved in the crisis that led
to war. In a forthright statement, W. J. McMurray, former surgeon with the
20th Tennessee Infantry Regiment, wrote in his unit's regimental history:

"We of the South believe that there were three great primary causes that brought on the war ... 1st—African slavery. 2nd—Constant encroachment by the Federal or Northern party upon the reserved rights of the Southern States. 3rd—The right to secede from the Federal Union." That McMurray would assign slavery the first position in a list of causes suggests a bold move on his part. It was a rare event indeed where a Confederate veteran would make such admissions. Outweighing even the vague "defense of rights" argument typically offered by most former Confederates, McMurray's position on slavery probably raised more than a few eyebrows. Yet his acknowledgment provided an opening to take a much more familiar tack in terms of outlining culpability and thus countering haughty northern claims of moral superiority—the war may have been over slavery, but blame rested on northern shoulders.[25]

McMurray made good on his promises to show how "the Southern States believed that their reserved rights had been invaded, their property was about to be destroyed, and their social fabric upturned by the Northern party." In so doing, he painted a tellingly negative portrait of his northern countrymen that fell precisely in line with numerous other critiques of antebellum and wartime northern society. A long and meticulously detailed argument concerning the right of secession preceded an instructive note for future generations: "The victors write the history of the vanquished and control public sentiment whether it be true or false, until it finds lodgment in the public mind and becomes settled as historical facts. Such is the course that our enemies at the close of the war, and since, have attempted to pursue." Yet rather than dwell on particular examples, McMurray chose to provide his own lesson as a rebuttal to the extensive "misrepresentation and bitter calumny." Slavery assumed center stage in this veteran's story, but northerners took the brunt of argument when he outlined the complexities of the issue. The antebellum crisis over slavery in the territories was exacerbated not by southern slaveholders, but by "Anti-slavery people in the New England States" and other "armed northerners." This seemed ironic to McMurray for the simple reasoning that New Englanders had not only reaped great financial rewards from the slave trade but had been the institution's primary accelerant. "Is not this a strange fact," questioned McMurray, " that these soldiers from Massachusetts—the State that bought and sold more negroes into slavery than all the others combined—should shed the first blood for the emancipation of the very negroes that she had brought from Africa and enslaved?"[26]

For all of the commemoration revealing the connections between slavery and the northern states, what leaps off the page is McMurray's unfiltered animosity toward his northern countrymen and his use of the abolition movement as the primary distinguishing characteristic. Referring to northern states such as Massachusetts and New Hampshire as "bitter" and "rabid," he painted a caricature illustrating all northerners as cut from the same abolitionist cloth. "The people who lived north of Mason and Dixon's line were against slavery," he argued in the most revealing terms. Moreover, drawing on the well-worn argument that slavery had been protected by the Constitution, if not expressly so then implicitly, McMurray summoned the memory of antislavery conventions in Ohio, New York, and elsewhere suggesting that they (referring not to abolitionists necessarily, but to northerners in general) had pledged "their *sacred honor*" to violate the Constitution. An act the amounted to nothing less than "treason against the laws of their country."[27]

In terms of recognizing slavery as the primary cause of the war, McMurray was atypical. But in other respects, his sentiments were characteristic—particularly those that furthered resentment toward the North during a period noted for its reconciliatory trends. Ranging from perverse attempts at humor such as one South Carolinian's wishes that his dog bite no person but "Yankees and free niggers"[28] to carefully argued treatments of the war in general, former Rebels seemed bent on destroying northern credibility, refuting misleading claims, and painting a negative image of northerners altogether. Slavery, emancipation, and the abolition movement often figured as the primary points of Confederate commemorative literature. Either singularly or in combination, Confederate veterans generally drifted back to this subject. One case criticized Union officers for their apparent reversal of opinion regarding the emancipation issue. Recalling a conversation with Federal officers captured at Tiptonville in 1862, Edward Young McMorries, a former private with the 1st Alabama Infantry and the author of the unit's regimental history, acknowledged that Union officers "repelled as an insult the least insinuation that the war, professedly for the Union, involved the emancipation of slaves." While "doubtless sincere at the time," McMorries censured the Union officers who could not "make good this declaration upon the issuance of Lincoln's Emancipation Proclamation." Such censures were not isolated, but rather part of a wider attempt by this author to portray Yankees in the most negative light.[29]

Virginia veteran William Henry Morgan's recollections further typify this phenomenon. Morgan had served under James L. Kemper in George Pickett's division and was captured in May 1864. After the war, he worked as one of Campbell County's most prominent lawyers. Published in 1911 and widely circulated, Morgan's reminiscences set out to commemorate a soldier's life, describing camp activities, incessant drilling and marching, and various military engagements. The early sections of the book, however, accent heated polemics where slavery figures centrally. "The question of slavery in the Southern States was not an issue at the beginning of the war, as many believe," he directly pointed out. Who exactly the "many" Morgan referred to is unknown, but one can surmise that he is challenging northern sentiments refuting his claims, particularly as he seems most willing to attack northerners at every turn. Point after point rebukes "New England Yankees" as the original perpetrators of African slavery and condemns Yankee shipping for the perpetration of the institution. While Morgan admitted that slavery became an issue as the war progressed, he did so in a way that highlighted the sectionalism of "rabid abolitionists" in New England who were "always jealous of the South [and] opposed everything that would extend the power and influence of the Southern States." The significance rests not so much with the accuracy of what Morgan said in regard to slavery, but why he felt the need to articulate his thoughts on the matter so far removed from the events. Reminding his readers that lingering anger continued to drive a wedge between sections—that northerners were determined still to control the South, Morgan reiterated that the "Yankees of New England will hold on to their pet policies ... abusing and vilifying the South."[30]

"And when they levied war to carry out their policy
they became traitors."

With striking similarity, authors of various commemorative forms worked tirelessly to refute vilifications of the South by underscoring causation, northern sectionalism, and the fanaticism of abolitionists. Northerners had initiated an era of slavery in America but had perverted the national founding documents in an attempt to subvert property rights enshrined in the Constitution. Northerners had thus committed treason. Further, they were the guilty party when it came to easing sectional tensions. Veterans' words such as those of Robert S. Bevier from 1879 reminded former Confederates that northerners had pushed the slavery issue on the South—that pretensions of nobility for emancipation and the Union cause were merely ways to destroy the South from within. Theirs was a cause of aggrandizement, suggested many, and a way for a tyrannical autocracy to force itself and impose its will on those who had resolutely expressed loyalty to the old Union. "It is with criminal negligence we permitted the foes to define the issue upon which we fought," suggested Bevier. "They proclaimed that it was the 'Irrepressible Conflict' between the ideas representing the freedom and the slavery of the African race. It was nothing of the kind, it was the very antipode of that question." Sectionalism guided Bevier's thoughts in this regard. While he may have singled out the ambitions of the "Abolitionists of the North, who recognized the extinction of slavery in the South as the essential object of the war," his harshest words attacked the federal government and manufacturers of the East—those not necessarily interested in slaves but in the submission of the South.[31]

Bevier's "educational" theme—presenting a Confederate interpretation of slavery while blaming outsiders for establishing and perpetuating the institution—resonated in the early twentieth century. Adding a touch of personal reminiscences to Confederate histories, many felt compelled to discuss slavery by challenging outside interpretations. Moreover, some would proceed to remind readers of the long-established and persistent sectionalism driving the nation further apart. Former Confederates such as Jabez Lamar Monroe Curry, a prominent attorney who had served the Confederacy both as Alabama's representative in the first Confederate Congress and as colonel of the 5th Alabama Cavalry, argued precisely these points in his 1901 publication, *Civil History of the Government of the Confederate States*. Curry was an extremely influential and powerful politician after the war. One of Alabama's favorite sons, he was active in postwar education and helped establish public school systems across the South. Although he claimed to support Jefferson Davis's notion that the Confederacy fought not for slavery, but independence, the peculiar institution figured prominently in Curry's depiction of the Confederate experiment. But like many other

former Confederates, Curry regarded the institution as only the "proxi-
mate cause" of the war. Quoting Alexander Stephens, Curry maintained
that slavery was "infinitely less important to the seceding states than the
recognition of the great principle of constitutional liberty. There was with
us no such thing as slavery in the true and proper sense of that word."[32]

"Our sole object," Curry argued, "is to present the Southern side of the
controversy as it existed in 1860, and to vindicate it from accusations and
aspersions which are based on ignorance and injustice." Although a self-
proclaimed reconciliationist, Curry touched nearly every sectional base. He
both acknowledged controversy between the sections and aligned the South
as a whole against outsiders, presumably "ignorant and unjust" Yankees. As
if to further the slavery debate in the twentieth century, Curry, consistent
with his fellow veteran commemorators, turned the table on northerners by
blaming them for the institution. Slavery, in Curry's words, was "fastened on
[the South] by New England." Implying that the southerners and ultimately
the Confederacy merely inherited the institution, Curry capitalized on and
perpetuated a recurring theme in Confederate reminiscences.[33]

Many, embracing commemorative efforts both in print and spoken in
public, believed they had an airtight case against northern accusations.
From a Confederate perspective, their logic was infallible—especially since
they generally observed history from a retrospective advantage and ignored
documents preserved from the secession crisis period. "The pious sons
of New England," Robert C. Cave sarcastically stated at the unveiling of
Richmond's Soldiers and Sailors monument in May 1894, "were slave owners and deterred by no conscientious scruples from plying the slave trade
with proverbial Yankee enterprise." Cave, a former Confederate private
who was called to the pulpit after the war, was the well-respected pastor of
the Seventh Street Christian Church and a member of R. E. Lee Camp in
Richmond. Addressing the throng, noted for being boisterous, if somewhat
"less imposing" than the gathering for the dedication of Richmond's Lee
statue four years earlier, Cave reasoned carefully. Northerners had essentially imposed slavery on the southern people, who not incidentally, had no
particular inclination toward it. Yet it became a southern institution, Cave
admitted, not because the "rights of others were dearer to the Northern
than to the Southern heart," but because slavery was better suited for the
southern climate. With slavery thus fastened on to them by circumstances,

southern people "sought to deal with it in the wisest and most humane way." In short, Cave responded to northern accusations in much the same way as many other former Confederates: the southerners were not fighting to preserve an institution they had never really wanted to begin with. Thus revealing the hypocrisy of his former foe, Cave used slavery as a means to underscore the distinctions between sections. His 1911 publication, *Defending The Southern Confederacy: The Men in Gray,* articulated precisely the same sentiment. Cave strongly opposed northern ideas regarding the centrality of slavery and emancipation in the war and spent the remainder of his life working to prove otherwise.[34]

Praising the work of Jefferson Davis, a veteran on the *Southern Historical Society Papers* editorial staff noted, "Our friends at the North were mainly instrumental in establishing [slavery]." This seemed particularly curious for a section that had mobilized against the institution. But, the author points out, the North only discovered that slavery was the "sum of all villainies *after* they had sold their slaves and pocketed the money." Only then did they proceed with their sectional agitation. "Slavery was not the cause," he notes, "but an incident of the separation, and that for the secession movement the North, and not the South, was responsible."[35] Even Joseph Wheeler, the consummate reconciliationist, looked northward when it came to the nagging problem of interpreting slavery. "The South had been opposed to the institution from the beginning, northern industry profited more from slavery than anyone and ultimately the North had nullified the Constitution in terms of property rights." For Wheeler, the South had sought to honor the Union and the Constitution while the North distorted the intentions of the founders and in the end destroyed the Union as it was.[36]

By the 1920s, this line of reasoning was written in stone, both figuratively and literally, all across the South. Former Confederates had essentially absolved themselves of any crimes—persistently denying culpability in terms of war causation. Veterans such as S. A. Steele, a former Confederate from Nashville, summed up succinctly what by now had become a Confederate truism. Insisting that at the formation of the republic the "South was more opposed to slavery than the North," Steel remarked that Confederates—descendants of the revolutionary fathers Washington, Jefferson, and Henry—could not possibly have been fighting to preserve the institution. Thus when northerners condemned the Confederacy as a "belligerent fighting to make slavery a permanent principle on which to establish and maintain a national life," Steel responded in heated fashion. Indeed, he referred to one Union veteran's words as the "bray of an ass mingling in the roar of the great wave that roils around the world." He further implied that those "up North" were in general agreement on the subject. Steel's archetypal words exactly mirrored those who had observed speeches and other commemorations radiating from the North for decades. They were equally typical of those who felt the pressures of outside commemorative interpretations of the war. The North, it seemed, was more responsible for slavery in North America, and ultimately for disunion, than those who eventually seceded to form their own republic.[37]

Even the more temperate writers of the day furthered this persistent commemorative trend and made sure to issue some sort of response to northern versions of history. They used commemorative publications such as the *Southern Historical Society Papers,* the immensely popular *Confederate Veteran,* and others periodicals to transmit their arguments. By the late nineteenth century, their words filled the southern commemorative press. "Northern writers and speakers," suggested prominent veteran John Lamb, "have attempted to show that the South plunged this country into desperate war for the purpose of perpetuating slavery." Lamb, former Confederate cavalryman, sheriff, county surveyor, and seven-term United States congressman who would eventually take the helm as superintendent of the Confederate Battle Abbey in Richmond, invited his audience to look for themselves in a 1910 speech commemorating the battle of New Market. "If any man will read the debates between Lincoln and Douglas just prior to the war, or the Emancipation Proclamation, he will see that slavery was not the cause of action or its abolition its intent." Assuring fellow ex-Rebels that the Confederacy would have soon emancipated slaves had they been successful, he simply asked, "Did you ever see a [Confederate] soldier who was fighting for slavery?"[38]

That was not all. Most, like Lamb, were certain that Yankees had ignored what actually happened and twisted history to their liking. Yet former Confederates also concluded that the North was to blame for the problems created by emancipation. They suggested that the fight resulting in slavery's demise only disrupted a natural system, one that northerners were now unable to fully comprehend. From the Confederate perspective, the invading armies of the Union had little interest in the plight of former slaves once they had secured victory. Ex-Rebels accepting this point were compelled to infuse their position on slavery and emancipation into postwar writings. Northern veteran authors insisted that they had fought the war to both preserve the Union and destroy slavery and likewise maintained that Confederates saw independence as the primary means to secure the institution. Why then, asked former Rebels, had the Yankees turned their backs on freedmen in the aftermath of war? They answered through elaborately detailed arguments nearly always asserting the slavery was the occasion and not the cause of the war, and that emancipation only weakened the Confederate war effort and ultimately undermined the southern way of life.

Ex-Rebels had lived in a society based on a well-grounded racial hierarchy—a society instituted by the founding generation and one that northern aggression had disrupted. Some former Confederates sought to reassert their authority after the war, at first with partial success. But social control especially in the first decades following the war was at best tenuous, at worst impossible. White people saw this control issue a serious problem, and many turned to extralegal, often violent means to assert authority. While groups of white renegades terrorized freed people in secret, others publicly called for northern "liberators" to do something in terms of correcting obstinate former slaves. "The crusade not only destroyed slavery, but entailed upon the South a social condition for which the crusaders suggest no relief, and a condition which seems to be without the hope of peaceful solution," suggested John Randolph Tucker in 1893. "Those who had no interest in the relation have inoculated the South with a social and political disease for which their statesmen have provided no remedy and can find no panacea. These were the issues upon which the Southern states seceded, and defended their imperiled rights with valor, constancy and fortitude which has made them immortal." Others would readily agree. Regarding the race problem, one irritated veteran claimed, "The north owes an unfulfilled duty to the south."[39]

Authors of commemorative war stories looked with dismay at the postwar southern landscape—especially at the travails of their former slaves and the corruption of northern agencies that from a Confederate perspective offered no real assistance or guidance in the chaotic aftermath of war. "What was called the 'Freedman's Bureau' caused most of our trouble" suggested

Georgia veteran and former prisoner of war Peter Pelham. He noted that other "dishonest northern men" did more "damage retarding reconstruction in many places than the corrupt Freedman Bureau." For Pelham, former Confederates were blacks' best allies: "Negroes generally were true to their former masters—until corrupted for plunder and office by corrupt [northern] whites." Gustavus W. Smith, former major general and Confederate secretary of war, shared these sentiments. When commemorating the life of the recently deceased Charles Jones Colcock, who had served as colonel with the 3rd South Carolina Cavalry and was noted to be a "typical citizen and soldier of the old regime," he included the dismal circumstances of his home county's former slaves. He observed, "It was the period of that demoralizing Federal agency, 'the Freedmen's Bureau,' with its false promises, 'forty acres and a mule,' and kindred follies."[40]

Gathering writings from across the former Confederacy, the editors of the *Southern Historical Society Papers,* with good reason, feared that future generations would fall under the spell of the victors. Reprinting vitriolic speeches, the *SHSP* reminded readers of such dangers, linking the defense of their cause to northern calumny. "They will be told that their fathers were oligarchs, aristocrats, slave drivers, rebels, traitors, who, to perpetuate the sin of human slavery, tried to throttle the life out of the nation. What if this be but false cant and calumny? Constant repetition will give it something of the authority of truth. Our descendants will see these slanders repeated in Northern publications." Similarly, an angry former Confederate asked the readers of *Confederate Veteran,* "How can the Northern people bring charges so infamous against such a record of loyalty and patriotism? The South was not responsible for slavery nor eager for its perpetuation.... We are not willing to be handed down to the coming generation as a race of slave-drivers and traitors. So let the North lay aside her prejudice and hatred, and seek the truth instead."[41]

Former Confederates had evidently found their version of the truth in opposition to northern authors, and it was this particular truth that they repeated: abolitionists had stirred the fires of hatred against the South and its institutions, and they had garnered the favor of the majority of the North even though southerners were well on the way to abolishing slavery on their own. With optimism, whatever "opinions scouted by northern historians," former Confederates anticipated the day when future generations would side with the South—when all would empathize with their cause and recognize the North for its fanaticism. "Future historians," suggested Randolph Harrison McKim at a gathering of veterans in 1904, "will see in the abolition crusade which was launched by William Lloyd Garrison, Jan. 1st, 1831, the real cause of this revolution in Southern sentiment on the subject of slavery."[42]

But during the last decades of the nineteenth century and the first of the twentieth, the victor of the battle over who would write the history of the war was yet to be determined. Ultimately, those who supported reconciliation could not resist exposing the failings of their former enemies in some fashion. Those who avowed that "this is an era of peace" seemed willing to embrace their former enemies only on terms of Confederate making. Former Confederate general John T. Morgan, a United States senator from Alabama, admitted that many in the North had not cared for abolitionist aims. However, "[Those] who denied the propositions on which the Abolition party was based followed its lead, believing it was safer to violate the Constitution than to lose power." Moreover, Union soldiers were simply doing the bidding of northern emancipationists. By his estimation, thousands of Union soldiers engaged in the destruction of slavery as their purpose, but they were assisted by tens of thousands who fought to save the Union alone.[43]

Confederate veterans were not always of the same opinion regarding slavery. Some played it down, and some implicitly or explicitly confessed that slavery caused the war. Most who recorded their thoughts on the matter, however, turned their words about slavery against the North, stood firmly behind the constitutional right of ownership and law, and in some cases, labeled those who had fought against them traitors. "When the people of the Northern States commenced their crusade for the abolition of slavery," argued one Confederate veteran, "they commenced a distinct violation of the Constitution and laws; they made themselves a lawless, revolutionary party. And when they levied war to carry out their policy they became traitors. Their pretense was that they were fighting to save the Union ... their purpose was to overthrow the Constitution."[44]

Former Confederates did not stand idly by while the victorious North assaulted their cherished heritage. As time distanced the attentions of some Americans from the events of war and Reconstruction, and as the federal government loosened reins of control over the defeated states, Confederate veterans regained much of the power over their former dominions and established a lasting, compelling, and purely Confederate commemorative culture. They did so in public with their own visions of reconciliation. In many cases, these men combined the symbols of rebellion with professions of loyalty to the United States—in seemingly contradictory ways. However conflicting such imagery may have been, former Confederates, now claiming to be proud Americans, flaunted their Confederate heritage in public ceremonies, often sporting Rebel gray and waving the Confederate battle flag. While Union veterans fought to preserve their memories, former Confederates did the same—quite frequently defending their cause with vehemence reminiscent of the 1860s.

LEGACIES UNDER PRESSURE

Hey it ain't over ... it's just the longest cease-fire in history.

—KEVIN DOLAN aka Johnny Reb,
reenactor on *Sabers and Roses,* Civil War reality show, 2008

One of the most heated displays of animosity reminiscent of veterans' commemorative cultures took place in April 2003. That spring, a statue of Abraham Lincoln and his son Tad was unveiled on the grounds of the old Tredegar Iron Works in Richmond, Virginia. The idea of Lincoln once again "invading" the Confederate capital city as he had done during the final days of the war made headlines in the Old Dominion. Sounding very much like their Confederate ancestors, a significant number of white southerners responded with sharp language. Virginia state delegate Richard H. Black concluded, "Putting a statue to [Lincoln] there is sort of like putting the Confederate flag at the Lincoln Memorial." Black even went so far as to accept a request from the local Sons of Confederate Veterans chapter to seek an injunction from state attorney general Jerry W. Kilgore until they could determine the legality of placing a statue at Tredegar. Bragdon Bowling, commander of the Virginia Division, SCV, whose great-grandfather John Stephen Cannon fought for the Confederacy, saw the statue as the definitive humiliation. Stating, "[Lincoln] sat at Jefferson Davis's desk and propped his feet up on the desk," Bowling was clearly incensed. Together with Black, Bowling and others argued that a Lincoln statue had no place in Virginia. "We've got a Lincoln Memorial not that distant," argued Bowling. "It's a huge memorial right across the Potomac. I suppose you could put a Lincoln memorial in every city of the United States. I'm not sure what that accomplishes."[1]

Even the proposition of a Lincoln statue in Richmond certainly had accomplished one thing: a response that included some stinging acts of opposition. Robert Kline, chairman of the Richmond-based nonprofit organization U.S. Historical Society Inc., had been considering a Lincoln statue for at least twenty of the fifty years he had spent in the former Confederate capital. Kline, who had helped raise $1 million for the Museum of the Confederacy, knew that a statue of the president would not be entirely embraced. He wished to avoid controversy by diplomatically situating the monument far from Richmond's famed Monument Avenue, a street that boasts some of the most celebrated figures of the Confederate war effort.[2] Discussing Lincoln, Kline noted: "He came down here as a gesture of reconciliation . . . he came as a peacemaker." Reconciliation notwithstanding, Kline admitted of his plans, "We've had more controversy [than anticipated] and it's been more vitriolic, attacking us and attacking Lincoln as a traitor and a vicious conqueror." Some even suggested that a Lincoln statue in Richmond would be comparable to an Osama Bin Laden statue at Ground Zero in Manhattan. Undeterred, Kline, along with the Richmond City Council, which approved $45,000 for the monument's site, along with supporters such as American University's American Studies professor Edward Smith, worked diligently to raise the estimated $250,000 for the monument. Throughout the planning process, Kline and his supporters confronted allegations of corruption and criminal activity alongside the usual taunts from incensed neo-Confederates. Kline and others who claimed to be "delighted that Lincoln is in Richmond again" came under intense fire from heritage groups and prominent Virginia state officials. State representative Virgil Goode, for example, called into question the society's nonprofit status in an effort to quash fundraising activities meant to pay for the monument.[3]

On the day of the unveiling of New York sculptor David Frech's statue depicting Lincoln and Tad sitting on a bench against a granite wall, those in attendance witnessed both applause and jeers. The statue was meant to convey sectional healing, yet while Lieutenant Governor Tim Kaine gave a dedication address, a small plane pulling a banner reading "*sic semper tyrannis*" flew overhead. Invoking the Virginia state motto, "thus always to tyrants," the words allegedly shouted by John Wilkes Booth to the audience at Ford's Theatre after he had shot the president in 1865, sent a rather clear message. If catcalls from the audience were not enough, several offered their words to the press in attendance. "When somebody does something as ignorant as put Abe Lincoln in the capital of the Confederacy," declared H. K. Edgerton, America's most well-known black neo-Confederate, "how can I not come to protest it? You don't put a criminal up and call it reconciliation, and Lincoln was a war criminal on top of it."[4]

The previous day, about one hundred members of the Virginia SCV had rallied in Hollywood Cemetery at the gravesite of Confederate president Jefferson Davis in protest of the Lincoln statue. There, Bragdon Bowling iterated his opposition: "They have no concept of history and how it might be the wrong place to put the statue. As a Southerner, I'm offended. You wouldn't put a statue of Winston Churchill in downtown Berlin, would you? What's next, a statue of Sherman in Atlanta?" The protest was the culmination of a year-long battle by Confederate sympathizers, including hundreds of reenactors and SCV members. But the activity during the unveiling itself overshadowed the earlier protest. One group of protesters displayed a large Confederate Navy Jack on a hilltop overlooking the ceremony, and a few scuffles ensued when officials barred attendants from bringing Confederate flags to the ceremony.[5]

Are such protestations the inheritors of Confederate veterans' commemorative culture? In many ways, those in the twenty-first century who follow the Confederate explanation of the war—its causes, consequences, and reasons for defeat—have adopted the commemorative rhetoric of their Rebel ancestors. Advocates of Confederate heritage, it seems, have found their identity in the past and follow precisely what an author writing in the 1930s called an "inescapable tradition."[6] But a tradition that once defined near-unity of white southerners now describes quickly diminishing, if exceptionally vocal, groups of heritage advocates and neo-Confederates. Feeling the pressure of the now dominant national sense that the Confederate States of America waged a war to protect slavery, these groups have lashed out in anger. Contributors to Confederate heritage Web sites and blogs are continually fueling the sectional fires—they defend their position that the war had nothing to do with slavery while referring to Yankees as tyrants, ruthless invaders, or cruel and vindictive conquerors—exactly as their Confederate ancestors did in the decades following the Civil War.[7]

In some cases, the movement to promote Confederate heritage lambasts the North in a tongue-in-cheek fashion. T-shirts emblazoned with the Stars and Bars (the first Confederate national flag) reading: "If at first you don't secede..." or "It's a Southern thing, you wouldn't understand," suggest good-natured humor at the expense of a few Yankees. Parking lot placards displaying the Confederate battle flag commanding: "Confederate parking only—all others go back North!" and posters showing a red "X" through an image of William Tecumseh Sherman or a battle flag stating "Occupied Since 1865" imply a message of slightly more animosity. Web sites broadcasting a clear message of hostility take wartime bitterness to an extreme. And finally, the perverse bumper sticker appearing here and there showing a grizzled veteran in Confederate gray admitting, "If I knew we were going to lose, I would have picked my own cotton," reveals the racialized undertones of contested memories (while curiously admitting that the war somehow involved slavery). Whatever method harnessed to make their points, heritage groups and neo-Confederates are clearly concerned that their history is under attack—perhaps rapidly fading. Regardless of heritage group protests, Confederate flags have come down from statehouses across the South, Confederate symbols have been banned in schools, and textbooks overwhelmingly cite slavery as the central cause for southern secession. The rest of the nation does indeed seem to be steadily closing in on the stalwart Confederate sympathizers. In this respect, it may appear that the Confederacy is perhaps on its last legs, especially in terms of slavery, emancipation, and Civil War memory.

Does this mean neo-Confederates are losing the peace? Would their Confederate ancestors be disheartened at such alarming news? Without question, more and more Americans now celebrate national unity with the acknowledgment that slavery was at the root of sectional conflict. This fact troubles neo-Confederates and heritage advocates as it troubled their forefathers. But does this suggest that sectional harmony is nearing realization on northern terms? This may not be the precise way to analyze commemorative activity in the twenty-first century. Historical events determined that many U.S. citizens now residing in the states constituting the loyal Union in 1860 have little or no perceived connection to the war. Vast waves of immigrants arriving on America's shores in the late nineteenth and early twentieth centuries and settling primarily in the Northeast and Midwest did not share the experiences of the war generation and thus did not share the same lived memories as their veteran neighbors. A significant number of white southerners, however, can (and happily will upon request) trace their roots to the war. Their identities as southerners and as Americans are in many cases inextricably bound both to the war and to its enduring legacy south of the Potomac. As such, many of the greatest battles over memory are waged in the former Confederacy—especially as southerners observe an inexorable domination of a Civil War narrative focused on a war to end slavery and a progressive celebration of emancipation. The modern battle over Civil War memory is largely a southern phenomenon.

But while these battles of words rage on Web logs, social media Web sites, and physical sites of memory, another vitally important strand of commemoration that the veterans themselves saw as paramount has slipped quietly beneath the surface. It is not the issue of slavery, but the issue of treason that has faded from the battle over Civil War memory. Union veterans steadfastly maintained that union *and* emancipation were noble causes—but the memory of union has all but disappeared. This is an odd state of affairs. Restoration of the Union motivated millions to flock to the colors. And during the commemorative period, veterans were sure to point out that the word "Union" meant suppression of rebellion. Confederate veterans naturally considered treason preposterous; they fought to preserve the Constitution of their forefathers, not destroy it. In their lifetimes, Civil War veterans commemorating the war waged a heated battle over this profound issue in conjunction with the fight over the meaning of slavery. But if the question of slavery is now at least edging closer to resolution, the issue of treason—supplanted by overwhelmingly racialized memory of the war—is far from resolved. In this respect, the Confederacy can claim one last interpretive victory, not because one side was right and the other wrong, but because the issue has yet to fully reemerge from below the surface.

As the last Civil War veterans passed away in the early and mid-twentieth century, the possibility that their memories would be relegated to obscurity seemed all too real to the few remaining. What would happen to these recollections—these reminiscences that had so perfectly informed two distinctly different visions of Civil War commemoration? The final few living veterans had every reason to worry. When the last of the veterans died, proponents of the national commemorative culture denoting progress and unity filed many of their memories away in archives around the nation. While living, veterans' sentiments had so infused the war generation's commemorative cultures that each side could claim that they had—without question—represented the true meaning of the conflict. They had served the founders well, and their visions of reconciliation reflected a living commitment to sectional perceptions of the founding generation. Their self-evident truths accompanied the commemorative markers left behind by veterans of the war. But in ways these were not silent sentinels. Although generations far removed from the conflict would greatly distance themselves from contentious issues when scripting the broader national commemorative ethos, causes of the past are not always so easily forgotten in the present. As opposing truths battled in the nineteenth century, their legacies would resurface on commemorative landscapes throughout the twentieth. They would meet again in conflict in the twenty-first. Civil War veterans have long passed, but their memories compete for dominance still.

NOTES

ABBREVIATIONS

GARM Grand Army of the Republic Museum, Philadelphia, Pennsylvania
GNMP Gettysburg National Military Park, Gettysburg, Pennsylvania
MOC   Eleanor S. Brockenbrough Library, Museum of the Confederacy, Richmond,
      Virginia
NYPL New York Public Library, New York, New York
UVA   Albert and Sidney Small Special Collections Library, University of Virginia,
      Charlottesville, Virginia
VHS   Virginia Historical Society, Richmond, Virginia
WVM   Wisconsin Veterans Museum, Madison, Wisconsin

INTRODUCTION

1. "Oration of W. T. Collins" in Ernest F. M. Faehtz, *The National Memorial Day: A Record of Ceremonies over the Graves of the Union Soldiers, May 29 and 30, 1869* (Washington City: Headquarters of the Grand Army of the Republic, 1870), 37; William R. Hanby, "Address of William R. Hanby," in *Unveiling and Dedication of Monument to Hood's Texas Brigade on the Capitol Grounds at Austin, Texas, Thursday, October Twenty-Seven, Nineteen Hundred and Ten and Minutes of the Thirty-Ninth Annual Reunion of Hood's Texas Brigade Association Held in Senate Chamber at Austin, Texas, October Twenty-Six and Twenty-Seven, Nineteen Hundred and Ten, Together with a Short Monument and Brigade Association History and Confederate Scrapbook* (Houston: F. B. Chilton, 1911), 36 [volume hereafter cited as *Hood's Texas Brigade Scrapbook*].

2. A good frame of reference for a "Reconciliation era" should include the 1885 publication of Ulysses S. Grant's nationally respected *Personal Memoirs of U. S. Grant* and the 1915 theatrical release of D. W. Griffith's *The Birth of a Nation*, a film with a decidedly reconciliationist bent. Both of these cultural landmarks offer a message of reconciliation while simultaneously leaning toward either a northern or southern interpretation of the conflict, respectively. The range of sectional tones intrinsic (as I argue) to the reconciliation period and the implications suggested by such sentiment will be discussed at length in the following chapters. Further, I recognize the problematic nature of strict periodization and thus reserve the right

to look beyond the borders of these dates. Scholars would surely agree that individuals uttered most expressions of reconciliation during the late nineteenth and early twentieth centuries. However, one can find seeds of the reconciliation period sown at such varied places as Appomattox Courthouse (in 1865), in the pages of the southern Reconstruction press, and in the studies authored by northern public figures immediately following the war. Likewise, while the troubling divisions embedded in reunion faded with the deaths of the last surviving Civil War veterans, they did not cease to exist. Indeed, the memories of those who killed one another in great profusion between 1861 and 1865 survive still. On loyal United States soldiers' and civilians' commitment to the notion of Union, see Gary W. Gallagher, *The Union War* (Cambridge, MA: Harvard University Press, 2011). On the Civil War in film, see Melvyn Stokes, "The Civil War in the Movies," in *Legacy of Disunion: The Enduring Significance of the American Civil War*, ed. Susan-Mary Grant and Peter J. Parish (Baton Rouge: University of Louisiana Press, 2003), 65–78; Gary W. Gallagher, *Causes Won, Lost, & Forgotten: How Hollywood and Popular Art Shape What We Know about the Civil War* (Chapel Hill: University of North Carolina Press, 2008).

3. Caroline E. Janney, *Remembering the Civil War: Reunion and the Limits of Reconciliation* (Chapel Hill: University of North Carolina Press, 2013).

4. By the 1890s, Republican Party leadership, including many Union veterans and others who lived through the tumult of the 1860s, discovered that voters had lost interest in sectional politics and instead focused on economic issues in a rapidly industrializing nation. Republicans, according to one historian, turned their backs on their southern wing—thus ignoring sectional issues concerning civil rights—and looked toward the national economy. See Charles W. Calhoun, *From Bloody Shirt to Full Dinner Pail: The Transformation of Politics and Governance in the Gilded Age* (New York: Hill & Wang, 2010). While it may be true that many distanced themselves from sectionalizing sweeping national movements in the name of expedient reunion, veterans from both parties held tight to their sectional war memories embedded within their commemorative cultures.

5. *Charleston News and Courier,* April 25, 1918; On William Gordon McCabe on reconciliation, see Ray Drinkwater, "War and Reconciliation in the 19th-Century American South: The Personal Journey of William Gordon McCabe," *Southern Historian* 15 (Spring 1994): 5–23; Armistead C. Gordon, *William Gordon McCabe: A Brief Memoir* (Richmond, VA: Old Dominion Press, 1920). See also Susan-Mary Grant, "'The Charter of Its Birthright': The Civil War and American Nationalism," in Grant and Parish, *Legacy of Disunion,* 188–206; Susan-Mary Grant, *North over South: Northern Nationalism and American Identity in the Antebellum Era* (Lawrence: University Press of Kansas, 2000).

6. *The Civil War,* directed By Ken Burns, produced by Ken Burns and Ric Burns, episode nine, "The Better Angels of Our Nature" (PBS Home Video, 1990). Scholars too have emphasized a prewar fragmented collection of loyalties. Joyce Appleby, Lynn Hunt, and Margaret Jacob examine the notion, explaining that the "nation" implied by the ratification of the Constitution was "a federal roof without federal walls. The United States was "a noun used with a plural verb at the time." "What a successful war for independence could not supply," the authors argue, "were the shared sentiments, symbols, and social explanations necessary

for an integrative national identity." The Civil War, for many, functions as a bloody catalyst in the national story—a horrible stage along the road to a new vision of national unity. See Joyce Appleby, Lynn Hunt, and Margaret Jacob, *Telling the Truth about History* (New York: W. W. Norton, 1994), 93–94. Analyses of a shift to an era defined by a new sense of national unity frames scholarship concerning this period of intensified national commemoration. Two examples of works outlining this cultural shift away from celebratory traditions steeped in localism are Michael Kammen's *Mystic Chords of Memory: The Transformation of Tradition in American Culture* and John Bodnar's *Remaking America: Public Memory, Commemoration, and Patriotism in the Twentieth Century*. While Kammen admits that many Civil War veterans for a time remained "unreconciled" due in large part to "regional chauvinism" and "spasmodic bursts of Northern aggressiveness," he suggests that, in time, "selective memory helped eventually to facilitate reconciliation." Bodnar frames his work in part around late nineteenth-century divisions between a growing class of entrepreneurs and ordinary people that trumped the sectional divisions embedded in disunion. Ultimately, argues Bodnar, this contest would reconfigure national traditions away from localism and ensure the "political and cultural power of the nation-state." Further, illuminating the selective nature of memory, many scholars have amplified how people in the present shape the vestiges of the past through today's predilections. David Lowenthal, for example, in *The Past Is a Foreign Country,* argues that Civil War remembrances illustrate how "past discord [was] simplified or played down, making times of violent strife seem remarkably benign and orderly." Kammen, *Mystic Chords of Memory* (New York: Knopf, 1991), 109–15, 121; Bodnar, *Remaking America* (Princeton, NJ: Princeton University Press, 1992), 21, 35–36; Lowenthal, *The Past Is a Foreign Country* (London: Cambridge University Press, 1985), xviii, 345. Ideas regarding individuals' selectivity in crafting commemorative traditions, especially in public settings, remain extremely influential. At the Southern Historical Association conference held in Richmond, Virginia, between October 31 and November 3, 2007, papers delivered by Karen L. Cox, Alisa Harrison, and Joan Marie Johnson all suggested a historical "redevelopment" at sites of historical memory along reconciliatory lines saving southern tourism from embarrassing tributes to anything recalling the contentions of war. After a brief question-and-answer exchange, members of the panel agreed that sectional divergence was negligible during this period. Rather, suggested one presenter, significant resonant sectional antipathy is merely a creation of scholars who mistakenly deem postwar sectionalism important. (Notes from panel discussion, "Southern Tours and Southern Tourism: Locating Postbellum Confederate Nationalism and Reconciliation," Seventy-third Annual Meeting of the Southern Historical Association, November 3, 2007, Richmond, Virginia.)

7. Pressly argues that by "the close of the 1890's, the war with Spain revealed the extent to which the Civil War was becoming 'history,' the extent to which the animosities of the 1860's were now being submerged in the emotional 'new nationalism' of a reunited North and South." Thomas J. Pressly, *Americans Interpret Their Civil War* (Princeton, NJ: Princeton University Press, 1954), 137. Historians have long noted President William McKinley's reconciliatory gestures implied by appointing former Confederates to top-ranking posts. McKinley wanted to demonstrate that sectional animosity was a thing of the past. See David F. Trask, *The War*

with Spain in 1898 (Lincoln: University of Nebraska Press, 1981), 157; Graham A. Cosmas, *An Army for Empire: The United States Army and the Spanish American War* (Columbia: University of Missouri Press, 1971), 142. Nina Silber's *The Romance of Reunion: Northerners and the South, 1865–1900* similarly offers the war with Spain as a conspicuous landmark in the reconciliation process. Extending her argument to include northern visions of a romantic South, Silber argues that gender served as the central metaphor that shaped northern society's image of the relationship between sections in the postwar years. On the one hand, reconciliation helped prop up declining Victorian standards in the North, while on the other, it provided the psychological means to alleviate a northern crisis in gender. The resulting "New Patriotism" produced by a metaphorical marital reunion of a masculine North to a feminine South minimized politics and *specific* values and principles. This focus on simple loyalty to nation triumphed in the 1890s against waves of immigration while Americans simultaneously began to look outside of the United States to the promises of imperial expansion. Meanwhile, this prospect placed a premium on American unity and encouraged northerners to accept southerners into the national family. The "marriage" complete, a fitting war fought against a foreign enemy by the sons born of a new nation underscored the distance between sectional divergence and Union. Silber, *The Romance of Reunion*, 6, 10, 162. For an essay on intersectional courtship and marriage effecting political reconciliation, see Karen A. Keely, "Marriage plots and national reunion: The trope of romantic reconciliation in postbellum literature[a]," *Mississippi Quarterly* 51 (Fall 1998).

8. Paul H. Buck tendered an affirming appraisal of veterans' efforts despite the overt racism apparent at commemorative gatherings. In 1937, his *The Road to Reunion, 1865–1900* lauded the "positive influences" paving the way for the "promise of ultimate peace" and applauded the breakdown of sectional animosity during the postwar years. He nevertheless admitted that reconciliation ushered in a "period where [black people] would no longer figure as the ward of the nation to be singled out for special guardianship or peculiar treatment." Buck paid tribute to reconciliation but observed "the tremendous reversal of opinion" regarding freed people. Paul H. Buck, *The Road to Reunion, 1865–1900* (Boston: Little, Brown, 1937), 114, 297, 283–84. Much later in the twentieth century, scholars challenged Buck's celebratory message by singling out and stressing the marginalization of black people during this period. Typical among these works is Edward Tabor Linenthal's analysis of American battlefields. In *Sacred Ground: Americans and Their Battlefields,* Linenthal examines Civil War commemorations through the lens of "tacit forgetfulness" and characterizes the "elaborate rituals of reconciliation" as a "moral myopia that ignored the real legacy" of the Civil War. Similarly, Gaines M. Foster's influential *Ghosts of the Confederacy: Defeat, the Lost Cause, and the Emergence of the New South* laments that the "sense of triumph derived from [the 1913 reunion at Gettysburg] involved little that had been at issue in the war," and Stuart McConnell's work on Union veterans, *Glorious Contentment: The Grand Army of the Republic, 1865–1900,* reminds readers that "the question of blacks and slavery received scant mention in celebrations of the war's outcome." Edward Tabor Linenthal, *Sacred Ground: Americans and Their Battlefields* (Urbana: University of Illinois Press, 1991), 91–93; Foster, *Ghosts of the Confederacy,* 193–94; McConnell, *Glorious Contentment,* 181. The most eloquently expressed and powerful account of the

implications surrounding the supposed enthusiastic and unmitigated support for national reconciliation appears in David W. Blight's *Race and Reunion: The Civil War in American Memory.* Blight, while curiously overlooking northern efforts to commemorate the fight to preserve the Union, examines how participants at events geared toward reconciliation, such as the fiftieth anniversary reunion at Gettysburg in 1913, ignored the principal issues leading to war and the Union war aim of emancipation. At these events, mentions of slavery or emancipation were conspicuously absent. Because of such testimony, Blight reasons, together with white supremacists, reconciliationists "locked arms" and "delivered a segregated memory of the Civil War on Southern terms." He concludes, "Forces of reconciliation overwhelmed the emancipationist vision in the national culture [and] the inexorable drive for reunion both used and trumped race." Blight, *Race and Reunion,* 2. Blight has inspired a legion of scholars who apply the "southern terms" argument to their analysis of specific localities, events, and people. For recent examples, see Michelle A. Krowl, "'In the Spirit of Fraternity': The United States Government and the Burial of Confederate Dead at Arlington National Cemetery, 1864–1914," *Virginia Magazine of History and Biography* 3 (2003):151–86; Susanna Michelle Lee, "Reconciliation in Reconstruction Virginia," in *Crucible of the Civil War: Virginia from Secession to Commemoration,* ed. Edward L. Ayers, Gary W. Gallagher, and Andrew J. Torget (Charlottesville: University Press of Virginia, 2006),189–208; Drew Gilpin Faust, "Battle over the Bodies: Burying and Reburying the Civil War Dead," in *Wars within a War: Controversy and Conflict over the American Civil War,* ed. Joan Waugh and Gary W. Gallagher (Chapel Hill: University of North Carolina Press, 2009), 184; Kevin M. Levin, *Remembering the Battle of the Crater: War as Murder* (Lexington: University of Kentucky Press, 2012).

9. Evidence suggests that white Union veterans went as far as to eagerly embrace their black comrades—veterans of the United States Colored Troops and other units—despite their shared racism. Recent work by scholars Barbara A. Gannon and Donald R. Shaffer reveal how postwar comradeship between black and white GAR veterans helped tear down any notions of a white-only war. Race, according to Gannon, was hardly an impediment to forming a commemorative group. Indeed, the GAR was the nation's first interracial organization. Donald R. Shaffer, *After the Glory: The Struggles of Black Civil War Veterans* (Lawrence: University Press of Kansas, 2004); Barbara A. Gannon, *The Won Cause: Black and White Comradeship in the Grand Army of the Republic* (Chapel Hill: University of North Carolina Press, 2011).

10. Historian John R. Neff examines those outside the reconciliation framework defined by most scholars. Basking in the light of the "cause victorious," Neff argues, many of the Union veterans mourning their fallen comrades harbored bitter resentment toward their former enemies. Reasoning that veterans could in no way imagine the memories of their dead apart from the contentions of war, he suggests their sentiments represent the key challenge to reconciliatory efforts in the late nineteenth century. This compelling study does more to expose the lingering bitterness than any of its predecessors. Yet it oversimplifies antagonisms by reinforcing a dichotomy of reconciled versus unreconciled veterans. Analyzing these individuals in terms of stark opposition—those who were committed to reconciliation and those who were not—may indeed be a dead end. John R. Neff, *Honoring the Civil War Dead: Commemoration and the Problem of Reconciliation* (Lawrence: University Press of Kansas, 2005).

11. Scholars more often than not situate commemorations as highly selective processes whereby participants choose memories that best reflected the given circumstances. As Pierre Nora notes in his seminal work on memory studies, "Memory always belongs to our time and forms a lived bond with the eternal present." Pierre Nora, *Les lieux de la mémoire,* 4 vols. (1984; reprint, Chicago: University of Chicago Press, 2001), 1:xix. But recent work by such scholars as Alon Confino and Peter Fritzsche point out that "a weakness of memory studies is the tendency to conceive of memory as an entity of symbols without actions, of culture without society, of representations without material goods and interests." Suggesting that memories *shape* the culture around them opens doors for the study of contestations by groups and individuals generally considered part of a unified (white) nation. See Alon Confino and Peter Fritzsche, eds., *The Work of Memory: New Directions in the Study of German Society and Culture* (Urbana: University of Illinois Press, 2002), 4, 1–2. William Blair, for instance, capitalizes on this idea by explaining how early Confederate commemorations set aside cemeteries as a means to distance the Confederate cause from United States identity. Further, black southerners celebrated Emancipation Days in stark contrast to the ubiquitous tributes to the Lost Cause. Blair's arguments offer valuable insights for future study. Numerous voices echoed through the postwar landscape, and each jockeyed for prominence in terms of war memories. Caroline E. Janney explains how white women engaged some of the most forthright and highly contentious commemorative activity in the postwar South. Janney at once challenges the idea that women were peripheral to the broader commemorative movement and reveals Ladies' Memorial Association activity as intensely political, underscoring the tensions inherent to postwar memories. Yet despite efforts to revise matters of Civil War commemorations, most follow easily recognizable paths of interpretation and analyze contested memories along a strictly racial axis. Ellen M. Litwicki at first accents the contestation of scripted American rituals. Building on the work of Benedict Anderson, she concludes that groups characterized by different "ideological persuasions" objected to the so-called "common and immutable history" in the United States. However, she ultimately follows familiar reasoning by suggesting that "federal holidays constructed America as a white nation," which did not extend "black victims" full citizenship. "This shared vision," she argues, "made it relatively easy for white Northerners and Southerners to reconcile after the end of Reconstruction." William Blair, *Cities of the Dead: Contesting the Memory of the Civil War in the South, 1865–1914* (Chapel Hill: University of North Carolina Press, 2004); Caroline E. Janney, *Burying the Dead But Not the Past: Ladies' Memorial Associations & the Lost Cause* (Chapel Hill: University of North Carolina Press, 2008); Ellen M. Litwicki, *America's Public Holidays 1865–1920* (Washington, DC: Smithsonian Institution Press, 2000), 2, 4–6; Benedict Anderson, *Imagined Communities: Reflections on the Origins and Spread of Nationalism* (1983; reprint, London: Verso, 1991). On the efforts to secure an emancipationist memory of the Civil War, see David W. Blight, *Frederick Douglass' Civil War: Keeping Faith in Jubilee* (Baton Rouge: Louisiana State University Press, 1989), 217–18.

12. Commonwealth of Pennsylvania, *Fiftieth Anniversary of the Battle of Gettysburg: Report of the Pennsylvania Commission* (Harrisburg: Commonwealth of Pennsylvania, ca. 1913), 175. Wilson's oratory was an example of a single strand of Civil War memory—one largely benign and written *specifically* to alleviate the still-present pains involved with reunion and reconcili-

ation. Much of this tradition of reconciliatory writing was authored by veterans during the 1880s and 1890s in an effort to promote bravery, honor, and fortitude of the fighting men of the Civil War. See Tim Goff, ed., *Under Both Flags: Personal Stories of Sacrifice and Struggle during the Civil War* (Chicago: C. R. Graham, 1896). The introduction reads: "The truth only, without bitterness or malice, finds place upon its pages; that no word or expression is used that could not with propriety be read by a Northern or Southern veteran, or to the children either.... Grant, Lee, Sherman, Jackson were Americans, and it is to our country's glory that their valor is known throughout the world; for such heroes is our land peopled from sea to sea. How noble, then, the motive that would bind in fraternal bonds the loyal veteran warriors of our land! Such is the sentiment that fills the heart of every true American."

13. Franklin Delano Roosevelt, "Address of Franklin Delano Roosevelt, Gettysburg, Pennsylvania, July 3, 1938." www.gettysburgdaily.com/?p=1482, accessed February 8, 2009. The "better angels" quotation refers to Abraham Lincoln's first inaugural address, in which he reminded his disaffected southern countrymen of the ties between sections and the "mystic chords of memory" that he hoped would prevail over sectional tensions. See Roy P. Basler, ed., *The Collected Works of Abraham Lincoln,* 9 vols. (New Brunswick, NJ: Rutgers University Press, 1955), 4:271.

14. State commemorative organizations dedicated a handful of other Confederate state monuments during the Civil War centennial (1960–65) and in 1998, a private organization helped provide the means for a James Longstreet equestrian statue in Pitzer's Woods.

15. William Carey Walker, *History of the Eighteenth Regiment Conn. Volunteers in the War for the Union* (Norwich, CT: published by the Committee, 1895), i–ii. See also Lyman Jackman, *History of the Sixth New Hampshire Regiment in the War for the Union* (Concord, NH: Republican Press Association, 1891), iii–iv; Charles Folsom Walcott, *History of the Twenty-First Regiment Massachusetts Volunteers in the War for the Preservation of the Union* (Boston: Houghton, Mifflin, 1882), v–viii; Earl Fenner, *The History of Battery H, First Regiment Rhode Island Light Artillery in the War to Preserve the Union* (Providence, RI: Snow & Farnham, 1894), v–vi. Veterans were painfully aware that their memories had faded with time and many noted the various embellishments in their regimental histories. For example, J. T. Gibson, editor of the 78th Pennsylvania's history, observed, "Many of the current stories concerning our army experiences have an element of truth in them, but they have been so embellished by the exuberant imagination of the narrators that they cannot now be accepted as veritable history." However, regimentals do offer valuable insights as to what weighed on veterans' minds at the time of writing. J. T. Gibson, ed., *History of the Seventy-Eighth Pennsylvania Volunteer Infantry* (Pittsburgh, PA: Pittsburgh Printing Co., 1905), 7–8.

16. James M. McPherson has illustrated the degree to which textbooks became a thorn in the postwar Confederate side, particularly among women's commemorative groups. See McPherson, "Long-Legged Yankee Lies: The Southern Textbook Crusade," in *The Memory of the Civil War in American Culture,* ed. Alice Fahs and Joan Waugh (Chapel Hill: University of North Carolina Press, 2004), 64–78.

17. Some scholars have suggested the opposite. Barbara J. Fields, for instance, has gone as far to suggest that during the war, "preserving the Union [was] a goal too shallow to be

worth the sacrifice of a single life." On the "shallow" goal of union, see Barbara J. Fields, "Who Freed the Slaves?" in *The Civil War: An Illustrated History, ed. Geoffrey C. Ward et al.* (New York: Knopf, 1990), 178. On the motivational factors behind Union enlistment, see James M. McPherson, *For Cause and Comrades: Why Men Fought in the Civil War* (New York: Oxford University Press, 1997). On "Union" as the primary motivating factor for United States soldiers, see Gallagher, *The Union War.*

18. The phrase "Lost Cause" holds a prominent position in the historiography of Civil War memory. While a great deal of the rhetoric typically associated with the Lost Cause memory of the war was deeply embedded in Confederate commemorative efforts, contemporaries varied in opinion regarding the phrase's meaning and application. For an compelling collection of essays illustrating the impact of the Lost Cause warriors see, Gary W. Gallagher and Alan T. Nolan, eds., *The Myth of the Lost Cause and Civil War History* (Bloomington: Indiana University Press, 2000).

19. For an intriguing analysis of soldiers' views of slavery, see Chandra Manning, *What This Cruel War Was Over: Soldiers, Slavery and the Civil War* (New York: Alfred A. Knopf, 2007). Manning concludes that during the war Union soldiers generally viewed the fight as a way to strike at the sin of slavery. This view is problematic. While soldiers may have seen emancipation as a helpful way to undermine the Confederate war effort, the overwhelming majority of Union volunteers originally enlisted and sustained the fight for the sole purpose of restoring the Union. Only retrospectively did most Union veterans include the demise of slavery among their principle war aims.

20. Ulysses S. Grant, for example, strongly suggested a moral dimension to the fight to end slavery. See Grant, *Personal Memoirs of U.S. Grant,* 2 vols. (New York: Charles L. Webster, 1885–86), 2:549, 489. On Grant and the Union cause, see Joan Waugh, "Ulysses S. Grant, Historian," in Fahs and Waugh, *The Memory of the Civil War in American Culture,* pp. 5–38.

21. In fact, many former Confederates observed that slaves were perfectly content and loyal to their masters. On crafting the image of the faithful slave in the Confederacy see, Mark E. Neely, Jr, Harold Holzer, and Gabor S. Boritt, eds., *The Confederate Image: Prints of the Lost Cause* (Chapel Hill: The University of North Carolina Press, 1987), 48–50. The figure of the loyal slave transcended Confederate memory and resonated throughout the twentieth century playing a powerful role in American culture. For a general overview of this phenomenon see, Micki McEyla, *Clinging to Mammy: The Faithful Slave in Twentieth-Century America* (Cambridge, MA: Harvard University Press, 2007).

22. Joseph W. Morton Jr., ed., *Sparks from the Campfire; or, Tales of the Old Veterans* (Philadelphia: Keeler & Kirkpatrick, 1899), 1.

CHAPTER ONE

1. James M. McPherson, *Battle Cry of Freedom: The Civil War Era* (New York: Ballantine Books, 1988), 853–54.

2. Numerous hangings took place during the war, generally as punishment for guerrilla activities or as retaliatory measures. With the exception of the hanging of Captain Henry Wirz,

the commandant of Andersonville Prison, the United States government hanged no Confederate soldiers for war crimes. A few, including Jefferson Davis, were imprisoned, and many high-ranking former Confederate officers had their voting rights temporarily suspended. For one account of hangings in Virginia's Shenandoah Valley, see James A. Ramage, *Gray Ghost: The Life of John Singleton Mosby* (Lexington: University Press of Kentucky, 1999), 199–200. For a compelling look at why Union officials decided not to pursue hangings for the crime of treason, see William Blair, *Why Didn't the North Hang Some Rebels? The Postwar Debate over Punishment for Treason* (Milwaukee, WI: Marquette University Press, 2004). Janney, *Remembering the Civil War,* esp. chap. 2.

3. For an example of veteran bitterness immediately following Appomattox and how it steeled resolve for sectionalism later in the nineteenth century, see Jason Phillips, *Diehard Rebels: The Confederate Culture of Invincibility* (Athens: University of Georgia Press, 2007), esp. "Conclusion: The Aftermath of Invincibility." James M. Gillispie has argued that veterans' postwar narratives, especially those concerning prisons, were greatly overstated and used for political advantage, profit, and to cast the veteran and his comrades as heroes. See Gillispie, "Postwar Mythmaking: Popular Writings on the Treatment of Prisoners, 1865–1920," *North & South: The Official Magazine of the Civil War Society* 6, no. 3 (March 2003): 40–49. While some veterans' narratives were indeed prone to hyperbole, this should not suggest that their stories failed to bolster one side against the other in the national commemorative culture. Veterans did a splendid and very convincing job illustrating their points.

4. Clement A. Evans, "Contributions of the South to the Greatness of the American Union, Delivered before the Association of the Army of Northern Virginia, October 10, 1895 at Richmond, Virginia," *Southern Historical Society Papers* 23 (January 1895): 4–5; Bradley T. Johnson, *The Founding of the Eastern Shore: An Address Delivered at the Centennial Celebration of Easton, July 26th, 1888* (Baltimore: The Sun Book and Job Printing Office, 1888), 4, 17–18.

5. Wallace Evan Davies, *Patriotism on Parade: The Story of Veterans' Hereditary Organizations in America, 1783–1900* (Cambridge, MA: Harvard University Press, 1955), 107.

6. Davies, *Patriotism on Parade,* 29–30, 101. Several stories pinpoint the origins of the GAR, including many testaments to an Illinois doctor named Benjamin Franklin Stephenson. Stephenson, together with a former United States Army chaplain, supposedly founded the group in the spring of 1866 as a way to provide for destitute former Union soldiers and their families as well as to protect the heroes from unscrupulous characters. Others, citing this story as mere legend, suggest Illinois governor Richard J. Oglesby and Union general John A. Logan formed the GAR as a political bloc to help elect Logan to the United States Senate. The exact details of the group's founding are insignificant compared to the power wielded by the GAR. The GAR eventually became one of the most powerful organizations in late nineteenth- and early twentieth-century United States politics. See Mary Harriet Stephenson, *Dr. B. F. Stephenson, Founder of the Grand Army of the Republic* (Springfield, IL: The H.W. Rokker Printing House,1894), 44–45; Robert B. Beath, *History of the Grand Army of the Republic* (New York: Bryan Taylor & Co., 1889), 47; Janney, *Remembering the Civil War,* 108.

7. This singular group of United States Army veterans comprised roughly .79 percent of the total United States population of 63 million in 1890.

8. Scholars refer to this first period of commemoration as the "memorial movement." Some suggest that members of women's groups, most notably the Ladies Memorial Associations in Virginia, South Carolina, Georgia, and elsewhere, developed a movement through which white southerners could pay tribute to the Confederate dead while distancing themselves from the cause. Their work presumably extricated Confederate images from day-to-day southern life and allowed southerners the opportunity to come to terms with defeat and move on with their lives. Men participated in such activities, but usually only as financial backers. Others offer an entirely different estimation. Women, some of the most resolute Confederate patriots, capitalized on gender customs and assumed the leadership of commemorative efforts during the years of Reconstruction. Precisely because occupying Union forces kept such a watchful eye on former Rebel soldiers, women worked diligently to preserve memories of the cause and fan sectional flames through the creation of Confederate national cemeteries and the celebration of Confederate Memorial Day. See Foster, *Ghosts of the Confederacy,* esp. chap. 3; Janney, *Burying the Dead But Not the Past,* 90–91, and *Remembering the Civil War,* esp. chap. 8. On the work of the United Daughters of the Confederacy and the preservation of Confederate heritage, see Karen L. Cox, *Dixie's Daughters: The United Daughters of the Confederacy and the Preservation of Confederate Culture* (Gainesville: University Press of Florida, 2003).

9. Foster, *Ghosts of the Confederacy,* 51. On the image of Lee after his death, see Thomas L. Connelly, *The Marble Man: Robert E. Lee and His Image in American Society* (Baton Rouge: Louisiana State University Press, 1977), 11–13, 28; Alan T. Nolan, *Lee Considered: General Robert E. Lee & Civil War History* (Chapel Hill: University of North Carolina Press, 1991), 171–72.

10. Foster, *Ghosts of the Confederacy,* 52–53.

11. On the growth and power of the United Confederate Veterans, see Foster, *Ghosts of the Confederacy,* 112–14; William Garrett Piston, *Lee's Tarnished Lieutenant: James Longstreet and His Place in Southern History* (Athens: University of Georgia Press, 1987), 163; Davies, *Veterans on Parade,* 40–43.

12. Scholars have thoroughly analyzed the experiences of Civil War prisoners and prison atrocities, but comparatively few have looked closely at the problematic nature of national reconciliation when veterans recalled their prison experiences later in life. For example, William Best Hesseltine suggested in 1962, "No controversy ever evoked such emotion as the mutual recriminations between Northern and Southern partisans over the treatment of prisoners of war." But Hesseltine offers no conclusions about how veterans fused their bitterness with a commemorative ethos founded on reunion. Hesseltine, ed., *Civil War Prisons* (Kent: Kent State University Press, 1962), 5. Recently, historians such as James R. Hall, Michael Horigan, and Kelly Pucci have added their works to the enormous collection of Civil War literature. Their focus, generally on northern prisons, offers little attention to postwar discussion and remains almost entirely on the war years. James R. Hall, *Den of Misery: Indiana's Civil War Prison* (Gretna, LA: Pelican, 2006); Michael Horigan, *Elmira: Death Camp of the North* (Mechanicsburg, PA: Stackpole Books, 2002); Kelly Pucci, *Camp Douglas: Chicago's Civil War Prison* (Charleston, SC: Arcadia, 2007).

13. Winthrop D. Sheldon, *"The Twenty-Seventh" (Connecticut): A Regimental History* (New Haven, CT: Morris & Benham, 1866), 65–68; Osceola Lewis, *History of the One Hundred and*

Thirty-Eighth Pennsylvania Volunteer Regiment (Norristown, PA: Wills, Iredell, & Jenkins, 1866), 110; William Watts Hart Davis, *History of the 104th Pennsylvania Regiment from August 22nd, 1861 to September 30th, 1864* (Philadelphia: Jas. B. Rogers, 1866), 149, 125, 106.

14. William Henry Locke, *The Story of the Regiment* (Philadelphia: J. B. Lippincott, 1868), 246, 363, 401; Thomas H. Parker, *History of the 51st Regiment of P.V. and V.V.* (Philadelphia: King & Baird, 1869), 439, 479; Charles H. Banes, *History of the Philadelphia Brigade* (Philadelphia: J. B. Lippincott, 1879), 211, 291.

15. Ezra D. Simon, *A Regimental History: The One Hundred and Twenty-Fifth New York State Volunteers* (New York: Ezra D. Simon, 1888), 186.

16. Leander W. Cogswell, *A History of the Eleventh New Hampshire Volunteer Infantry in the Rebellion War, 1861–1865* (Concord, NH: Republican Press Association, 1891), 457. Nearly all regimental histories that mentioned prisons discussed the barbarities of prison life. See Luther S. Dickey, *History of the 103d Regiment, Pennsylvania Veteran Volunteer Infantry, 1861–1865* (Chicago: L. S. Dickey, 1910), 290.

17. John Anderson, *The Fifty-Seventh Regiment of Massachusetts Volunteers in the War of the Rebellion* (Boston: E. B. Stillings & Co., 1896), 348, 349.

18. Charles M. Clark, *The History of the Thirty-Ninth Regiment, Illinois Volunteer Veteran Infantry (Yates Phalanx) in the War of the Rebellion* (Chicago: Veteran Association of the Regiment, 1880), 342, 343, 530; George Lewis, *The History of Battery E, First Regiment Rhode Island Light Artillery in the War of 1861 and 1865 to Preserve the Union* (Providence, RI: Snow & Farnham, 1892), 333; James Harvey McKee, *Back "In War Times," History of the 144th Regiment, New York Volunteer Infantry* (New York: Horace E. Bailey, 1903), 246; Mary Genvie Green Brainard, *Campaigns of the One Hundred and Forty-Sixth Regiment New York State Volunteers* (New York: G. P. Putnam Sons, 1915), 193, 256, 258.

19. George Francis Dawson, *Life and Services of Gen. John A. Logan* (Chicago: Belford, Clarke & Company, 1887), 120.

20. John A. Logan, *The Volunteer Soldier of America* (Chicago: R. S. Peale, 1887), 341–42; John A. Logan, *The Great Conspiracy: Its Origin and History* (New York: A. R. Hart, 1886), 588.

21. John G. B. Adams, *Reminiscences of the Nineteenth Massachusetts Regiment* (Boston: Wright & Potter Printing Co., 1899). On life in prison, Adams's book mirrored works such as Kellogg's stinging account of Confederate cruelty published soon after the war. See Robert H. Kellogg, *Life and Death in Rebel Prisons* (Hartford, CT: L. Stebbins, 1867).

22. "Address of Comrade Jones," *Journal of Proceedings of the Eleventh Annual Encampment of the Department of Minnesota, Grand Army of the Republic, Under the New Organization, February 17, 18 and 19, 1891* (Minneapolis: Co-operative Printing Company, 1891), 112.

23. "Address of Comrade Halstead," *Journal of Proceedings of the Twelfth Annual Encampment of the Department of Minnesota, Grand Army of the Republic, Under the New Organization, February 17, 18 and 19, 1892* (St. Paul: Pioneer Press Co., 1892), 184. GAR departments kept meticulous records of their various reunions. Their published accounts, made available by subscription, offered transcriptions of formal speeches, debates, toasts, and other talks. Memories of prison life was a favorite topic among veterans. See *Proceedings of the First to Tenth Meetings, 1866–1876 (inclusive) of the National Encampment, Grand Army of the Republic*

(Philadelphia: Samuel P. Town, 1877), 20, 240; *Journal of the Nineteenth Annual Session of the National Encampment, Grand Army of the Republic, Portland Maine, June 24th and 25th, 1885* (Toledo, OH: Montgomery & Vrooman, 1885), 240, 264, 284, 288; *Journal of the Twentieth Annual Session of the National Encampment, Grand Army of the Republic, San Francisco, California, August 4th, 5th, and 6th, 1886* (Washington: Gibson Bros., 1886), 289; Journal *of the Twenty-Sixth National Encampment, Grand Army of the Republic, Washington, D.C., September 21st and 22nd, 1892* (Albany, NY: S. H. Wentworth, 1892), 216, 274; *Journal of the Twenty-Seventh Annual Encampment, Department of Massachusetts, Grand Army of the Republic, February 7 and 8, 1894* (Boston: E. B. Stillings & Co., 1894), 129, 180, 186, 253; *Journal of the Forty-First Annual Encampment of the Department of Rhode Island, G-A-R, Thursday, February 13, 1908* (Providence: Department of Rhode Island, Grand Army of the Republic Headquarters, 1908), 27.

24. "Rebel Prisons," *National Tribune*, May 19, 1904.

25. Edward P. Kimball, ed., *Brimley Hall Album and Post 10 Sketch Book* (Worchester, MA: F. S. Blanchard & Co., ca 1896), 147.

26. Harrison C. Hobart, "Libby Prison—The Escape," *War Papers Read Before the Commandery of the State of Wisconsin,* 4 vols. (Milwaukee, WI: A. Ross Houston, 1891), 1:402; Author unknown, "My Experiences as a Prisoner of War," *War Papers Read Before the Commandery of Michigan,* 2 vols. (Detroit: Winn & Hammond, 1893), 1:31.

27. James L. High, "My Hero," *Military Essays and Recollections Read Before the Commandery of the State of Illinois,* 8 vols. (Chicago: Dial Press, 1899), 3:166; Henry A. Castle, "The Boys in Blue Brown Gray," *Glimpses of Our Nation's Struggle: Papers Read Before the Minnesota Commandery* (St. Paul: H. L. Collins, 1898), 476; Robert Stoddard Robertson, "From the Wilderness to Spotsylvania," 1:270; and Owen Price, "Afield with the Eleventh Corp at Chancellorville, 361, in *Sketches of War History: Papers Read Before the Ohio Commandery,* 9 vols. (Cincinnati: Robert Clarke & Co., 1888).

28. J. Ogden Murray, *The Immortal Six Hundred: A Story of Cruelty to Confederate Prisoners of War* (Roanoke, VA: Stone Printing and Manufacturing Co., 1911), 13. In an unusual account of Andersonville, Union veteran James Madison Page agreed with Confederate assertions that the United States government had to share the blame for the horrors of Andersonville. Page's published writings drew sharp rebuke from his GAR comrades and his personal letters reveal how his work stirred controversy in the North. James Madison Page and M. J. Haley, *The True Story of Andersonville: A Defense of Major Henry Wirz* (New York: Neale Publishing Co., 1908); For a brief analysis of the reactions to Page's memoir and Page's rebuttal, see Spencer Wilson, "Andersonville: A Civil War Legacy of Hatred in Far-Off Montana," *Montana: The Magazine of Western History,* 27 (January 1977): 52–57.

29. Charles T. Loehr, *War History of the Old First Virginia Infantry Regiment* (Richmond: Wm. Ellis Jones, 1884), 61.

30. Frank Stovall Roberts, "An Echo of Johnson's Island," *Confederate Veteran* 30 (November 1922): 406.

31. L.T. Dickerson, "The Negro on Guard," in *Campfires of the Confederacy,* ed. Benjamin LaBree (Louisville: Courier-Journal Job Printing Co., 1898), 71. See also, W. J. McMurray, *His-*

tory of the Twentieth Tennessee Regiment Volunteer Infantry, C.S.A. (Nashville: W. J. McMurray, Deering J. Roberts, & Ralph J. Neal, 1904), 475.

32. Mauriel Phillips Joslyn, *Immortal Captives: The Story of Six Hundred Confederate Officers and the United States Prisoner of War Policy* (Shippensburg, PA: White Mane, 1996).

33. "Minutes of the Immortal 600 Society," in Joslyn, *Immortal Captives, 278.* For biographical info on the Immortal 600 Society, see Joslyn, *The Biographical Roster of the Immortal 600* (Shippensburg, PA: White Mane, 1992).

34. For example, Union captain Webster of transfer ship *Crescent City* refused to let prisoners above deck or allow their quarters cleaned, stating that it was "good enough for Rebels." Further, veterans described at length the "brutal white officers of the nigger regiment" and the cruelty of the African American guards (Murray, *The Immortal Six Hundred,* 9, 80, 96).

35. *Acts and Joint Resolutions, Amending the Constitution, of the General Assembly of the State of Virginia* (Richmond: Davis Bottom, 1910), 324. Despite a concerted effort to establish such a tribute, no monument exists honoring the Immortal Six Hundred on Morris Island.

36. McHenry Howard, *Recollections of a Maryland Confederate Soldier and Staff Officer under Johnston, Jackson, and Lee* (Baltimore: Williams & Wilkins, 1914), 326; Yates Snowden, *History of South Carolina* (Chicago: Lewis Publishing, 1930), 98; "The Immortal Six Hundred," *Confederate Veteran* 30 (June 1922): 216–17.

37. *Confederate Veteran* 20 (September 1912): 327.

38. *Minutes of the First Annual Meeting and Reunion of the United Confederate Veterans Held in the City of Chattanooga, Tenn., July 3rd 1890* (New Orleans: Hopkins' Printing, 1891), 137; *Minutes of the Sixth Annual Meeting and Reunion of the United Confederate Veterans Held in the City of Richmond, Va. June 30th & July 1st & 2nd, 1896* (New Orleans: Hopkins' Printing, 1897), 75, 94; *Minutes of the Ninth Annual Meeting and Reunion of the United Confederate Veterans Held in the City of Charleston, S. C. May 10th, 11th, 12th & 13th, 1899* (New Orleans: Hopkins' Printing, 1900), 3, 250; *Official Proceedings of the Fifth Annual Reunion of Missouri Division United Confederate Veterans, Springfield, Mo., August 8, 9, and 10, 1901* (St. Louis: C. C. Rainwater, 1901), 81.

39. W. A. Hemphill, "Address of W. A. Hemphill," *Proceedings of the Sixth Annual Meeting and Reunion of the United Confederate Veterans Held at Richmond Virginia, June 30 and July 1st and 2nd, 1896* (New Orleans: Hopkins' Printing Office, 1897), 21; R. Prosper Landry, "The Donaldsonville Artillery at the Battle of Fredericksburg," *Southern Historical Society Papers* 19, no. 23 (1895): 198–202 [journal hereafter cited as *SHSP*]; John Lamb, "The Battle of Fredericksburg," *SHSP* 27 (1899): 231–40. The *Papers* are a particularly good source for recollections in this regard. In addition to publishing speeches and editorials, the editors compiled and republished newspaper articles from across the South.

40. "Battle of Fredericksburg," *SHSP* 19 (May 1891): 262–63, For a postwar account of the Fredericksburg "exodus of terror," see Heros Von Borke, *Memoirs of the Confederate War for Independence,* 2 vols. (London: William Blackwood & Sons, 1866), 2:99–100. For a modern account of the civilian response to the shelling and Federal occupation of Fredericksburg, see George C. Rable, *Fredericksburg! Fredericksburg!* (Chapel Hill: University of North Carolina Press, 2002), 181–83.

41. "Barksdale's Mississippi Brigade at Fredericksburg," *SHSP* 36 (January 1908): 20–21. On the burning of Columbia, see, *SHSP* 9 (June 1881): 380; "The Burning of Columbia—Affidavit of Mrs. Agnes Law," *SHSP* 12 (April 1884): 233; "General Sherman's Method of Making War," *SHSP* 13 (September 1885): 439–53; Joseph Tyrone Derry, *Story of the Confederate States* (Richmond: B. F. Johnson, 1898), 403. Suggesting that Sherman was to blame for the burning of Columbia, the United Daughters of the Confederacy developed a "Confederate Catechism" to test the younger generation on Civil War "facts." See "Who Burned Columbia?" *Confederate Veteran* 24 (February 1916): 61. Witnesses to such scenes did not likely forget Union attacks on Confederate civilians. One veteran recollected about the shelling and evacuation of Fredericksburg early in the twentieth century, "The scenes incident to the evacuation of Fredericksburg are well remembered to the present day. They are indelibly impressed upon the mind and can never be forgotten" (J. S. Quinn, *The History of the City of Fredericksburg, Virginia* [Richmond: Hermitage Press, 1908], 81–82).

42. Historians debate whether or not the Civil War was a "total war." For those living in and around northern Virginia, for example, where armies camped and marched—taking with them what they needed, and where some of the East's biggest battles took place, the war surely must have seemed total. For a study that suggests the war was not total, see Mark Grimsley, *The Hard Hand of War: Union Military Policy toward Southern Civilians, 1861–1865* (Cambridge: Cambridge University Press, 1995). Others have suggested that scholars have gone too far drawing comparisons between nineteenth-century warfare and twentieth-century total war. See, Mark E. Neely Jr., *The Civil War and the Limits of Destruction* (Cambridge, MA: Harvard University Press, 2007). For a view chronicling the destructive nature of the Civil War, see Charles Royster, *The Destructive War: William Tecumseh Sherman, Stonewall Jackson, and the Americans* (New York: Knopf, 1991). On the burning of Darien, Georgia, see Spencer B. King Jr., *Darien: The Death and Rebirth of a Southern Town* (Macon, GA: Mercer University Press, 1981).

43. Sherman's exploits continued to anger former Confederates well into the reconciliation period. Particularly in regimental histories, personal recollections, and other writings, Sherman stood apart from other Union generals, with the possible exception of Phillip Sheridan, as the most vindictive and ruthless. See "Sherman in Atlanta," *SHSP* 10 (May 1882): 332–33; McMurray, *History of the Twentieth Tennessee,* 454–55; B. L. Eidley, "Coming Home from Greensboro," *Confederate Veteran* 3 (December 1895): 366; A. M. Keiley, *In Vinculis; or, The Prisoner of War* (New York: Blelock & Co., 1866), 40, 88; George S. Bernard, ed., *War Talks of Confederate Veterans* (Petersburg: Penn & Owen, 1892), 287–88; Charles C. Jones, "Sherman's March from Atlanta to the Coast," *SHSP* 12 (July 1884):294–309. The memories of the burning of Atlanta in particular resonated among former Confederates until the end of their lives. Suggests one British observer, "such deeds are not forgotten in a day, and until they are forgotten, they will never be forgiven." William Hepworth Dixon, *White Conquest,* 2 vols. (London: Chatto &Windus, Piccadilly, 1876), 1:126.

44. "Opinion of a United States Officer on the Depopulation of Atlanta," *SHSP* 9 (April 1881): 272–73; "Diary of Captain Robert E. Park, Twelfth Alabama Infantry," *SHSP* 2 (April 1876): 306–7. For contemporary reactions to Sherman by Confederate civilians, see Jacqueline

Glass Campbell, *When Sherman Marched North from the Sea: Resistance on the Confederate Home Front* (Chapel Hill: University of North Carolina Press, 2003).

45. On contemplating a campaign through Georgia in 1864, Sherman understood that maintaining a base of operation and supply lines would tie down thousands of soldiers. The occupation of Georgia was not Sherman's objective. Rather, he planned "the utter destruction of its roads, houses and people [so to] cripple [the Confederacy's] military resources." Sherman concluded that he could sustain a march and in so doing, "make Georgia howl." See William T. Sherman, *Memoirs of William T. Sherman,* 2 vols. (London: Henry S. King, 1875), 2:152; *SHSP* 9 (1881), 380.

46. Charles C. Jones, *The Siege of Savannah in December 1864* (Albany, NY: Joel Munsell, 1874), 116–17; *SHSP* 1 (1876), 424–26; Robert Preston Brooks, *History of Georgia* (Boston: Atkinson, Mentzer & Co., 1913), 287–98; Joel Chandler Harris, *Stories of Georgia* (New York: American Book Co., 1896), 297. Modern scholars have recently reassessed the memories concerning Sherman's campaigns in Georgia and the Carolinas and the campaigns themselves. See Campbell. *When Sherman Marched North from the Sea; Edward Caudill and Paul Ashdown, Sherman's March in Myth and Memory* (Lanham, MD: Rowman & Littlefield, 2008).

47. R. J. Harding, "Address of R. J. Harding," *Unveiling and Dedication of Monument to Hood's Texas Brigade on the Capitol Grounds at Austin, Texas, Thursday, October Twenty-Seven, Nineteen Hundred and Ten and Minutes of the Thirty-Ninth Annual Reunion of Hood's Texas Brigade Association Held in Senate Chamber at Austin, Texas, October Twenty-Six and Twenty-Seven, Nineteen Hundred and Ten, Together with a Short Monument and Brigade Association History and Confederate Scrapbook* (Houston: F. B. Chilton, 1911), 176, 179, 177 (book hereafter cited as *Hood's Texas Brigade Scrapbook*).

48. Harding, "Address of R. J. Harding," 177. Both Sherman and Philip H. Sheridan received severe criticism from Confederate veteran authors. For reminiscences of Sheridan and "the Burning" of the Shenandoah Valley in 1864, see Clement A. Evans, ed., *Confederate Military History,* 12 vols. (Atlanta: Confederate Publishing Co., 1899), 1:626; William Worthington Goldsborough, *The Maryland Line of the Confederate Army, 1861–1865* (Baltimore: Guggenheim, Weil & Co., 1900), 291; Hunter McGuire, *The Confederate Cause and Conduct of the War Between the States* (Richmond: L. H. Jenkins, 1907), 90–92; M. S. Watts, "General Battle and the Stolen Colt," *Confederate Veteran* 30 (May 1922):169. Among the most notable unreconstructed Rebels, Jubal A. Early berated Sheridan, along with Sherman, Nathaniel P. Banks, and Benjamin F. Butler for "plundering and rendering utterly desolate the houses of thousands of women and children" (Jubal Anderson Early, *Autobiographical Sketch and Narrative of the War between the States* [Philadelphia: J. B. Lippincott, 1912], 299).

49. *Proceedings of the 39th Annual Encampment, Department of Pennsylvania, Grand Army of the Republic, June 7 and 8, 1905* (Harrisburg, PA: Harrisburg Publishing Co., 1905), 59; *The Daily Inter Ocean,* January 15, 1881. For a contemporary account of the burning, see Thomas A. Wilson, *Sufferings Endured for a Free Government; or, A History of the Cruelties and Atrocities of the Rebellion* (Washington, DC: Thomas A. Wilson, 1864), 242.

50. Jubal A. Early, *A Memoir of the Last Year of the War for Independence in the Confederate States of America* (Lynchburg: Charles W. Button, 1867), 56–59.

51. Charles C. Coffin, *Redeeming the Republic: The Third Period of the War of the Rebellion* (New York: Harper & Bros., 1889), 438; A. Bayard Nettleton, "How the Day Was Saved at the Battle of Cedar Creek," in *Glimpses of the Nation's Struggle: A Series of Papers Read Before the Minnesota Commandery, MOLLUS* (St. Paul: St. Paul Book and Stationary, 1887), 259; Alexander K. McClure, *Old Time Notes of Pennsylvania*, 2 vols. (Philadelphia: John C. Winston Co., 1905), 2:149; Alfred Nevin, *Men of Mark of Cumberland Valley, Pa, 1776–1876* (Philadelphia: Fulton Publishing, 1876), 52; Alexander K. McClure, *Abraham Lincoln and Men of War-Times* (Philadelphia: Times Publishing Co., 1892), 390. Confederate veterans naturally refuted accusations of wanton destruction and cruelty. See J. Scott Moore, "A Southern Account of the Burning of Chambersburg," *Richmond (VA) Dispatch*, February 5, 1899.

52. "Oration of Comrade Collyer," *National Memorial Day: A Record of the Ceremonies over the Graves of the Union Dead* (Washington: Gill Withekow, 1870), 148.

53. "Oration of Dan J. Wilson," *Journal of the Twenty-Fifth Annual Encampment G.A.R. Department of Michigan June 10–11, 1903* (n.p: 1903), 22.

54. Fitzhugh Lee, "The Unveiling of the Monument to the Confederate Dead of Alexandria, Va.," in *Speeches of Capt. Raleigh T. Daniel, and Gov. Fitzhugh Lee, May 24th 1889* (n.p.: n.p., ca. 1889), 10. This monument dedication is generally cited for its reconciliatory context. See Krowl, "In the Spirit of Fraternity."

55. Wm. C. P. Breckinridge, "The ex-Confederate and What He Has Done in Peace: An Address Delivered before the Association of the Army of Northern Virginia, October 36, 1892," *SHSP* 20 (1892): 236, 228.

56. W. W. Ballew, *Historical Address to Confederate Veterans, Corsicana, Texas, July 23, 1913* (n.p.: n.p., ca. 1913), 60: Surry Light Artillery & Deal-Crenshaw Minute Book, Mss4C708a1, VHS, 58.

57. George L. Christian, *The Confederate Cause and Its Defenders. An Address Delivered Before the Grand Army of Confederate Veterans of Virginia, at the Annual Meeting Held at Culpepper C.H., Va., October 4, 1898* (Richmond: Wm. Ellis Jones, Book and Job Printer, 1898), 3, 4, 26.

58. *National Tribune*, September 25, 1890; *Journal of the Twenty-Sixth National Encampment, Grand Army of the Republic* (Albany, NY: S. H. Wentworth, 1892), 356.

59. Hosea W. Rood letters, box 8, folder 2, "Grand Army of the Republic, Department of Wisconsin Records, 1861–1986," WVM. On children's literature, see Alice Fahs, "Remembering the Civil War in Children's Literature of the 1880s and 1890s," in Fahs and Waugh, *The Memory of the Civil War*, 79–93.

60. Hosea W. Rood letters, box 8, folder 2, WVM.

61. Lymon G. Wilcox, "The South in War Times," *War Papers Read Before the Michigan Commandery, MOLLUS*, 2 vols. (Detroit: James H. Stone, 1898), 2:32, 27; James A. Beaver, "Address of James A. Beaver," *Ceremonies at the Twenty-fifth Anniversary, MOLLUS* (Philadelphia: n.p., 1890), 39. Concerns regarding posterity were a common theme at Union veterans' meetings throughout the reconciliation period. See Richard Robins, ed., *Toasts and Responses Given at Banquets [Honoring] Lieut-Gen P. H. Sheridan* (Chicago: Knight & Leonard, 1883), 17; W. H. L. Browning, "Address of W. H. L. Browning," *Records of Members of the Grand Army of the Re-*

public with a Complete Account of the Twentieth National Encampment (San Francisco: H. S. Crocker, 1886), 21; C. H. J. Woodbury, "Address of C. H. J. Woodbury," *Journal of the Twenty-Seventh Annual Encampment, Department of Massachusetts, GAR* (Boston: E. B. Stillings & Co., 1894), 211; Charles H. Browning, ed., *The American Historical Register and Monthly Gazette of Patriotic-Hereditary Societies of the United States of America*, 4 vols. (Philadelphia: Historical Register Publishing Co., 1895), 4:806; *Memorials of Deceased Companions of the State of Illinois, MOLLUS*, 2 vols. (Chicago: n.p., 1913), 2:361.

62. John Lamb, "The Battle of Fredericksburg," *Richmond (VA) Dispatch*, November 26, 1899.

CHAPTER TWO

1. Robert G. Ingersoll, *The Works of Robert G. Ingersoll*, 12 vols. (New York: Dresder Publishing Co., 1907), 9:157–60; Ed Bradley, "The House, The Beast, and the Bloody Shirt: The Doorkeeper Controversy of 1878," *Journal of the Gilded Age & Progressive Era* 3 (January 2004), 15–34. Those who could nominate insisted that maimed veterans fill available positions such as doorkeeper. For an essay concerning the body as a metaphor for the consequences of war, see Brian Matthew Jordan, "'Living Monuments': Union Veteran Amputees and the Embodied Memory of the Civil War," *Civil War History* 57, no. 2 (June 2011): 121–52; Edward McPherson, "Address of Edward McPherson," *Michigan at Gettysburg, July 1st, 2nd, 3rd, 1863. June 12th 1889. Proceedings incident to the Dedication of the Michigan Monuments upon the Battlefield of Gettysburg, June 12th, 1889* (Detroit: Winn & Hammond, Printers and Binders, 1889), 50. For a look at the manipulation of symbols in Republican Party bloody shirt political campaigns that were reflective of veterans' sentiments, see "Beyond the Battle: The Flags of the Iron Brigade, 1863–1918," *Wisconsin Magazine of History* 69 (Fall 1985): 36–66. For political rhetoric emphasizing a "renewed nationalism," see Patrick J. Kelly, The Election of 1896 and the Restructuring of Civil War Memory," in Fahs and Waugh, *The Memory of the Civil War*, 180–212.

2. For a comprehensive single-volume study on the fighting at Gettysburg, see Noah Andre Trudeau, *Gettysburg: A Testing of Courage* (New York: HarperCollins, 2002). For the fighting at McPherson's Ridge on July 1, 1863, see chap. 12.

3. C. L. Sumbardo, "Address of Captain C. L. Sumbardo," in *Glimpses of the Nation's Struggle: Papers Read Before the Minnesota Commandery of the Loyal Legion of the United States, 1889–1892*, ed. Edward D. Neill (New York: D. D. Merrill Co., 1893), 41, and "Incidents of Prison Life, with Causes of Confederate Cruelty," in Neill, *Glimpses of the Nation's Struggle*, 367.

4. Commemorative efforts taking place at or concerning Fort Sumter especially resounded with this message. Veterans offering reconciliatory gestures at the "historic fort" would often note its significance in regard to the treasonous aims of their southern countrymen. See Robert Burns Beath, *History of the Grand Army of the Republic* (New York: Bryan, Taylor & Co., 1889), 688; H. B. Carrington, "Resolution," *Journal of the Twenty-Seventh Annual Encampment, Department of Massachusetts, Grand Army of the Republic, February 7 and 8, 1894* (Boston: E. B. Stillings, 1894), 267; Samuel P. Towne, "Report of Patriotic Instructor," *Proceedings of the 48th Annual Encampment Department of Pennsylvania, Grand Army of the Republic, June 11th and*

12th, 1914 (Harrisburg: Wm. Stanley Ray, 1914), 179. The "last best hope" remark refers to Lincoln's Annual Message to Congress, delivered December 1, 1862.

5. *National Tribune*, September 24, 1891.

6. George W. Johnson, "Address of George W. Johnson," *Proceedings of the Twenty-Second Annual Encampment Department of Maryland, Grand Army of the Republic, February 21 and 22, 1898* (Baltimore: John R. Shane & Co., 1898), 20–21. The passage of time weighed heavily on Civil War veterans, especially those actively involved with the preservation of memories. As time passed, veterans redoubled their commemorative efforts so as to ensure that they not be forgotten. See "Report of the Inspector," *Journal of the Thirty-Second Annual Encampment of the Grand Army of the Republic, Department of Rhode Island, G-A-R, February 2nd, 1899* (Providence: Head-Quarters, Department of Rhode Island, 1899), 29; *Journal of the Thirty-Fourth National Encampment of the Grand Army of the Republic, August 29th and 30th, 1900* (Philadelphia: Towne Printing Co., 1900), 309; Department Commander Pilcher, "Address of Department Commander Pilcher," *Abstract of General Orders and Proceedings of the Fifty-Third Annual Encampment, Department of New York, G.A.R., June 24th, 25th, 26th, 1919* (Albany, NY: J. B. Lyon Co., 1919), 63.

7. Luther Tracy Townsend, *History of the Sixteenth Regiment, New Hampshire Volunteers* (Washington, DC: Norman T. Elliott, Printer & Publisher, 1897), 15; Robert M. Green, *History of the One Hundred and Twenty-Fourth Regiment in the War of the Rebellion, 1862–1863* (Philadelphia: Ware Bros., 1907), 297. Scholars have noted the problematic nature of personal reminiscences written long after the fact. Among the most pressing concerns is the subjectivity of memory, which shapes perceptions of "truth." See Reardon, *Pickett's Charge*, 1–2.

8. Charles L. Holstein, "Address of Major Charles L. Holstein," *Journal of the Seventh Annual Session of the Grand Army of the Republic, Department of Indiana, February 17 & 18, 1886* (Indianapolis: Hasselman-Journal Co., 1886). 148. The inevitability of "right" triumphing over "wrong" is a recurring theme in Grand Army of the Republic literature. See *Proceedings of the 43rd National Encampment, Department of Pennsylvania, Grand Army of the Republic, June 9 and 10, 1909* (Harrisburg: C. F. Aughinbaugh, 1909), 56

9. Unknown news clipping, ca. May 1893, volume title "GAR C.C. Washburn Post no. 11 (Madison) Minute Book and Journal, January 1887—December 1993," GAR Papers, WVM.

10. Author unknown, "Memorial Day Address," n.d., box 1, folder title "Post # 2, Philadelphia, Department of Pennsylvania," GAR papers, GARM.

11. Simons, *History of the One Hundred Twenty-Fifth, New York State Volunteers*, 145.

12. William Henry Newlin, *A History of the Seventy-Third Regiment of Illinois Infantry Volunteers* (n.p.: Regimental Reunion Association of Survivors of the 73d Illinois Infantry Volunteers, 1890), 677. Truth and right were central components in commemorations of the Union cause. Beginning with the earliest commemorative efforts, Union veterans never flagged in this regard. See *The National Memorial Day: A Record of Ceremonies over the Graves of Union Soldiers, May 29 and 30, 1869* (Washington City: Headquarters Grand Army of the Republic, 1870), 848; *Journal of the Forty-First National Encampment of the Department of Rhode Island, G-A-R, Thursday, February 13, 1908* (Providence: Head-quarters Department

of Rhode Island Grand Army of the Republic, 1908), 32; Bowdoin S. Parker, *What One Grand Army Post Has Accomplished: History of the Edward W. Kinsley Post, No. 13, Department of Massachusetts* (Norwood, MA: Norwood Press, 1913), 206.

13. J. L. Grimm, "Address of J. L. Grimm," *Proceedings of the Twenty-Third Annual Encampment Department of Maryland, Grand Army of the Republic, February 21 and 22, 1899* (Baltimore: John R. Shane & Co., 1899). 30; Author unknown, *Proceedings of the 32nd Annual Encampment Department of Maryland, Grand Army of the Republic, April 9 and 10, 1908* (Baltimore: Press of N. C. Killam, 1908), 44.

14. Sheldon, *The "Twenty-Seventh": A Regimental History*, 11. Union veterans were likely to compare their cause to that of the revolutionary generation. See, *The National Memorial Day: A Record of Ceremonies, 1869*, 133; "Report of Allan H. Dougall," *Journal of the Twenty-Eighth National Encampment, Grand Army of the Republic, Pittsburgh, Pa. September 12th and 13th, 1894* (Boston: E. B. Stillings, 1894), 135; *Observances of the Centennial Anniversary of the Birth of Abraham Lincoln, February Twelfth, 1909, Under the Inspiration of the Grand Army of the Republic* (n.p.: National Committee, GAR, 1909), 93.

15. *Beaver Falls (PA) Tribune*, September 12, 1882; Robert M. Green, ed., *History of the One Hundred and Twenty-Fourth Regiment Pennsylvania Volunteers in the War of the Rebellion, 1862–1863* (Philadelphia: Wane Bros. Co., 1907), 222. On the connections between Lincoln and the founding generation, see Merrill D. Peterson, *Lincoln in American Memory* (New York: Oxford University Press, 1994), 27–29.

16. Thomas H. McKee, "Views and Reviews of the Civil War of 1861–65" (read April 4, 1906), *War Papers Being Papers Read Before the Commandery of the District of Columbia Military Order of the Loyal Legion of the United States*, 4 vols. (1906; reprint, Wilmington, NC: Broadfoot, 1993), 3:343; Genevieve Poyneer Hendricks, *Handbook of the Social Resources of the United States* (Washington, DC: American Red Cross, 1921), 141. *Proceedings of the 42nd Annual Encampment Department of Pennsylvania, Grand Army of the Republic, June 3rd and 4th, 1908* (Harrisburg, PA: Harrisburg Publishing Co., 1908), 48.

17. Simons, *A Regimental History*, v; Author unknown, "Resolution, January 2 1894," box 1, folder title, "Grand Army of the Republic," Abraham Gilbert Mills Papers, NYPL [collection hereafter cited as Mills Papers, NYPL]; George M Carpenter, *History of the Eighth Regiment Vermont Volunteers, 1861–1865* (Boston: Press of Deland & Barta, 1886), 251.

18. A. H. Mills, "Address of A.H. Mills, October 10, 1889," *New York Monuments Commission for the Battlefields of Gettysburg and Chattanooga*, 2:832.

19. John H. Maxwell, "Address of John H. Maxwell," box 2, unpublished volume title, "Proceedings of Annual Encampment G.A.R. Department of New York, 1907," 52–53, Mills Papers, NYPL; John W. Storrs, *The "Twentieth Connecticut": A Regimental History* (Ansonia, CT: Press of the Naugatuck Valley Sentinel, 1886), 18, 168.

20. Abraham Gilbert Mills, "Address of Abraham Gilbert Mills," box 1, folder title, "Writings," Mills Papers, NYPL. On the question of the rise of the United States as a world power and the legacy of the Civil War, see Richard N. Currant, "From Civil War to World Power: Perceptions and Realities, 1865–1914," in Grant and Parish, *Legacy of Disunion*, 205–21.

21. Blight, *Race and Reunion*, 65; Bodnar, *Remaking America*, 28; Alan Jabbour and Karen Singer Jabbour, *Decoration Day in the Mountains: Traditions of Cemetery Decorations in the Southern Appalachians* (Chapel Hill: University of North Carolina Press, 2010), 119.

22. Earnest F. M. Faehtz, *The National Memorial Day: A Record of Ceremonies over the Graves of the Union Soldiers, May 29 and 30, 1869* (Washington City: Headquarters of the Grand Army of the Republic, 1870), 37.

23. Faehtz, *National Memorial Day*, 37. Veterans contended that all Americans should observe Memorial Day. However, they generally noted only the trials endured by northern soldiers in an effort to preserve the Union. Veterans thus commemorated the Union cause alone. Former Confederates may have been welcome, in reconciliatory fashion, to join the celebrations. But they were welcomed on northerner terms—terms that included the suppression of treason. See Charles Theodore Russell Jr., ed., *Speeches and Addresses of William E. Russell* (Boston: Little, Brown, & Co., 1894), 103; Faehtz, *The National Memorial Day*, 20, 37, 45, 74; David P. Jones, "Something about Our Navy," *Military Essays and Recollections: Papers Read Before the Commandery of the State of Illinois, MOLLUS*. 8 vols. (Chicago: Dial Press, 1899), 3:338–39; Comrade Sprague, "Communications from Departments," *Proceedings of the First to Tenth Meetings, 1866–1876, of the National Encampment, GAR* (Philadelphia: Samuel P. Town, 1877), 298; Thayer, "Address of Joseph W. Thayer," *Journal of the Twenty-Seventh Annual Encampment, Department of Massachusetts, GAR, February 7 and 8, 1894* (Boston: E. B. Stillings, 1894), 53.

24. *New York Times*, May 31, 1895.

25. Thayer, "Address," 23; Wilfred Weatherby, "Address of Wilfred Weatherby," *Journal of the Thirtieth National Encampment, Department of Massachusetts, GAR* (Boston: E. B. Stillings, 1896), 270.

26. Lucy S. Stewart to "patriotic citizens of America," January 30, 1932, box 13, folder 7, GAR Papers, WVM.

27. Comrade Castle, "Address of Comrade Castle," *Journal of Proceedings of the Eleventh Annual Encampment of the Department of Minnesota, Grand Army of the Republic, Under the New Organization, February 17, 18 and 19, 1891* (Minneapolis: Co-operative Printing Co., 1891), 232. Other Union veterans considered honoring the Confederate war effort through monuments an "insult to every man who wore the blue." See Thayer, "Address,"), 53; Comrade Tressler, "Resolution," *Proceedings of the 34th National Encampment of the Department of Pennsylvania, GAR, Gettysburg, June 6–7, 1900* (n.p.: William Stanley Ray, 1900), 251.

28. Donald E. Collins, *The Death and Resurrection of Jefferson Davis* (Lanham, MD: Rowman & Littlefield, 2005); Foster, *Ghosts of the Confederacy*, 158–59; GAR officials seldom tolerated any favorable recognition of the former Confederate executive. The GAR court-martialed and removed one post commander, Jacob Gray, for honoring Davis's funeral procession. *New York Times*, August 9, 1890.

29. Lyman G. Wilcox, "The South in War Times," *War Papers Read Before the Michigan Commandery, MOLLUS*, 2 vols. (Detroit: James H. Stone & Co., 1898), 2:28; Charles Devens, "Address of Charles Devens," *Military Essay and Recollections of the Pennsylvania Commandery of the Loyal Legion of the United States*, 2 vols. (1890; reprint, Wilmington, NC: Broadfoot,

1995), 1:84; *Grand Army Record* 4 (December 1889): 4. Davis was attacked especially for his government's neglect of Union prisoners of war. See Joseph E. Moody, "Life in Confederate Prisons," *Civil War Papers Read Before the Commandery of the State of Massachusetts, Military Order of the Loyal Legion of the United States,* 3 vols. (Boston: Printed for the Commandery, 1890), 2:354, 360–61.

30. No author, "Resolution," *Journal of Proceedings of the Sixteenth Annual Encampment of the Department of Minnesota, Grand Army of the Republic, Under the New Organization, March 11th and 12th 1896* (Minneapolis: Co-operative Printing Co., 1896), 132.

31. Blair, *Why Didn't the North Hang Some Rebels;* Collins, *The Death and Resurrection of Jefferson Davis,* 18–21.

32. Asa B. Isham, "Address of Asa B. Isham," *Sketches of War History 1861–1865: Papers Read Before the Ohio Commandery of the Military Order of the Loyal Legion of the United States 1883–1886,* 9 vols. (Cincinnati: Robert Clarke & Co, 1888), 2:215, 232. GAR veterans generally detested honoring any of the Confederate heroes. On the suggested of lowering the flag to half-mast in reverence to one deceased secessionist, Jacob Thompson, GAR comrades responded with bitter acrimony, citing "treason is not dead yet, but lived in the act of lowering the flag at half-mast for a damned and damnable traitor" (William H. Ward, *Records of Members of the Grand Army of the Republic* [San Francisco: H. S. Crocker & Co., 1886], 100).

33. C. L. Sumbardo, "Incidents of Prison Life: With Causes of Confederate Cruelty," in *Glimpses of the Nation's Struggle,* 376; *Grand Army Record* 5 (December, 1889): 4; *Grand Army Record* 11 (January, 1896): 7; *National Tribune,* September 19, 1889.

34. "Rebel Monuments," *Grand Army Record* 6 (August 1891): 5; "Andersonville," *Grand Army Record* 6 (December 1891): 4; "Statue of Robert E. Lee," *The Sabbath Recorder* 69 (July 1910): 357; "Resolution," *Journal of the Forty-Third Annual Convention of the Department of Massachusetts Women's Relief Corps April 11 and 12, 1922* (Boston: William J. Walsh, 1922), 195.

35. "Montgomery Sustained," *Grand Army Record* 11 (January 1896): 7. Alan T. Nolan proposes that the North, whose people "had to acknowledge the honor of the South," fully embraced the Lee tradition. "Revisionism," especially in terms of Lost Cause interpretations of the war where Lee figured centrally, argues Nolan, "could not become part of the Civil War legend without northern acceptance, and the North did accept the South's rewriting of the record" (Nolan, *Lee Considered,* 165); *Grand Army Record* 5 (June 1890): 4.

36. Robert Kissick, "False Patriotism," *Journal of the Forty-First Encampment of the Grand Army of the Republic, September 11th and 12th 1907* (Zanesville, OH: Courier Company, 1907), 183–84; *Proceeding of the 56th Annual Encampment, Department of Pennsylvania, Grand Army of the Republic* (Harrisburg, PA: J. L. L. Kuhn, Printer to the Commonwealth, 1922), 195; For other protestations against commemorations honoring Robert E. Lee, see *National Tribune,* September 19, 1889; *Proceedings of the 44th Annual Encampment, Department of Pennsylvania, GAR, June 8th and 9th, 1910* (Harrisburg, PA: C. E. Aughinbaugh, 1910), 210.

37. Author unknown, "Resolutions of Post 480, Department of Ohio, GAR," quoted in Mary R. Dearing, *Veterans in Politics,* 345.

38. For a comprehensive look at the political career of Grover Cleveland, see Alyn Brodsky, *Grover Cleveland: A Study in Character* (New York: Truman Talley Books, 2000). For a study

of how Civil War rivalries influenced state politics, especially the 1888 presidential campaign, see James H. Madison, "Civil War Memories and 'Pardnership Forgittin',' 1865–1913," *Indiana Magazine of History* 99, no. 3 (September 2003): 198–230.

39. "War Produces Awful Horrors," *Wisconsin Democrat*, ca. June 5, 1905.

40. Author unknown, entry for March 6, 1905, volume title, "G.A.R. N.Y. Department, Brooklyn City Post 233, Minutes, 1898–1909," p. 412, NYPL, 412.

41. "G.A.R. N.Y. Department, Brooklyn City Post 233, Minutes, 1898–1909," entry for March 11, 1905, 413, 419, 424. Angering surviving GAR veterans, President Roosevelt signed a bill returning all captured Confederate battle flags to the South in 1905. For Roosevelt's reconciliatory message, see Theodore Roosevelt, "Charleston Exposition Address, April 9, 1902," in *Addresses and Presidential Messages of Theodore Roosevelt* (New York: G. P. Putnam's Sons, 1904), 3–4.

42. The Confederate battle flag has seen a great deal of controversy since the end of the war. Many (generally white southern) people interpret the flag as a soldier's emblem detached from ideological connections to slavery. Rather than depicting the flag as a symbol of treason, many envision it as a second American flag, symbolizing the virtues of all American fighting men. Many others disagree with these sentiments and wish to see the flag banned in government buildings, public schools, and at civic gatherings. See John M. Coski, *The Confederate Battle Flag: America's Most Embattled Emblem* (Cambridge, MA: Harvard University Press, 2005). For a sympathetic view of the flag, see Don Hinkle, *Embattled Banner: A Reasonable Defense of the Confederate Battle Flag* (Paducah, KY: Turner, 1997).

43. *Journal of Proceedings of the Twelfth Annual Encampment of the Department of Minnesota, Grand Army of the Republic, Under the New Organization, February 17, 18 and 19, 1892* (St. Paul: Pioneer Press Company, 1892), 236. Grand Army veterans recognized that "treasonable sentiments uttered and the display of the symbols of treason at every meeting of the Confederate Veterans and the Daughters of the Confederacy can only lead to weaken loyalty and inspire treason in the hearts of participants and onlookers and those who read about these doings in the newspapers." GAR men worked diligently to eradicate this practice, citing the *National Tribune* as the principal organ for this purpose. See *Abstract of General Orders and Proceedings of the Fortieth Annual Encampment, Department of New York, G.A.R.* (Albany, NY: Brandow Printing Co., 1906), 251.

44. Alan Kraut, *The Huddled Masses: The Immigrant in American Society, 1880–1922* (Wheeling, IL: Harlan Davidson, 1982); Ivan N. Walker, "Address of Ivan N. Walker," *Journal of Proceedings of the Sixteenth Annual Encampment of the Department of Minnesota, Grand Army of the Republic, Under the New Organization, March 11th and 12th 1896* (Minneapolis: Co-operative Printing Co., 1896), 213. For other contemporary condemnations of the Confederate battle flag, see Edward Livermore Burlingame et al., *Scribner's Magazine* 19 (January–June 1896): 75; *Journal of the Fortieth National Encampment of the Grand Army of the Republic at Minneapolis, Minnesota August 16th and 17th, 1906* (Philadelphia: Town Printing Co., 1906), 99; Henry M. Nevius, "Address of Henry M. Nevius," *Proceedings of the 43rd Annual Encampment, Department of Pennsylvania, GAR, June 9 and 10, 1909* (Harrisburg, PA: C. E. Aughinbaugh, 1909), 239–40.

45. Orlando B. Potter, "Address of Hon. Orlando B. Potter," *New York Monuments Commission for the Battlefields of Gettysburg and Chattanooga—Final Report on the Battlefield of Gettysburg*, 2 vols. (Albany, NY: J. B. Lyon Co., Printers, 1900), 2:670. For nearly identical remarks, see also John R. Strang, "Address of John R. Strang," *New York Monuments Commission*, 750.

46. Entry for May 7, 1906, box 15, folder 10 "Post 11 Meeting Book," GAR Papers, WVM. On commemorations to the Civil War dead and the problems with reconciliation, see Neff, *Honoring the Civil War Dead*. On the culture of reverence surrounding Civil War deaths, see Drew Gilpin Faust, *The Republic of Suffering: Death and the American Civil War* (New York: Knopf, 2008).

47. Comrade Craig, "Resolution," *Proceedings of the 34th Annual Encampment of the Department of Pennsylvania, GAR, Gettysburg, June 6th and 7th, 1900* (n.p.: William Stanley Ray, 1900), 251.

48. Mark D. Flower, "Address of Mark D. Flower," *Journal of Proceedings of the Thirty-second Annual Encampment of the Department of Minnesota, Grand Army of the Republic, March 2–3. 1898* (Minneapolis: Co-operative Printing Co., 1898), 62. For a recent study on the dialogue between Confederate sympathizers and Unionists in a postwar border state, see Anne E. Marshall, *Creating a Confederate Kentucky: The Lost Cause and Civil War Memory in a Border State* (Chapel Hill: University of North Carolina Press, 2010).

49. The notion that the Union victory at the battle of Gettysburg sealed the fate of the Confederacy stands out as a recurring theme in veterans' recollections. A. M. Mills, "Address of A. M. Mills," *New York Monument Commission for the Battlefields of Gettysburg and Chattanooga*, 2:832. See also Neill, *Glimpses of the Nation's Struggle*, 435, 498; J. A. Watrous, "General George Gordon Meade," in *War Papers Read Before the Commandery of the State of Wisconsin, Military Order of the Loyal Legion of the United States*, 4 vols. (Milwaukee, WI: Burdick & Allen, 1914), 4:445; Richard S. Thompson, "A Scrap at Gettysburg," *Military Essays and Recollections: Papers Read Before the Commandery of the State of Illinois, Military Order of the Loyal Legion of the United States*, 8 vols. (Chicago: Dial Press, 1899), 3:106–7.

50. William Glenny, "Address of General William Glenny, July 2, 1890," *New York Monuments Commission for the Battlefields of Gettysburg and Chattanooga*, 2:521. Glenny, after the war, served as the postmaster of Ithaca, New York. See "Gen. William Glenny Dead, *New York Times*, January 8, 1900.

51. Clinton Spencer, "Address of Captain Clinton Spencer," *Michigan at Gettysburg, July 1st, 2nd, 3rd, 1863. June 12th 1889. Proceedings Incident to the Dedication of the Michigan Monuments upon the Battlefield of Gettysburg, June 12th, 1889* (Detroit: Winn & Hammond, Printers and Binders, 1889), 72–73.

52. Miller "Address of Captain Miller," *Michigan at Gettysburg*, 89. The "Angle" at Gettysburg holds a powerful place in Civil War memory as the "High Water Mark of the Confederacy" and thus the turning point of the war. Much of the mythology surrounding this particular point stems from the work of John B. Bachelder and his efforts to enshrine Gettysburg National Military Park as the premier Civil War battlefield. His intentions were to accent the Angle as the exact spot where the Civil War was lost and won. Most Americans would come

to view the battle as the decisive event of the war. See David Ladd and Audrey Ladd, eds., *The Bachelder Papers*, 3 vols. (Dayton, OH: Morningside Bookshop, 1994). On the importance of John B. Bachelder and the prominence of the Gettysburg battlefield, see Thomas A. Desjardin, *These Honored Dead: How the Story of Gettysburg Shaped American Memory* (Cambridge, MA: De Capo Press, 2003); Barbara L. Platt, *"This is Holy Ground": A History of the Gettysburg Battlefield* (Harrisburg, PA: Barbara L. Platt, 2001).

53. Clarendon E. Adams, "Address of Clarendon E. Adams," *Abstract of General Orders and Proceedings of the Fifty-Third Annual Encampment Department of New York, GAR, Held at Elmira, June 24, 25, 26, 1919* (Albany, NY: J. B. Lyon Co., 1919), 249.

54. I. M. Cravath, "Oration of I. M. Cravath," *The National Memorial Day: A Record of Ceremonies over the Graves of the Union Dead, May 29 and 30, 1869* (Washington City: Headquarters of the GAR, 1870), 474; Comrade Cole, "Address of Comrade Cole," *Journal of the Forty-Eighth Encampment, Grand Army of the Republic, Detroit Michigan, September 8 and 9, 1914* (Washington, DC: Government Printing Office, 1915), 264; Theodore Roosevelt, "Address of Theodore Roosevelt," *Two Hundredth Anniversary of the Old Dutch Church of Sleepy Hollow, October 10 and 11, 1897* (Tarrytown, NY: De Vinne Press, 1898), 103; Charles Dick, "Speech of Charles Dick," *Congressional Record*, January 5, 1904.

55. Wilbur F. Brown, ed., *Lafayette Post No. 140, Department of New York, Grand Army of the Republic* (New York: Wilbur F. Brown, 1900), 19, 93, 59.

56. Thomas H. McKee, "Views and Reviews of the Civil War of 1861–65," in *War Papers* 3:328–29.

CHAPTER THREE

1. Thomas Neville Waul, "Address of General T. N. Waul, Reunion of Hood's Texas Brigade, Brenham, Texas, June 22, 1881," in *Hood's Texas Brigade Scrapbook*, 12, 239; J. W. Stevens, "Address of J. W. Stevens," in *Hood's Texas Brigade Scrapbook*, 33.

2. *Hood's Texas Brigade Scrapbook*, 34; Charles Joyner, "'Forget Hell': The Civil War in Southern Memory," in Grant and Parrish, *Legacy of Disunion*, 17–29.

3. James N. Dunlop, "Address of James N. Dunlop," in *Annual Reunion of Pegram Battalion Association in the Hall of the House of Delegates, Richmond, Va., May 21st, 1886: When the Battle-flag of the Battalion Was Presented by Capt. W. Gordon McCabe, Adjutant.* (Richmond, VA: Wm. Ellis Jones, 1886), 23. Historians have effectively misplaced this form of commemoration. The majority of white southerners, historians suggest, distanced themselves from efforts to revitalize the divisive aspects of Confederate memory and rejected bitter former Rebels. In his most influential work, Gaines M. Foster equates such bitter Rebels with Native American Ghost Dancers of the late nineteenth century. "They clung to the past, defended old values, and dreamed of a world untouched by defeat." Very few southerners, Foster argues, joined the ghost dance. By the 1880s, "Confederate celebration did not foster a revival of rabid sectionalism." Historians Thomas L. Connelly and Barbara L. Bellows agree. Their work focuses on commemorations during the late nineteenth and early twentieth centuries and emphasizes how the "passing of time quieted the roar of Rebel yells." Such observations obscure the

intentions of those who considered themselves reconciled. Foster, *Ghosts of the Confederacy,* 3–8, 60–61; Thomas L. Connelly and Barbara L. Bellows, *God and General Longstreet: The Lost Cause and the Southern Mind* (Baton Rouge: Louisiana State University Press, 1982), 3.

4. Historians have a tendency to explain Confederate commemorations as if they were generally accepted across the nation—as if former Confederates ultimately won the war with the pen. In 1973, historian Rollin G. Osterweis attempted to elucidate this phenomenon. Osterweis analyzed images, literary and otherwise, of moonlight and magnolias, the "obliging old Uncle Remus," and, the "good, gray Confederate veteran." He observed a persistent sense of "southerness" despite a humiliating Confederate defeat and several years of infuriating Reconstruction politics. White southerners, Osterweis suggests, used these images as part of their efforts to romanticize and pay tribute to the antebellum South. He further notes, former Confederates clung fervently to a new American nationalism and, ironically, the righteous, fiercely sectional account of the Confederate States of America "[was] continually belied by the conduct of Southerners themselves." In this way, veterans involved in Civil War commemorations seemingly connected the New South—characterized by "progress," industry, and steadfast devotion to reunion—to a benign past that, while virtuous, inevitably gave way to modern America. They carefully recalled a few scattered memories that helped southerners come to terms with their greatest failure, retain a sense of regional dignity, and embrace a reunited nation. Rollin W. Osterweis, *The Myth of the Lost Cause 1865–1900 (Hamden, CT: Archon Books, 1973),* x–xi.

5. On setting an example of submission to authority, particularly while considering his acceptance of the presidency of Washington College, see Robert E. Lee to Gentlemen, n.d., #L51c737, microfilm, Lee Family Letterbook, VHS [collection hereafter cited as Lee Family Letterbook, VHS]. On promoting prosperity through reconciliation, see Robert E. Lee to Mr. A. M. Keiley, September 4, 1865, Lee Family Letterbook, VHS; Robert E. Lee to James Longstreet, October 29, 1867, Lee Family Letterbook, VHS. Treatments on Lee throughout much of the twentieth century were favorable in terms of his willingness to submit to authority. One study suggested that Lee "emerged from the searing fire, not destroyed but refined." See Marshall W. Fishwick, *Lee after the War* (Westport: Greenwood, 1963), 207. For a critical study of Lee in the aftermath of war and as college president, see Connelly, *The Marble Man,* 209–11.

6. Robert E. Lee to Jubal A. Early, October 15, 1866, November 22, 1865; Lee to C. M. Wilcox, December 25, 1865; Lee to Lord John Dalberg Acton, December 15, 1866, Lee Family Letterbook, VHS. On Lee's inability to adjust to the radical changes during the Reconstruction Period and his reactionary views on race, see Michael Fellman, *The Making of Robert E. Lee* (New York: Random House, 2000).

7. John T. Goolrick, *Historic Fredericksburg: The Story of an Old Town* (Richmond, VA: Whittet & Shepperson, 1922), 10, 37, 194, 196; John T. Goolrick to William Berkeley, November 29, 1921, Box 1-a, #6769, folder 11, Berkeley Minor Papers, UVA.

8. Fitzhugh Lee Address, 1876, recalled by reporter, *New York Tribune,* August 29, 1905, quoted in James L. Nichols, *General Fitzhugh Lee: A Biography* (Lynchburg, VA: H. E. Howard, 1989), 119; John Warwick Daniel Address, 1907, box 16, folder title "Speeches: Confederate Veterans, 1907," #5383, John Warwick Daniel Papers, UVA; John Warwick Daniel Address,

undated typescript, box 16, folder title "Speeches: Confederate Veterans," #5383, John Warwick Daniel Papers, UVA.

9. Fitzhugh Lee to Jubal A. Early, July 6, 1875, quoted in Nichols, *General Fitzhugh Lee,* 119; John Warwick Daniel to Eppa Hutton, September 30, 1909, box 1, folder 1, #9267a, Hutton Family Papers, VHS.

10. John Randolph Tucker, *The Old and New South: Baccalaureate Address before the South Carolina College, Commencement, 1887* (Columbia: Presbyterian Publishing House, 1887), 3.

11. Jos. R. Stonebraker, *A Rebel of '61* (New York: Wynkoop Hallenbeck Crawford Co., Printers, 1899), 1; Frank Edwards, *Army Life of Frank Edwards* (n.p.: n. d.; reprint: Bibliolife, 2009), 90, 93.

12. G. B. Harris, "The Heritage of a Son," *Confederate Veteran* 24 (November 1916): 523; Hunter McGuire, ed., *The Confederate Cause and Conduct in the War Between the States* (Richmond, VA: L. H. Jenkins, 1907), 144.

13. McGuire, *The Confederate Cause and Conduct,* vii.

14. Remarks of G[eorge] L. Christian at "General Jubal A. Early Memorial Address by Hon. John Warwick Daniel before the Association of the Army of Northern Virginia at the Annual Meeting Held at Richmond December 13, 1894," *SHSP* 22 (June 1894):283, and *The Confederate Cause and Its Defenders: An Address Delivered before the Grand Army of Confederate Veterans of Virginia, at the Annual Meeting Held at Culpepper C.H., Va., October 4, 1898* (Richmond, VA: Wm. Ellis Jones, Book and Job Printer, 1898), 25.

15. J. W. Ward, "General M. C. Butler of South Carolina," *Confederate Veteran* 2 (February 1895): 42; Author unknown, "Memorial Day at Savannah Georgia," *Confederate Veteran* 2 (May 1895): 130; Author unknown, "The Lost Dispatch," *The Land We Love* 1 (May 1867): 272; John Herbert Claiborne "The Last Days of Lee and His Paladins," in *War Talks of Confederate Veterans: Addresses Delivered before A. P. Hill Camp of Confederate Veterans, of Petersburg Va.,* ed. George S. Bernard (Petersburg, VA: Fenn & Owen, 1892), and *Seventy-Five Years in Old Virginia* (New York, Neale Publishing Co., 1904).

16. John S. Beard, *Address of Hon. John S. Beard of Pensacola at Defuniak Springs, Florida, March 16, 1901 at Reunion of First Florida Brigade, United Confederate Veterans* (n.p., ca. 1901), 1; Entry for August, 1912, "Seventeenth Reunion," Surry Light Artillery & Deal-Crenshaw Minute Book, Mss4C708a1, VHS, 31.

17. J. L. Underwood, *The Women of the Confederacy* (New York: Neale Publishing Company, 1906), 262.

18. Bradley T. Johnson, "Oration of General Bradley T. Johnson," *SHSP* 23 (October 1895): 364–72, and *Address before the Association of Confederate Soldiers and Sailors of Maryland, June 10, 1874* (Baltimore: Kelly Piet & Co.), 1874), 4.

19. Robert E. Lee Jr., *Address of R. E. Lee, Jr. to the Veterans: Delivered during the Confederate Reunion Held at Richmond, Virginia, 1907* (n.p.: n.p., ca. 1907), 7.

20. Clement A. Evans, "Contributions of the South to the Greatness of the American Union: Delivered before the Association of the Army of Northern Virginia, October 10, 1895 at Richmond, Virginia," *SHSP* 23 (January 1895): 17. Not simply the right of secession, but the right of secession in the face of northern slander and abuse pervades the commemora-

tive press. See Jonathan H. Savage, "Schoolmasters at Chickamauga," *Confederate Veteran* 3 (December 1895): iii; B. B. Munford, "The Vindication of the South," *SHSP* 27 (January 1899), 67; Charles C. Hemming, "Confederate Dead of Florida," *SHSP* 27 (January 1899): 119.

21. Beard, *Address of Hon. John S. Beard of Pensacola at Defuniak Springs,* 12, 10, 13, 1. For a similar message, see Bradley T. Johnson, *The Maryland Confederates: An Address before the Confederate Society of St. Mary's at Leonardtown March 1894* (Baltimore: J. Harry Drechsler, ca. 1894), 3.

22. P. McGlashan, "Memorial Day Oration," *Address Delivered before the Confederate Veterans Association of Savannah, 1898–1902* (Savannah, GA: Published by the Association, 1902), 15; John Warwick Daniel, "Oration of Senator Daniel," *Minutes of the First Annual Meeting and Reunion of the United Confederate Veterans* (New Orleans: Hopkins' Printing, 1891), 31.

23. George Moorman, "Address of George Moorman," *Minutes of the Sixth Annual Meeting of the United Confederate Veterans Held in the City of Richmond, Va.* (New Orleans: Hopkins' Printing, 1897), 50; R. T. W. Duke, "Address of R. T. W. Duke," *Memorial History of the John Bowie Strange Camp, United Confederate Veterans* (n. p.: n. p., ca. 1891), 15.

24. D. Gardner Tyler, "Address of D. Gardner Tyler," in *Addresses Delivered at the Unveiling of the Monument to Confederate Soldiers of Charles City County, Virginia, at Charles City Courthouse, November 21, 1900* (Richmond: Whittet & Shepperson, 1901), 41, 44–45; Lee, "The Unveiling of the Monument to the Confederate Dead of Alexandria," 8, 17. On Tyler's rise in national politics, see *New York Times,* November 14, 1892.

25. Speaker unknown, "The Jackson Monument at Charlottesville," *Confederate Veteran* 30 (February 1922): 44; Law, *The Confederate Revolution,* 5.

26. Beard, *Address of Hon. John S. Beard of Pensacola at Defuniak Springs,* 1, 14–15; Ballew, *Historical Address to Confederate Veterans,* 20.

27. Author unknown, "Report of History Committee, Grand Camp, C.V.," *SHSP* 28 (June 1899): 192; Tucker, *The Old and New South,* 7; Evans, "Contributions of the South to the Greatness of the American Union." In a compilation of records concerning the "illegal" imprisonment of United States citizens from the border states, John A. Marshal summed up the sentiments of Confederate sympathizers—even those initially opposed to secession—in constitutional terms. Many, such as George William Brown of Baltimore, believed that the "constitutional rights of the southern states had been persistently violated by the northern states" and the war "was waged for the purpose of subjugation." John A. Marshall, *American Bastille* (Philadelphia: Thomas W. Hartley & Co., 1881), 254.

28. R. J. Harding, "Annual Address of Colonel R. J. Harding, President of Hood's Texas Brigade Association, at Corsica Texas Reunion, June 28, 1905," *Hood's Texas Brigade Scrapbook,* 177.

29. James H. M'Neilly, "What Did President Lincoln's Statesman-ship Accomplish?" *Confederate Veteran* 25 (October 1917): 453, and *The Failure of the Confederacy: Was It a Blessing?* (Nashville: n. p., ca. 1911).

30. James M. Mullen, "The Last Days of Johnston's Army," in *War Talks of Confederate Veterans: Addresses Delivered before A.P. Hill Camp of Confederate Veterans, of Petersburg Va.,* ed. George S. Bernard (Petersburg, VA: Fenn & Owen, 1892), 298; John R. Reagan, "Address of John R. Reagan," *Hood's Texas Brigade Scrapbook,* 320.

31. Charles C. Jones, "Oration Pronounced by Col. Charles C. Jones, Jr. on the 31st October, 1878 Upon the Occasion of the Unveiling and Dedication of the Confederate Monument erected by the Ladies Memorial Association of Augusta in Broad Street in the City of Augusta, Georgia," *Augusta Evening Sentinel* October 31, 1878; Ballew, *Historical Address to Confederate Veterans*, 1. On denunciations of the accusation of treason, see Arthur B. Jennings, "That Lincoln Resolution—and Some Other Things," *Confederate Veteran* 30 (August 1922): 285. Those reflecting on accusations of treason implied an impediment to reconciliation during the time of writing. Suggested one veteran, the use of the term was part of an "ignorant and venomous spirit of persecution." R. L. Dabney, "Memoir of the Narrative Received of Colonel John B. Baldwin, of Staunton, Touching on the Origin of the War" *SHSP* 1 (June 1876); 450; M.T. Hunter, "The Origin of the Late War," *SHSP* 1 (January 1876): 11; Clement A. Evans, "Jefferson Davis Home Association," *Confederate Veteran* 17 (January 1909): 2; John S. Robson, *How a One-Legged Rebel Lives*, (Durham, NC: The Educator Co., 1898), 81; "Southern Veterans Protest," *New York Times*, September 20, 1900.

32. William L. Calhoun, *History of the 42nd Regiment, Georgia Volunteers, Infantry* (Atlanta: n. p., 1900), 3; Wayland Fuller Dunaway, *Reminiscences of a Rebel* (New York: Neale Publishing Co., 1913), 127; Author unknown, "The 9th of April, 1865," *SHSP* 28 (November 1899): 376–77. Both Alexander Stephens and Jefferson Davis wrote extensively on republicanism and the Confederacy as the true inheritors of republican ideals. See Stephens, *A Constitutional View of the Late War between the States*, 1:521; Davis, *The Rise and Fall of the Confederate Government*, 2:300–303.

33. Author unknown, "Sketch of the First Kentucky Brigade," *The Land We Love* 2 (December 1867): 98. For a similar perspective, see Robson, *How a One-Legged Rebel Lives*, 35; McKim, "The Vindication of the South"; T. S. Garrett, "Address of T. S. Garrett" *SHSP* 28 (January 1899), 154.

34. B. H. Hill, "Address of Honorable B. H. Hill" *SHSP* 14 (November 1886): 487–88; *New York Times*, April 11, 1861.

35. Joseph Wheeler, "Causes of the War" *SHSP* 22 (January 1894): 36.

36. Henry A. Wise, "Career of Wise's Brigade, 1861–65" *SHSP* 25 (January 1898): 20–21.

37. Captain Park, "Address of Captain Park" *SHSP* 25 (June 1898): 357–58; R. M. T. Hunter, "The Republic of Republics" *SHSP* 13 (July 1885): 344–45; B. B. Munford, "The Vindication of the South" *SHSP* 27 (January 1899): 61.

38. Foster, *Ghosts of the Confederacy*, 106, 91–92.

39. *Confederate Veteran* 3 (June 1895): 179; *Confederate Veteran* 3 (October 1895): 316.

40. *Confederate Veteran* 11 (September 1903): 389.

41. *Confederate Veteran* 2 (June 1894): 174; *Confederate Veteran* 11 (June 1903): 252.

42. *Confederate Veteran* 24 (October 1916): 447; Edwin A. Alderman, "The Jackson Monument at Charlottesville," *Confederate Veteran* 30 (February 1922): 44; *Confederate Veteran* 30 (August 1922): 285; Giles B. Cooke, "Endorsement of Committee," *Confederate Veteran* 30 (November 1922): 437.

43. *Confederate Veteran* 2 (January 1894): 2. John Brown Gordon, a devout reconciliationist, insisted that he dedicated his career as UCV commander to the "truth of history" and "justice

to the South." Even though Gordon made such claims, a number of Confederate veterans, including the entire roster of the Confederate Association of the Army of Tennessee, censured him for his amiable relations with members of the GAR. See "Gen. Gordon's Statement," *New York Times,* August 21, 1900.

CHAPTER FOUR

1. Charles A. Fuller, "Address of Charles A. Fuller," *New York Monuments Commission for the Battlefields of Gettysburg and Chattanooga,* 2 vols. (Albany: J. B. Lyon Co., Printers, 1900), 2:456.

2. Henry M. Rogers, "The Inspiration of the Loyal Legion," *Vermont War Papers and Miscellaneous States Papers and Addresses for Military Order of the Loyal Legion of the United States* (1915; reprint, Wilmington, NC: Broadfoot, 1994), 249.

3. John J. Ingalls, "Address of John J. Ingalls," *Journal of Proceedings of the Thirteenth Annual Encampment of the Department of Minnesota, Grand Army of the Republic, Under the New Organization, February 21 and 22, 1893* (St. Paul: Press of Zander Bros., 1893), 210. On Ingalls's illustrious political career, see Burton J. Williams, *Senator John J. Ingalls: Kansas' Iridescent Republican* (Lawrence: University Press of Kansas, 1972).

4. Regimental histories, for example, are explicit on this issue—a point that scholars such as David Blight all but ignore. Recalling the various battles of the war, veterans would proclaim, "The war [would] go on until the South should be hopelessly crippled, and would of necessity, yield all claim to slavery" (Simons, *A Regimental History of the One Hundred and Twenty-Fifth New York State Volunteers,* 147). Further, victorious Union veterans rejoiced in a "holy trinity of results: the saving of the Nation's life, the extinction of the blot of slavery from the National escutcheon, and the establishment of the principle of the equality of all" (Robert Laird Stewart, *History of the One Hundred and Fortieth Pennsylvania Volunteers* [n.p.: Franklin Bindery, 1912], 288); Janney, *Remembering the Civil War,* esp. chap. 7.

5. Gannon, *The Won Cause,* see especially Appendix I: African American GAR Posts, 201–7; Appendix II: Integrated GAR Posts, 209–20.

6. M. P. Larry to "Dear sister," February 16, 1863, in *Yankee Correspondence: Civil War Letters between New England Soldiers and the Home Front,* ed. Nina Silber and Mary Beth Sievens (Charlottesville: University Press of Virginia, 1996), 98; Charles Fesseden Morse, *Letters Written during the Civil War, 1861–1865* (n. p.: privately printed, 1898), 98; Jeffrey L. Patrick, ed., *Three Years with Wallace's Zouaves: The Civil War Memoirs of Thomas Wise Durham* (Macon, GA: Mercer University Press, 2003), 98.

7. As historian Thomas Pressly suggests, the "position of abolitionists was enhanced after the war and their viewpoints given greater prestige." In his 1954 publication, *Americans Interpret Their Civil War,* Pressly asserted that supporters of the Union had "confident assurance of the evil of their late foes and of their own virtual faultlessness. The victorious Unionists of 1865 would have been less than human," Pressly remarks, "if their triumph of arms had not strengthened their belief in the rightness of their opinions." Even leniency toward the former Confederate states could not diminish many Unionists' moral rectitude. Union vet-

erans were well aware that they put down an act of rebellion intricately linked with slavery. Pressly, *Americans Interpret Their Civil War,* 31–33, 38, 44, 47–48. See also George Grenville Benedict, *Vermont in the Civil War: A History of the Part Taken by the Vermont Soldiers and Sailors in the War for the Union, 1861–65* (Burlington, VT: Free Press Association, 1886), 71. Benedict's words affirmed Pressly's assessment that "the Unionists of 1865 taught a moral lesson: the forces of darkness had attempted, unsuccessfully, to destroy the best government in the world with the purpose of erecting a new nation founded upon slavery." Had they succeeded, suggested the Vermonter, "another civil war would have become necessary before slavery and secession were destroyed."

8. Charles E. Curtis Post no. 34, GAR, Whitewater, Wisconsin, Meeting Minute Book, folder 6, box 23, GAR Records, Dept. of Wisconsin, WVM.

9. George E. Sutherland, "Address of George E. Sutherland," *War Papers Read Before the Commandery of the State of Wisconsin, Military Order of the Loyal Legion of the United States,* 4 vols. (Milwaukee, WI: Burdick & Allen, 1914), 3:102.

10. Charles Devens, "Address Delivered at the Celebration of the Twenty-Fifth Anniversary of the Founding of the Military Order of the Loyal Legion of the United States," read: April 15, 1890, *Military Essay and Recollections of the Pennsylvania Commandery of the Loyal Legion of the United States,* 2 vols. (1903; reprint, Wilmington, NC: Broadfoot, 1995), 1:80–81.

11. Entry for July 5, 1887, box 15, folder 8, "C.C. Washburn Post no. 11, Madison, Wisconsin, Meeting Minute Book," GAR Papers, WVM. The entry for July 5, 1887, further illuminates the voice of the Confederate cause as a "language of ingratitude and a disregard of the facts of history."

12. Anonymous letter to Fairchild Post, no. 11, GAR, March 10, 1930, box 18, folder 2, GAR Papers, WVM.

13. Benjamin F. Butler, *Autobiography and Personal Reminiscences of Major-General Benjamin F. Butler; Butler's Book* (Boston: A. M. Thayer, 1892), 961–62, 128–29; James Laughery Paul, *Pennsylvania's Soldiers' Orphan Schools* (Harrisburg, PA: Lanes Hart, 1877), 17.

14. *National Tribune,* April 8, 1915.

15. Thomas M. Woodruff, "Early War Days in the Nation's Capital," *Glimpses of the Nation's Struggle, Papers Read Before the Minnesota Commandery of the Military Order of the Loyal Legion of the United States, 1889–1892,* 6 vols. (St. Paul: D. D. Merill), 3:88–89.

16. J. B. Foraker, "Address of J. B. Foraker," in E. R. Monfort, H. B. Furness, and Fred. H. Alms, eds., *G.A.R. War Papers: Papers Read Before Fred. C. Jones Post, No. 401, Department of Ohio, G.A.R.* (Cincinnati: Fred. C. Jones Post, No. 401, 1891), 388.

17. The vast collection of war papers read before the various commanderies of the Military Order of the Loyal Legion of the United States attest to this statement. Many recognized that Union soldiers fought to suppress rebellion conceived upon the cornerstone of slavery. For example, see Irving M. Bean, "The Glover Rescue," *War Papers Read Before the Commandery of Wisconsin, Military Order of the Loyal Legion of the United States,* 4 vols. (Milwaukee, WI: Burdick & Allen, 1914), 4:222, 230; James L. Foley, "With Frémont in Missouri," *Sketches of War History 1861–1865: Papers Read for the Commandery of the State of Ohio, Military Order of the Loyal Legion of the United States,* 9 vols. (Cincinnati: Robert Clarke Co., 1903), 5:484.

18. George B. Loring, *An Oration Delivered at the Dedication of the Soldiers Monument In North Weymouth, Mass. On July 4th, 1868* (Weymouth, MA: C. G. Kasterbrook, 1869), 23; *Proceedings at the Dedication of the Soldiers' and Sailors' Monument, in Providence* (Providence, RI: A. Crawford Greene, 1871), 24, 36; Charles Devens, "Address of Charles Devens," *Dedication of the Monument on Boston Common Erected to the Memory of the Men of Boston Who Died in the Civil War* (Boston: Boston City Council, 1877), 133–34; *Ceremonies at the Dedication of the Soldiers' Monument in West Roxbury Mass.* (Boston: Hollis & Gunn, 1871), 29.

19. Daniel Clark, "Address of Daniel Clark," *Ceremonies at the Dedication of the Monument Erected by the City of Manchester, N. H., to the Men Who Periled Their Lives to Save the Union in the Late Civil War* (Manchester, NH: Mirror Steam Printing Press, 1880), 68; J. W. Patterson, "Address of J. W. Patterson," *Ceremonies at the Dedication,* 98.

20. Seth Low, "Dedication of Monument to the Eighty-Fourth Regiment Infantry: 'Fourteenth Brooklyn,'" *New York Monuments Commission for the Battlefields of Gettysburg and Chattanooga,* 2:683.

21. H. N. Shepard, "Address of H. N. Shepard," *The Record of the Processions and of the Exercises of the Dedication of the Monument Erected by the People of Pembroke, Mass.* (Plymouth, MA: Avery & Doten, 1890), 37; R. C. Griffit, ed., *Report of the Unveiling and Dedication of the Indiana Monument at Andersonville* (n. p., 1909), 26.

22. D. Scott Hartwig and Anne Marie Hartwig, *Gettysburg: The Complete Pictorial of Battlefield Monuments* (Gettysburg, PA: Thomas, 1995). If flank markers are also counted, the number of monuments, broadly defined, exceeds thirteen hundred.

23. Turning points are a recurring theme in Civil War literature, especially that which concerns the conspicuous place of contingency in academic analysis. See, for example, James M. McPherson, *Battle Cry of Freedom: The Civil War Era* (New York: Oxford University Press, 1988), and *Crossroads of Freedom: Antietam, the Battle That Changed the Course of the Civil War* (New York: Oxford University Press, 2002).

24. John W. Phillips, "Address of John W. Phillips," in *Pennsylvania at Gettysburg: Ceremonies of the Dedications of the Monuments,* ed. John P. Nicholson, 2 vols. (Harrisburg, PA: E. K. Meyers, 1893), 2:863; Robert Laird Stewart, *History of the One Hundred Fortieth Regiment, Pennsylvania Volunteers* (n. p., 1912), 93–145.

25. Comrade Cole, *Journal of the Forty-Eighth National Encampment, Grand Army of the Republic, Detroit, Michigan* (Washington, DC: Government Printing Office, 1915), 263; William Hobson, "Hobson's Oration," *Maine at Gettysburg: Report of the Maine Commissioners* (Portland, Maine: Lakeside Press, 1898), 220; By the World War I era, veterans were comparing the achievements at Gettysburg with fights all around the world. See *Journal of the Thirty-Eighth National Encampment of the Grand Army of the Republic, Department of Oregon* (Salem. OR: State Printing Dept., 1919), 87.

26. A. J. Sellers, "Address of A. J. Sellers," *Pennsylvania at Gettysburg,* 1:482.

27. John A. Danks, "Address of John A. Danks," *Pennsylvania at Gettysburg,* 359; Cornelius R. Parsons, "Address of Cornelius R. Parsons," *Final Report on the Battlefield at Gettysburg,* 2 vols. (Albany: J. B. Lyon, 1902), 2:786.

28. J. H. H. Love, "Dedication of the Monument to the Thirteenth New Jersey Volunteers, July 1, 1887: Address of General F. H. Harris, read by J. H. H. Love," in *State of New Jersey, Final Report of the Gettysburg Battle-field Commission, 1891*(Trenton: John L. Murphy, 1891), 35; John Ramsey, "Dedication of the Monument to the Eighth New Jersey Infantry, June 30, 1888, John Ramsey: Address on Behalf of the Eighth Regiment," in *State of New Jersey, Final Report*, 48.

29. Asa B. Isham, "Care of Prisoners of War, North and South," *Sketches of War History 1861–1865 Papers Read Before the Ohio Commandery of the Military Order of the Loyal Legion of the United States 1883–1886*, 9 vols. (Cincinnati: Robert Clarke & Co„ 1888), 2:214. For a wartime account of how emancipation struck a blow against the Confederacy, see John Fitch, *Annals of the Army of the Cumberland* (Philadelphia: J. B. Lippincott & Co., 1864), 683. For a postwar account praising the eradication of slavery in terms of progress and the growth of nation, see William H. Ward, *Records of Members of the Grand Army of the Republic* (Washington, DC: H. S. Crocker & Co., 1886), 48. On soldiers' realignment in favor of emancipation, see McPherson, *For Cause and Comrades*, esp. chap. 9.

30. Benjamin F. Taylor, "Address of Benjamin F. Taylor, Dedication of the Monument to the Seventy-Sixth Regiment Infantry, July 1, 1888," *New York Monuments Commission for the Battlefields of Gettysburg and Chattanooga*, 2:611.

31. N. M. Crane, "Address of General N. M. Crane, Dedication of Monument to the 107th New York Infantry Regiment, September 17, 1888," *New York Monuments Commission for the Battlefields of Gettysburg and Chattanooga*, 764; T. L. Barhydt, "Address of T. L. Barhydt, Dedication of the Monument to the 134th New York Infantry Regiment, July 22, 1888," *New York Monuments Commission*, 911.

32. James H. Potts, "Address of James H. Potts," *Michigan at Gettysburg, July 1st, 2nd, 3rd, 1863. June 12th 1889. Proceedings Incident to the Dedication of the Michigan Monuments upon the Battle-field of Gettysburg, June 12th, 1889* (Detroit: Winn & Hammond, Printers and Binders, 1889), 65.

33. L. S. Towbridge, "Address of General L. S. Trowbridge," *Michigan at Gettysburg*, 29, 39. Many used the Battle of Gettysburg to illustrate the culmination of an inevitable war against slavery. See, S. S. Neely's address on behalf of the borough of Gettysburg in *Proceedings of the 43rd Annual Encampment, Grand Army of the Republic, Gettysburg* (Harrisburg, PA: C. E. Aughinbaugh, 1909), 55. For veterans' recollections proclaiming the war represented nothing less than the culmination of long-contested contentions between a slave and free society, see George H. Washburn, *A Complete Military History and Record of the 108th Regiment N.Y. Volunteers from 1862 to 1864* (Rochester, NY: E. R. Andrews, 1894), 462.

34. "Boston's Noble Tribute," *New York Times*, September 17, 1877.

35. "Dedication of the Soldiers' Monument in the National Cemetery," *New York Times*, July 2, 1869.

36. "Honor Veterans of Fight at Antietam," *New York Times*, September 22, 1912.

37. "Veteran Navy Services," *New York Times*, May 21, 1900.

38. Horace Potter, "Speech of General Horace Porter," in *Birthday Banquet by U.S. Grant Post Number 327, Department of New York, Grand Army of the Republic, April 28, 1890* (New York: George J. Collins, 1890), 31; "The Great Dinner Last Night," *Brooklyn Eagle*, April 29, 1890. Reproduced in *Birthday Banquet by U.S. Grant Post Number 327, Department of New*

York, Grand Army of the Republic, April 28, 1890, 4. On the issue of textbooks, see Dearing, *Veterans in Politics,* 402–4, 480–86. Dearing suggests that the GAR was extremely anxious regarding the "proper and patriotic" education of schoolchildren. This would naturally include the centrality of slavery to the war, something southern veterans' organizations and women's groups tried desperately to purge from textbooks. In the state of Pennsylvania, for example, the GAR was successful. See Matthew Page Andrews, *History of the United States* (Philadelphia, J. B. Lippincott, 1914), esp. chaps. 26–28., *Grand Army of the Republic, held at Washington D.C. February, 1918* (Washington, DC: R. Beresford, February 6, 1918), 66.

39. Nelson Miles, "Address of Nelson Miles," *Journal of the Proceedings of the Fiftieth Annual Encampment of the Department of the Potomac, Grand Army of the Republic, held at Washington D.C. February, 1918* (Washington, D.C.: R. Beresford, February 6, 1918), 66.

40. *Journal of the Proceedings of the Forty-second Annual Encampment of the Department of the Potomac, Grand Army of the Republic, held at Washington D.C. February, 1910* (Washington, DC: R. Beresford, February 15, 1910), 47.

41. William E. Chandler, *Decoration Day Address of William E. Chandler* (Concord, NH: Republican Press Association, 1889), 4; John S. Maxwell, "Address of John S. Maxwell, May 1, 1907," Box 2, Mills Papers, NYPL.

42. Author unknown, *Services for the Use of the Grand Army of the Republic* (Toledo: Headquarters of the Grand Army of the Republic, 1884), 16.

43. Nelson Monroe, *The Grand Army Button: A Souvenir* (Boston: Rockwell & Churchill Press, 1893), 37.

44. "Toast of Comrade Castle," *Journal of Proceedings of the Eleventh Annual Encampment of the Department of Minnesota, Grand Army of the Republic, Under the New Organization, February 17, 18 and 19, 1891* (Minneapolis: Co-operative Printing Co., 1891), 232.

45. Samuel Fallows, "Address of Bishop Samuel Fallows," *War Papers Read Before the Commandery of the State of Wisconsin, Military Order of the Loyal Legion of the United States,* 3 vols. (Milwaukee, WI: Burdick, Armitage & Allen, 1891–1903), 2:377–78; Warren Hewitt Mead, "Address of Warren Hewitt Mead" in Neill, *Glimpses of the Nation's Struggle,* 240.

46. Richard Robins, ed., *Toasts and Responses at Banquets Given Lieut. Gen P. H. Sheridan by the Military Order of the Loyal Legion of the United States, Commandery of the State of Illinois* (Chicago: Knight & Leonard, 1883), 64, 53, 32.

47. *Journal of the Proceedings of the Twenty-Nine Annual Meeting of the Commandery-In-Chief* (Philadelphia: n. p., 1913), 38; Rutherford B. Hayes, *Military Order of the Loyal Legion of the United States, Address of Brevet Maj-General Rutherford B. Hayes at the Fifth Quadrennial Congress* (Chicago: n. p., 1885), 4; Arthur Edwards, "Address of Arthur Edwards," *Military Essays and Recollections, Military Order of the Loyal Legion of the United States, Commandery of the State of Illinois,* 8 vols. (Chicago: A. C. McClurg, 1891), 1:446; James A. Beaver, "Lincoln and the People," *Abraham Lincoln: Memorial Meeting, Commandery of the State of Pennsylvania* (n. p.: John P. Nicholson, 1907), 32. See also Jim Cullen, *The Civil War in Popular Culture: A Reusable Past* (Washington, DC: Smithsonian Institution Press, 1995), esp. chap. 1; Harold Holzer, *Emancipating Lincoln: The Proclamation in Text, Context, and Memory* (Cambridge, MA: Harvard University Press, 2012).

48. Albert Gallitin Riddle, *Recollections of War Times, Reminiscences of Men and Events in Washington, 1860–1865* (New York: G. P. Putnam's Sons, 1895), 131–32, 159; Le Grand B. Cannon, *Personal Reminiscences of the Rebellion, 1861–1866* (New York: Burr Printing House, 1895), 9–10; Charles Nelson Kent, *History of the Seventeenth Regiment, New Hampshire Volunteer Infantry, 1862–1863* (Concord, NH: Seventeenth New Hampshire Veteran Association, 1898), 8.

49. Simons, *A Regimental History of the One Hundred and Twenty-Fifth New York State Volunteers,* 147. Robert Laird Stewart, *History of the One Hundred and Fortieth Pennsylvania Volunteers* (n. p.: Franklin Bindery, 1912), 288; D. Lathrop, *The History of the Fifty-Ninth Regiment Illinois Volunteers* (Indianapolis: Hall & Hutchinson, 1865), 37–38; John Gregory Bishop Adams, *Reminiscences of the Nineteenth Massachusetts Regiment* (Boston: Wright & Potter, 1899), 152; George H. Washburn, *A Complete Military History and Record of the 108th Regiment N. Y. Vols. From 1862 to 1864* (Rochester, NY: E. R. Andrews, 1894), 225; John W. Storrs, *The "Twentieth Connecticut": A Regimental History* (Ansonia, CT: Press of the Naugatuck Valley Sentinel, 1886), 150.

50. Charles Bryant Fairchild, *History of the 27th N. Y. Vols.* (Binghampton, NY: Carl & Matthews, 1888), 132; Robert McCay Green, *History of the One Hundred Twenty-Fourth Regiment, Pennsylvania Volunteers* (Philadelphia: Ware Brothers, 1907), 176; Simons, *Regimental History,* 37.

51. Peter Cozzens and Robert L. Girardi, eds., *The Military Memoirs of General John Pope* (Chapel Hill: University of North Carolina Press, 1998), 85; Carl Schurz, *The Reminiscences of Carl Schurz,* 3 vols. (New York: McClure, 1907), 2:278, 36, 320. Pope's memoirs are an edited collection of articles that appeared in the *National Tribune* during the 1880s and 1890s; Theodore Ayrault Dodge, *A Bird's-Eye View of Our Civil War* (Boston: Houghton Mifflin, 1883), 1–4; John M. Schofield, *Forty-Six Years in the Army* (New York: The Century Co., 1897), 74–75, 235; John A. Logan, *The Volunteer Soldier of America* (Chicago: R. S. Peale, 1887), 86; Abner Doubleday, *Chancellorsville and Gettysburg* (New York: Charles Scribner's Sons, 1889), 77, 108.

52. Ulysses S. Grant, *Personal Memoirs of U.S. Grant,* 2 vols. (New York: Charles L. Webster, 1885), 2:553.

53. Julia Lorrilard Butterfield, ed., *A Biographical Memorial of General Daniel Butterfield* (New York: Grafton Press, 1904), 163; Grant, *Personal Memoirs,* 2:549, 489. On Grant's far-reaching reconciliatory legacy, see Joan Waugh, "'Pageantry of Woe': The Funeral of Ulysses S. Grant," *Civil War History* 51(June 2005):151–74. On the significance of Grant's memoirs illustrating the causes of union and freedom, see Waugh, "Ulysses S. Grant, Historian," in Fahs and Waugh, *The Memory of the Civil War in American Culture,* 5–38. Grant was also praised internationally for the positive conclusion to the Union war effort. L. T. Remlap predicted that future generations "will remember that he acted a foremost part in the most notable events of the century; supporter and right hand of Lincoln in the emancipation of the slaves [and] restorer of peace." See L. T. Remlap, *General U.S. Grant's Tour Around the World* (Chicago: J. Fairbanks, 1879), 21.

54. Citing the significance of national progress, Grant argues, "We are better off now than we would have been without [the war], and have made more rapid progress than we otherwise should have made." Grant, *Personal Memoirs,* 2:544.

55. *National Tribune,* December 1, 1887.

56. Theda Skocpol, *Protecting Soldiers and Mothers: The Political Origins of Social Policy in the United States* (Cambridge, MA: Harvard University Press, 1995), 127.

57. Davies, *Patriotism on Parade,* 197. On the Republican Party ideology that carried over into the postwar period, see Eric Foner, *Free Soil, Free Labor, Free Men: The Ideology of the Republican Party before the Civil War* (London: Oxford University Press, 1970); Martin J. Hershock, *The Paradox of Progress: Economic Change, Individual Enterprise, and Political Culture in Michigan, 1837–1878* (Athens: Ohio University Press, 2003), esp. chap. 4; Adam I. P. Smith and Peter J. Parish, "A Contested Legacy: The Civil War and Party Politics in the North," in Grant and Parish, *Legacy of Disunion,* 81–99.

58. John Hay, "Fifty Years of the Republican Party," *Addresses of John Hay* (New York: The Century Co., 1906), 264–65.

59. Edward P. Kimball, ed., *Brimley Hall Album and Post 10 Sketch Book* (Worchester, MA: F. S. Blanchard & CO, ca. 1896), 271; Grand Army of the Republic, Department of Wisconsin, Phil Sheridan Post #10, Meeting Minute Book, Nov. 18, 1873-Sept. 18, 1884, entry for September 1, 1884, Oshkosh Public Museum, Oshkosh, Wisconsin; *Grand Army of the Republic, Department of Ohio, Fred C. Jones Post, No. 401, Cincinnati, G.A.R. War papers* (Cincinnati: Fred C. Jones Post, No. 401, 1891), 237–38; G.A.R. N.Y. Department, Brooklyn City Post 233, Minutes, 1898–1909, entry for January 16, 1905.

60. Meeting Minute Book, entry for May 19, 1900, Charles Graves Post no. 139, Department of Wisconsin, folder 6, box 41, WVM.

61. Meeting Minute Book, entry for March 20, 1921, Charles E. Curtis Post no. 34, Department of Wisconsin, folder 6, box 23, WVM.

62. Stuart Taylor, "Address of Colonel Stuart Taylor," *Official Manual Grand Army of the Republic: New York City, 1887* (n.p.: n.p., ca. 1887), 119.

63. Red Emerson Brooks, "All hail to the North! And all hail to the South!" *Official Manual,* 107.

64. Author unknown, *History of the 121st Regiment Pennsylvania Volunteers: A View From the Ranks* (Philadelphia: Catholic Standard and Times, 1906), 174; William P. Hogarty, "A Medal of Honor," *War Talks in Kansas* (Kansas City, MO: Franklin Hudson Publishing Co., 1906), 357.

CHAPTER FIVE

1. J. T. L. Preston, "The Execution of John Brown," *Southern Bivouac* 5 (August 1886): 188; M. J. W., "The Trial of John Brown: Its Impartiality and Decorum Vindicated," *SHSP* 16 (December 1888): 357–65.

2. John H. Reagan, "Address of John H. Reagan," *Confederate Veteran* 5 (July 1897): 343–44. An analysis of John Brown's Raid worked for many as a way to equate the "Abolition Party" with a growing sentiment in all of the free states for universal emancipation. See R. M. T. Hunter, "Origins of the Late War," *SHSP* 1 (January 1876): 7. For an analysis of the execution of John Brown, see Stephen B. Oates, *To Purge This Land with Blood: A Biography of John Brown* (Amherst: University of Massachusetts Press, 1984).

3. John Singleton Mosby to Sam Chapman, June 4, 1907, quoted in *Take Sides with the Truth: The Postwar Letters of John Singleton Mosby*, ed. Peter A. Brown (Lexington: University Press of Kentucky, 2007). Mosby's postwar position made him very unpopular among former Confederates, a point he mentioned frequently in his correspondence. Mosby also mentioned that uncontested sectional reconciliation, considering the unyielding sentiments of most white southerners, seemed unlikely. See John Singleton Mosby to Joseph Bryan, March 5, 1904, folder 4, Mss1B8047a47-106, VHS. Confederate regimentals would often connect the demise of slavery to Federal invasion. See Noel Crowson and John V. Brogden, *Bloody Banners and Barefoot Boys: A History of the 27th Regiment Alabama Infantry, CSA* (n.d., reprint: Shippensburg, PA: Burd Street Press, 1997), 1.

4. James Taylor Ellyson, "Address of James Taylor Ellyson," *SHSP* 23 (June 1895): 336.

5. *The Land We Love* 3 (June 1867): 100.

6. *Confederate Veteran* 30 (April 1922): 128.

7. Robert Stiles, "Monument to the Confederate Dead at the University of Virginia, June 7, 1893," reproduced in *SHSP* 21 (January 1894): 20; W. Gordon McCabe, "Address of W. Gordon McCabe," printed in *Richmond (VA) Dispatch,* June 7, 1890.

8. Benjamin Washington Jones, *Under the Stars and Bars: A History of the Surry Light Artillery; Recollections of a Private Soldier in the War between the States* (1909; reprint: Dayton, OH: Press of the Morningside Bookshop, 1975), v.

9. "Major J. Scheibert on Confederate History," *SHSP* 27 (January–December 1889): 424–27; Edward McGrady, "Address of Colonel Edward McGrady, Jr.," *SHSP* 16 (January–December 1888): 248; *Confederate Veteran* 3 (June 1895): 165.

10. Isaac Gordon Bradwell, "Address of Isaac Gordon Bradwell," *Confederate Veteran* 31 (October 1923): 382. Paul F. Hammond, "Campaigns of General E. Kirby Smith in Kentucky in 1862," *SHSP* 9 (January–December 1881): 237. On fissures within the Democratic Party during the antebellum years, see Michael F. Holt, *The Political Crisis of the 1850s* (New York: W. W. Norton, 1978); William W. Freehling, *The Road to Disunion, Volume II: Secessionists Triumphant 1834–1861* (New York: Oxford University Press, 2007).

11. *Confederate Veteran* 13 (March 1905): 119.

12. In the 1830s, southern authors developed the theory, spearheaded by John C. Calhoun, that the institution of slavery benefited the slave. Slavery offered elements of civilization to black people including, most importantly, Christianity. Postwar southerners used such arguments when trying to justify their involvement in the institution. See Larry E. Tise, *Proslavery: A History of the Defense of Slavery in America, 1701–1840* (Athens: University of Georgia Press, 2004).

13. *Confederate Veteran* 1 (May 1893): 136.

14. McEyla, *Clinging to Mammy*; Hale, *Making Whiteness*, esp. chap. 3.

15. McPherson, "Long Legged Yankee Lies," in Fahs and Waugh, *The Memory of the Civil War in American Culture*, 64–78 (see esp. p. 67); Cox, *Dixie's Daughters*, 120–21; Janney, *Remembering the Civil War*, 183–85.

16. Author unknown, "Was Slavery a Crime and the Slaveholder a Criminal?" *Confederate Veteran* 23 (October 1915): 233.

17. Hunter McGuire, "School Histories in the South," *Confederate Veteran* 7 (November 1899): 500–509; James H. M'Neilly, "History as It Should Be Written," *Confederate Veteran* 30 (January 1922): 12–14; "The Rouss Memorial Committee," *Confederate Veteran* 3 (November 1895): 341.

18. William Allan, "Is the 'Eclectic History of the United States a Proper Book to Use In Our Schools?" *SHSP* 12 (May 1884): 235–36: Lyon C. Tyler, "The South and Germany," *Confederate Veteran* 25 (November 1917): 506; *Confederate Veteran* 3 (June 1895): 166.

19. Apparently, Confederate veterans were not nearly as opposed to northern authors as they were to northern sentiment. George Lundt, author of *The Origin of the Late War,* as well as a "Mr. Ropes," another historian, were both Bostonians, but clearly held southern opinions. For former Confederates, reconciliation with northerners who agreed with their positions seemed perfectly acceptable.

20. "Abolition Crusade and Its Consequences," *Confederate Veteran* 20 (May 1912): 245; Robert White, "Abolition Crusade and Its Consequences," *Confederate Veteran* 20 (July 1912): 347.

21. George Wilson Booth, *A Maryland Boy in Lee's Army: Personal Reminiscences of a Maryland Soldier in the War Between the States, 1861–1865* (Baltimore: Privately Published, 1898), 6; C. I. Walker, "The Reunion in Richmond," *Confederate Veteran* 30 (July 1922): 244. Calls to "write, transmit, and speak of truth" recurred with great frequency in Confederate commemorative literature, often acknowledging that others would deem their truth dubious (*Confederate Veteran* 23 [January 1916]: 17, 39; *Confederate Veteran* 3 [September 1895]: 276).

22. Waylon Fuller Dunaway, *Reminiscences of a Rebel* (New York: Neale Publishing Co., 1913), 130. On subjugation by the Lincoln administration of the North in general, see John C. Stiles, "Brave Words, My Masters!" *Confederate Veteran* 24 (October 1916):435, 448; J. A. Chalaron, "Vivid Experiences at Chickamauga," *Confederate Veteran* 3 (September 1895): 280.

23. The editor of this former Confederate's reminiscences maintains that Bevens recalled the northern soldier as a wicked foe. This is important because it illustrates not only what mattered to Bevens during the war but also how his sentiment resonated at the time of writing. (Daniel E. Sutherland, *Reminiscences of a Private: William E. Bevens of the First Arkansas Infantry* [Fayetteville: University Press of Arkansas, 1992], 119, xiii).

24. Ferdinand Eugene Daniel, *Recollections of Rebel Surgeon and Other Sketches: Or, In the Doctor's Sappy Days (1899)* (Chicago: Clinic Publishing Co., 1901), 10. Daniel, a former slave owner, claimed to have always promoted ultimate emancipation. Other former Confederates found such sentiment "hypocritical" and the "language of a demagogue." (*The Land We Love* 3 [May–October, 1867], 85). See also John H. Reagan, "First Day's Proceedings," *Thirteenth Annual Meeting and Reunion of the United Confederate Veterans, May 19, 1903* (New Orleans: Hopkins' Printing, 1903): 23; Kate DeRossett Mears, "Opposition to Secession in the South," *Confederate Veteran* 20 (April 1912): 164.

25. McMurray, *History of the Twentieth Tennessee Regiment,* 9.

26. McMurray, *History of the Twentieth Tennessee Regiment,* 16, 50; James H. M'Neilly, "Was the Failure of the Confederacy a Blessing?" *Confederate Veteran* 24 (February 1916): 68. Tacitly acknowledging the centrality of slavery in the conflict, others attacked Lincoln,

Harriett Beecher Stowe, and John Brown for leading the nation to war. R. S. Ward, "A Candid Address to G.A.R. Veterans," *Confederate Veteran* 18 (December 1910): 135.

27. McMurray, *History of the Twentieth Tennessee* Regiment, 50, 54.

28. Jessie Watson Reid, *History of the Fourth Regiment of S.C. Volunteers, from the Commencement of War to Lee's Surrender* (Greenville, SC: Shannon & Co., 1892), 50.

29. Edward Young McMorries, *History of the First Regiment Alabama Volunteer Infantry, C.S.A.* (Montgomery: Brown Printing Co., 1904), 41.

30. William Henry Morgan, *Personal Reminiscences of the War of 1861–5* (Lynchburg, MS: J. P. Bell Co, Inc., 1911), 29–31.

31. Robert S. Bevier, *History of the First and Second Missouri Confederate Brigades 1861–1865* (St. Louis: Bryan, Brand & Co., 1879), 456, 53.

32. Jabez Lamar Monroe Curry, *Civil History of the Government of the Confederate States* (Richmond, VA: B. F. Johnson Publishing Co., 1901), 25, 26.

33. Curry, *Civil History*, 185, 186, 242.

34. "Address of R. C. Cave," *Richmond (VA) Dispatch*, May 21, 1894; Cave, *Defending The Southern Confederacy: The Men In Gray* (1911; reprint, Shippensburg, PA: White Mane Publishing, 2001).

35. "Literary Notice," *SHSP* 9 (May 1881): 286.

36. No author, *SHSP* 9 (June 1881): 286; "Causes of the War: Great Speech of Hon. Joseph Wheeler, of Alabama," *Virginia Dispatch* July 31, 1894; M. F. Maury, A Vindication of Virginia and the South," *SHSP* 1 (February 1876): 52–53.

37. S. A. Steele, "From the Pelican Pines," *Confederate Veteran* 30 (July 1922): 256. See also William R. Cox, "Stephen D. Ramseur: His Life and Character," *SHSP* 17 (January–December 1889): 219; Thomas Smith, "Brilliant Eulogy on Gen. W. H. Payne from Good Old Rebels Who Don't Care," *News Leader* (Richmond), January 28, 1909. The consensus among these individuals was that "New England forced slavery" upon the South.

38. John Lamb, "Address of Hon. John Lamb at the Twelfth Annual Reunion of the Neff-Rice Camp, U. C. V., No. 94, near New Market, Va., on Friday, August 19, 1910." Reprinted in *SHSP* 38 (1910): 301–3; *Confederate Veteran* 3 (June 1895): 165.

39. *Confederate Veteran* 1 (August 1893): 238; *Confederate Veteran* 9 (May 1903): 213.

40. Peter Pelham, "An Unfortunate Shot," *Confederate Veteran* 30 (May 1922):172; William A. Courtenay, "Charles Jones Colcock: A Typical Citizen and Soldier of the Old Regime, as told by Gen. Gustavus W. Smith," *SHSP* 25 (January 1897): 32–39; "The Decay of Religion in the South," *The Land We Love* 5 (May–October 1867–68): 212.

41. R. E. Colston, "Address of Gen. R. E. Colston, May 10, 1870," *SHSP* 21 (January 1893):40; *Confederate Veteran* 1 (November 1893): 323.

42. Randolph Harrison McKim, *The Motives and Aims of the Soldiers of the South in the Civil War* (Nashville: UVC, ca. 1904), 23, 25.

43. John T. Morgan, "Address of General John T. Morgan," *SHSP* 5 (January 1877): 2–3, 15; James H. M'Neilly, "The Mission of the Veteran," *Confederate Veteran* 25 (November 1917): 502.

44. *Confederate Veteran* 11 (May 1903): 216.

EPILOGUE

1. "Another Rebel Stand: Lincoln Statue Causes Uproar in Richmond," *Washington Post,* January 9, 2003.

2. Monument Avenue, home to tributes to famed Confederates Robert E. Lee, Stonewall Jackson, and Jefferson Davis. Also, a twelve-foot bronze statue to African American humanitarian, activist, and tennis star Arthur Ashe sits (in some ways incongruously) at the corner of Monument Avenue and Roseneath Road. When the Ashe statue was dedicated in July 10, 1996, Confederate flag-waving protesters demonstrated at the site. "Ashe Statue Joins Those of Confederates," *New York Times,* July 11, 1996.

3. Frank James, "Lincoln Statue Fuels Controversy," *Baltimore Sun,* March 13, 2003.

4. "Lincoln Statue Unveiled," *Richmond Times-Dispatch,* April 6, 2003; "Lincoln Statue is Unveiled, and Protesters Come Out," *New York Times* April 6, 2003. H. K. Edgerton, an African American who supports the delusional notion that thousands of black people willingly served in the Confederate ranks, spends a good deal of his time traveling throughout the South dressed in a Confederate uniform and waving a Confederate battle flag at various Civil War–themed events.

5. "Lincoln Statue Is Unveiled, and Protesters Come Out," *New York Times,* April 6, 2003; "Lincoln Statue Unveiled," *Richmond Times-Dispatch,* April 6, 2003; Bob Moser, "Conflicts Arise over Lincoln Statue in Richmond, Va., Cemetery" *Southern Poverty Law Center Intelligence Report* 110 (Summer 2003).

6. Sara Haardt, "Southern Credo," *American Mercury,* May 1930, 102–10. For a study of Confederate "Lost Cause" rhetoric surfacing at sites of memory throughout the twentieth and into the twenty-first centuries, see W. Stuart Towns, *Enduring Legacy: Rhetoric and Ritual of the Lost Cause* (Tuscaloosa: University of Alabama Press, 2012). Towns's conclusions emphasize the notion of a useful past, in which individuals not only adopt the language of their ancestors when applicable at events spanning commemorative activity to political movements, but also understand Confederate rhetoric as the truth of history. While accurate, Towns fails to thoroughly discuss two other important pieces of the commemorative story. First, the near ubiquity of Confederate rhetoric remains in the past. Such widespread Confederate support reminiscent of the nineteenth century is not a modern phenomenon. Reasons for this are worthy of discussion. Second, Confederate veterans did not invent all of the rhetoric they so deftly employed, but in fact adopted much of it from their forefathers—in much the same way as modern heritage groups. Thus the language we hear today at modern Confederate-themed events is part of a longer legacy. For a brief look at Confederate symbolism and Lost Cause history surfacing in the past and present, see Grace Elizabeth Hale, "The Lost Cause and the Meaning of History," *OAH Magazine of History* 27, no. 1 (January 2013): 13–17. Hale outlines the reactions to Ru Paul's Confederate flag sequined dress alongside efforts of Confederate veterans' groups to connect Lost Cause mentality to white cultural identity in the South. On Confederate identity, see Bruce Collins, "Confederate Identity and the Southern Myth since the Civil War," in Grant and Parish, *Legacy of Disunion,* 30–47.

7. Civil War animosities are alive and well on the Internet. Members of SCV comment frequently about their concerns in the face of mounting opposition, generally reiterating their Confederate ancestors' words. See sonsofconfederateveterans.blogspot.com/, accessed March 12, 2009; Blog entry, AmericaBlog.com, January 18, 2008, "'Preacher' Huckabee says Confederate flag opponents can shove flag pole up their ass," www.americablog.com/2008/01/ huckabee-gave-speech-to-white.html, accessed March 12, 2009. Flag controversies resonate in a variety of settings, from the workplace to government municipal buildings. Typical stories include: "Confederate Flag Display Ignites Florida Dispute," *Seattle Times,* March 18, 2007; "Confederate Flag Supporters Picket S.C. Utility," *The State* (Columbia, South Carolina), August 21, 2002; "Flying in the Face of Controversy," *Washington Post,* March 22, 2008; "A New Confederate Flag Fight," *Richmond Times-Dispatch,* September 11, 2007; "Flag Lovers Find Cause at Dead End," *Atlanta Journal-Constitution,* March 4, 2004.

BIBLIOGRAPHY

PRIMARY SOURCES

Manuscripts

Adams County Historical Society, Gettysburg, Pa.
    50th Anniversary File
    Family files
    Donald McPherson Papers
    Newspapers (hardcopy, microfilm, and electronic access)
Albert and Shirley Small Special Collections Library, University of Virginia, Charlottesville, Va.
    Berkeley Minor Papers
    Isaac Kimber Moran Papers, 1864–1914
    James Longstreet Letters
    James Mercer Garnett Papers, 1861–1919
    James Taylor Ellyson Papers
    John Warwick Daniel Papers
    Letters of Benjamin Washington Jones, 1902–1913
    Micajah Woods Papers, 1909
    United Confederate Veterans, Virginia Division, John Bowie Strange Camp
Butler Library, Columbia University, New York, N.Y.
    The Grand Army of the Republic in New York State, 1865–1898 (microfilm)
Eleanor S. Brockenbrough Library, Museum of the Confederacy, Richmond, Va.
    Archer Anderson Papers
    Battle Abbey Papers
    Confederate Memorial Association Papers
    Confederate Veterans Collection
    Ellyson-Hotchkiss Family Collection
    Hunt-Morgan-Hill Family Collection
    Monuments and Memorials Collection

Gettysburg National Military Park, Gettysburg, Pa.
 50th Anniversary, Grand Reunion 1913: Participant Accounts
 75th Anniversary, Grand Reunion 1938: Participant Accounts
 Gettysburg 1913 Reunion Records
 Gettysburg Battlefield Memorial Association Files, 1864–1895
 Gregory A. Coco Collection
 Jacqueline Thibaut Collection (monument commissions)
 John B. Bachelder Correspondence
 Military Order of the Loyal Legion of the US Papers: Gettysburg Subjects
 Newspapers
 Presidential Visits
 Veterans' Organizations Files: GAR, UCV, etc.
Grand Army of the Republic Museum, Philadelphia, Pa.
 Post No. 2 of Philadelphia Records
 Ellis Post No. 6 of Germantown, Philadelphia Records
 G.A.R. Posts of New York (miscellaneous Information)
 Meade Post 1, Philadelphia Records
 Post 41, New York State Records
 Winfield Scott Post No. 114, Philadelphia Records
Leyburn Library, Washington and Lee University, Lexington, Va.
 Lee-Jackson Collection, 1778–1914
 Robert E. Lee Collection, 1792–1935
 Robert E. Lee Papers
Library of Virginia, Richmond, Va.
 Christian Family Papers, 1888–1919
 Lee Monument Association Records
 United Confederate Veterans, Stonewall Jackson Camp, Staunton Records
 United Confederate Veterans, Virginia Division Records, 1890–1903
 United Confederate Veterans Records, 1932–1953
New York Public Library, New York, N.Y.
 Abraham Gilbert Mills Papers
 Brooklyn City Post 233 Minute Book
 Charles W. Cowtan Papers
 Daniel E. Sickles Papers
 Grand Army of the Republic, Department of California Records
 Grand Army of the Republic, Department of Illinois Records
 Grand Army of the Republic, Department of Indiana Records
 Grand Army of the Republic, Department of Nevada Records

Lafayette Post no. 140, Department of New York Records

Zook Post no. 11, Department of Pennsylvania Records

Virginia Historical Society, Richmond, Va.

Association of the Army of Northern Virginia Papers

Association of the Maryland Line Papers

Bagby Family Papers

"F" Company Association Minute and Scrap Book

Hutton Family Papers

John Singleton Mosby Letters

Lee Family Letterbook

Lee Monument Association Papers

Pegram Johnson McIntosh Family Papers

Surry Light Artillery & Deal-Crenshaw Minute Book

W. Gordon McCabe Papers

William Ruffin Cox Papers

Wisconsin Veterans Museum, Madison, Wisc.

Grand Army of the Republic, Department of Wisconsin Records

Grand Army of the Republic Memorial Hall Records

Grand Army of the Republic Papers

Women's Relief Corps, Department of Wisconsin Records

Printed Sources

Abstract of General Orders and Proceedings of the Fifty-Third Annual Encampment, Department of New York, G.A.R. June 24th, 25th, 26th, 1919. Albany, NY: J. B. Lyon Co., 1919.

Abstract of General Orders and Proceedings of the Fortieth Annual Encampment, Department of New York, G.A.R. Albany, NY: Brandow Printing Co., 1906.

Acts and Joint Resolutions: Amending the Constitution, of the General Assembly of the State of Virginia. Richmond, VA: Davis Bottom, 1910.

Adams, John G. B. *Reminiscences of the Nineteenth Massachusetts Regiment.* Boston: Wright & Potter Printing Co., 1899.

———. "Sunshine and Shadows of Army Life," *Civil War Papers Read Before the Commandery of the State of Massachusetts, Military Order of the Loyal Legion of the United States.* Boston: Published for the Commandery, 1900.

Address of the Commander-in-Chief, Reports of National Officers, also Reports of Committees of the Forty-Sixth National Encampment, Grand Army of the Republic, Los Angeles California, September 9 to 14, 1912. N.p., ca. 1912.

Addresses Delivered at the Unveiling of the Monument to Confederate Soldiers of Charles City County, Virginia, at Charles City Courthouse, November 21, 1900. Richmond, VA: Whittet & Shepperson, 1901.

Anderson, Archer. *Address on the Opening of Lee Camp Soldiers' Home, May 20, 1885.* Richmond, VA: R. E. Lee Camp No. 1, 1885.

Anderson, John. *The Fifty-Seventh Regiment of Massachusetts Volunteers in the War of the Rebellion.* Boston: E. B. Stillings & Co., 1896.

Annual Reunion of Pegram Battalion Association in the Hall of the House of Delegates, Richmond, Va., May 21st, 1886: When the Battle-flag of the Battalion Was Presented by Capt. W. Gordon McCabe, Adjutant. Richmond: Wm. Ellis Jones, 1886.

Arnold, Isaac Newton. *The History of Abraham Lincoln and the Overthrow of Slavery.* Chicago: Clarke & Co., 1866.

Avery, Myrta Lockett, ed. *Recollections of Alexander H. Stephens.* New York: Doubleday, Page & Co., 1910.

Ballew, W. W. *Historical Address to Confederate Veterans, Corsicana, Texas, July 23, 1913.* N.p., ca.1913.

Banes, Charles H. *History of the Philadelphia Brigade.* Philadelphia: J. B. Lippincott & Co., 1879.

Beard, John S. *Address of Hon. John S. Beard of Pensacola at Defuniak Springs, Florida, March 16 1901 at Reunion of First Florida Brigade, United Confederate Veterans.* N.p., ca. 1901.

Beath, Robert B. *History of the Grand Army of the Republic.* New York: Bryan Taylor & Co., 1889.

Beaver, James A. *Abraham Lincoln: Memorial Meeting, Commandery of the State of Pennsylvania.* N.p., 1907.

Benedict, George Grenville. *Vermont in the Civil War: A History of the Part Taken by Vermont Soldiers in the War for Union, 1861–65.* Burlington, VT: Free Press Association, 1886.

Bernard, George S., ed. *War Talks of Confederate Veterans: Addresses Delivered before A.P. Hill Camp of Confederate Veterans, of Petersburg, Va.* Petersburg, VA: Fenn & Owen, 1892.

Bevier, Robert S. *History of the First and Second Missouri Confederate Brigades, 1861–1865.* St. Louis: Bryan, Brand, & Co., 1879.

Birthday Banquet by U.S. Grant Post Number 327, Department of New York, Grand Army of the Republic, April 28, 1890. New York: George J. Collins, 1890.

Booth, George Wilson. *A Maryland Boy in Lee's Army: Personal Reminiscences of a Maryland Soldier in the War Between the States, 1861–1865.* Baltimore: Privately Published, 1898.

Borke, Heros von. *Memoirs of the Confederate War for Independence*. 2 vols. London: William Blackwood & Sons, 1866.

Brainard, Mary Genvie. *Campaigns of the One Hundred and Forty-Sixth Regiment, New York State Volunteers*. New York: G. P. Putnam Sons, 1915.

Brown, Wilbur F., ed. *Lafayette Post No. 140, Department of New York, Grand Army of the Republic*. New York: Wilbur F. Brown, 1900.

Butler, Benjamin F. *Autobiography and Personal Reminiscences of Major-General Benjamin F. Butler: Butler's Book*. Boston: A. M. Thayer, 1892.

Butterfield, Julia Lorriland, ed. *A Biographical Memorial of General Daniel Butterfield*. New York: Grafton Press, 1904.

Cannon, Le Grand B. *Personal Reminiscences of the Rebellion, 1861–1866*. New York: Burr Printing House, 1895.

Carpenter, George M. *History of the Eighth Regiment Vermont Volunteers, 1861–1865*. Boston: Press of Deland & Barta, 1886.

Ceremonies at the Dedication of the Soldiers' Monument in West Roxbury, Mass. Boston: Hollis & Gunn, 1871.

Chamberlain, Joshua Lawrence. *The Passing of the Armies*. 1915; reprint, New York: Bantam Books, 1993.

Champlin, John Dennison. *Orations, Addresses, and Speeches of Chauncey M. Depew*. 8 vols. New York: Privately Printed, 1910.

Chandler, William E. *Decoration Day Address of William E. Chandler*. Concord, NH: Republican Press Association, 1910.

Christian, George L. *Abraham Lincoln: An Address Delivered at Richmond, Virginia, October 29, 1909*. 1909; reprint, Richmond: Richmond Press, 1927.

———. *The Confederate Cause and Its Defenders: An Address Delivered Before the Grand Army of Confederate Veterans of Virginia at the Annual Meeting Held at Culpepper C.H., Va., October 4 1898*. Richmond: Wm. Ellis Jones, Book and Job Printer, 1898.

Civil War Papers Read Before the Commandery of the State of Massachusetts, Military Order of the Loyal Legion of the United States. 3 vols. Boston: Printed for the Commandery, 1890.

Claiborne, John Herbert. *Seventy-Five Years in Old Virginia*. New York: Neale Publishing Co., 1904.

Clark, Charles M. *The History of the Thirty-Ninth Regiment, Illinois Volunteer Veteran Infantry (Yates Phalanx) in the War of the Rebellion*. Chicago: Veteran Association of the Regiment, 1880.

Clark, Daniel. *Ceremonies at the Dedication of the Monument Erected by the City of Manchester, N. H., to the Men Who Periled Their Lives to Save the Union in the Late Civil War*. Manchester: Mirror Steam Printing Press, 1880.

Coffin, Charles C. *Redeeming the Republic: The Third Period of the War of the Rebellion.* New York: Harper & Bros., 1889.

Cogswell, Leander W. *A History of the Eleventh New Hampshire Volunteer Infantry in the Rebellion War, 1861–1865.* Concord, NH: Republican Press Association, 1891.

Commonwealth of Pennsylvania. *Fiftieth Anniversary of the Battle of Gettysburg: Report of the Pennsylvania Commission.* Harrisburg: Commonwealth of Pennsylvania, 1913.

Compton, James R. *Andersonville: The Story of Man's Inhumanity to Man.* Des Moines: Iowa Printing Company, 1887.

Cox, William Ruffin. *The Southern Cause Was Noble and Just: Address Delivered before the Oakwood Memorial Association, Richmond, Va., May 10, 1911.* Richmond: F. J. Printing Corp., ca. 1911.

Crowson, Noel, and John V. Brogden. *Bloody Banners and Barefoot Boys: A History of the 27th Alabama Infantry, CSA.* Reprint, Shippenburg, AL: Burd Street Press, 1997.

Curry, Jabez Lamar Monroe. *Civil History of the Government of the Confederate States.* Richmond, VA: B. F. Johnson Publishing Co., 1901.

Daniel, Ferdinand Eugene. *Recollections of a Rebel Surgeon and Other Sketches: Or, In the Doctor's Sappy Days (1899).* Chicago: Clinic Publishing Co., 1901.

Daniel, Frederick S. *Richmond Howitzers in the War.* Richmond, VA: n.p., 1891.

Davis, Jefferson. *The Rise and Fall of the Confederate Government.* 2 vols. New York: D. Appleton & Co., 1881.

Davis, William Watts Hart. *History of the 104th Pennsylvania Regiment from August 22nd, 1861 to September 30th, 1864.* Philadelphia: Jas. B. Rogers, 1866.

Dawson, George Francis. *Life and Services of General John A. Logan.* Chicago: R. S. Peale & Co., 1887.

Derry, Joseph Tyrone. *Story of the Confederate States.* Richmond: B. F. Johnson, 1898.

Devens, Charles. *Dedication of the Monument on Boston Common Erected to the Men of Boston Who Died in the Civil War.* Boston: Boston City Council, 1877.

Dickey, Luther S. *History of the 103d Regiment, Pennsylvania Veteran Volunteer Infantry, 1861–1865.* Chicago: L. S. Dickey, 1910.

Dinkins, James. *1861–1865: Recollections and Experiences in the Confederate Army, by an Old Johnnie.* Cincinnati: R. Clarke Company, 1897.

Dixon, William Hepworth. *White Conquest.* 2 vols. London: Chatto & Windus, Piccadilly, 1876.

Dodge, Theodore Ayrault. *A Bird's-Eye View of Our Civil War.* Boston: Houghton Mifflin, 1883.

Doubleday, Abner. *Chancellorsville and Gettysburg.* New York: Charles Scribner's Sons, 1889.

Drake, J. Madison. *The History of the Ninth New Jersey Veteran Vols.* Elizabeth, N.J.: Journal Printing House, 1889.

Duke, R. T. W. *Memorial History of the John Bowie Strange Camp, United Confederate Veterans.* N.p., ca. 1891.

Dunaway, Wayland Fuller. *Reminiscences of a Rebel.* New York: Neale Publishing Co., 1913.

Early, Jubal Anderson. *Autobiographical Sketch and Narrative of the War Between the States.* Philadelphia: J. B. Lippincott Co., 1912.

———. *A Memoir of the Last Year of the War for Independence in the Confederate States of America.* Lynchburg, VA: Charles W. Button, 1876.

Edwards, Frank. *Army Life of Frank Edwards.* Reprint, Charleston, SC: Bibliolife, 2009.

Evans, Clement A., ed. *Confederate Military History.* 12 vols. Atlanta: Confederate Publishing Co., 1899.

Faehtz, Earnest F. M. *The National Memorial Day: A Record of Ceremonies Over the Graves of the Union Soldiers, May 29 and 20, 1869.* Washington City: Headquarters of the Grand Army of the Republic, 1870.

Fairchild, Charles Bryant. *History of the 27th N. Y. Vols.* Binghampton, NY: Carl & Matthews, 1888.

Fenner, Earl. *The History of Battery H, First Regiment Rhode Island Light Artillery in the War to Preserve the Union.* Providence: Snow & Farnham, 1894.

Fitch, John. *Annals of the Army of the Cumberland.* Philadelphia: J. B. Lippincott & Co., 1864.

Gibson, J. T., ed. *History of the Seventy-Eighth Pennsylvania Volunteer Infantry.* Pittsburgh, PA: Pittsburgh Printing Co., 1905.

A Glimpse of Washington in 1892: Souvenir of the Twenty-sixth Encampment of the Grand Army of the Republic Beginning September 20, 1892. Washington, DC: Capitol Publishing Co., 1892.

Goldsborough, William Worthington. *The Maryland Line of the Confederate Army, 1861–1865.* Baltimore: Guggenheim, Weil & Co., 1900.

Goolrick, John T. *Historic Fredericksburg: The Story of an Old Town.* Richmond, VA: Whittet & Shepperson, 1921.

Gordon, John Brown. *Reminiscences of the Civil War.* 1903; reprint, Baton Rouge: Louisiana State University Press, 1993.

Grant, Ulysses S. *Personal Memoirs of U. S. Grant.* 2 vols. New York: Charles L. Webster, 1885.

Green, Robert M. *History of the One Hundred and Twenty-Fourth Regiment Pennsylvania Volunteers in the War of the Rebellion, 1862–1863.* Philadelphia: Wane Bros. Co., 1907.

Griffit, R. C., ed. *Report of the Unveiling and Dedication of the Indiana Monument at Andersonville.* N.p., 1909.

Halstead. "Address of Comrade Halstead," *Journal of Proceedings of the Eleventh Annual Encampment of the Department of Minnesota, Grand Army of the Republic, Under the New Organization, February 17,18 and 19, 1892.* St Paul: Pioneer Press Co., 1892.

Harris, Joel Chandler. *Stories of Georgia.* New York: American Book Co., 1896.

Harrison, Walter. *Pickett's Men: A Fragment of War History.* New York: D. Van Nostrand, 1870.

Hay, John. *Addresses of John Hay.* New York: Century Co., 1906.

Hayes, Rutherford B. *Military Order of the Loyal Legion of the United States, Address of Brevet Maj-General Rutherford B. Hayes at the Fifth Quadrennial Congress.* Chicago: n.p., 1885.

Hendricks, Genevieve Poyneer. *Handbook of the Social Resources of the United States.* Washington, DC: American Red Cross, 1921.

Herbert, Hilary Abner. "Address of Hilary Abner Herbert," *Programme of the Ceremonies at the Unveiling of the Arlington Confederate Monument, Arlington, Virginia, June fourth, nineteen hundred and fourteen.* N.p., 1914.

History of the 121st Regiment Pennsylvania Volunteers: A View from the Ranks. Philadelphia: Catholic Standard and Times. 1906.

Hoole, William Stanley, *Address Delivered at the Centennial Celebration of the Unveiling of the Darlington County Confederate Monument, Darlington South Carolina, May 10, 1980.* University, AL: Confederate Publishing Co., 1980.

Howard, McHenry. *Recollections of a Maryland Confederate Soldier and Staff Officer Under Johnson, Jackson, and Lee.* Baltimore: Williams & Wilkins Co., 1914.

Hughes, Nathaniel Cheairs, Jr., ed. *The Civil War Memoirs of Philip Daingerfield Stephenson, D.D.* Conway, AR: UCA Press, 1995.

Ingersoll, Robert G. *The Works of Robert G. Ingersoll.* 12 vols. New York: Dresder Publishing Co., 1907.

Jackman, Lyman. *History of the Sixth New Hampshire Regiment in the War for the Union.* Concord, NH: Republican Press Association, 1891.

Johnson, Bradley T. *Address before the Association of Confederate Soldiers and Sailors of Maryland June 19, 1874.* Baltimore: Kelly Piet & Company, 1874.

———. *Address Delivered at the Dedication of the Confederate Memorial Hall, Va., February 22, 1896.* Richmond: Wm. Ellis Jones, 1896.

———. *The Constitution of the Confederate States, Montgomery 1861.*

———. *The Founding of the Eastern Shore: An Address Delivered at the Centennial Celebration of Easton, July 26th 1888.* Baltimore: Sun Book and Job Printing Office, 1888.

——. *The Maryland Confederates: An Address before the Confederate Society of St. Mary's at Leonardtown, March 1894.* Baltimore: J. Harry Drechsler, ca. 1894.

Johnson, George W. "Address of George W. Johnson," *Proceedings of the Twenty-Second Annual Encampment Department of Maryland, Grand Army of the Republic, February 21 and 22, 1898.* Baltimore: John R. Shane & Co., 1898.

Jones, Benjamin Washington. *Under the Stars and Bars: A History of the Surry Light Artillery; Recollections of a Private Soldier in the War Between the States.* 1909; reprint, Dayton, OH: Press of the Morningside Bookshop, 1975.

Jones, Charles C. *The Siege of Savannah in December 1864.* Albany: Joel Munsell, 1874.

Journal of the Fifty-Fourth National Encampment of the Grand Army of the Republic, Indianapolis, Indiana, September 10 to 25, 1920. Washington, DC: Government Printing Office, 1921.

Journal of the Forty-Eighth National Encampment, Grand Army of the Republic, Detroit, Michigan. Washington, DC: Government Printing Office, 1915.

Journal of the Forty-First Encampment of the Grand Army of the Republic, September 11th and 12th 1907. Zanesville, OH: Courier Co., 1907.

Journal of the Nineteenth Annual Session of the National Encampment, Grand Army of the Republic, Portland Maine, June 24th and 25th, 1885. Toledo, OH: Montgomery & Vrooman, 1885.

Journal of the Proceedings of the Eleventh Annual Encampment of the Department of Minnesota, Grand Army of the Republic, Under the New Organization, February 17, 18 and 19, 1891. Minneapolis: Co-operative Printing Co., 1891.

Journal of the Proceedings of the Fiftieth Annual Encampment of the Department of the Potomac, Grand Army of the Republic, held at Washington D.C., February, 1918. Washington, DC: R. Beresford, 1918.

Journal of the Proceedings of the Forty-Second Annual Encampment of the Department of the Potomac, Grand Army of the Republic, held at Washington, D.C. Washington, DC: R. Beresford, 1910.

Journal of the Proceedings of the Sixteenth Annual Encampment of the Department of Minnesota, Grand Army of the Republic, Under the New Organization, March 11th and 12th 1896. Minneapolis: Co-operative Printing Co., 1896.

Journal of the Proceedings of the Thirteenth Annual Encampment of the Department of Minnesota, Grand Army of the Republic, Under the New Organization, February 21 and 22, 1893. St. Paul: Press of Zander Bros., 1893.

Journal of the Proceedings of the Thirty-Second Annual Encampment of the Department of Minnesota, Grand Army of the Republic, March 2–3, 1898. Minneapolis: Co-operative Printing Co., 1898.

Journal of the Proceedings of the Twelfth Annual Encampment of the Department of Minnesota, Grand Army of the Republic, Under the New Organization, February 17, 18, and 19, 1892. St. Paul: Pioneer Press Co., 1892.

Journal of the Proceedings of the Twenty-Ninth Annual Meeting of the Commandery-In-Chief. Philadelphia: n.p., 1913.

Journal of the Seventh Annual Session of the Grand Army of the Republic, Department of Indiana, February 17 & 18, 1886. Indianapolis: Hasselman-Journal Co., 1886.

Journal of the Thirty-Eighth National Encampment of the Grand Army of the Republic, Department of Oregon. Salem: Oregon State Printing Department, 1919.

Journal of the Thirty-Fourth National Encampment of the Grand Army of the Republic, August 29th and 30th, 1900. Philadelphia; Towne Printing Co., 1900.

Journal of the Thirty-Second Annual Encampment of the Grand Army of the Republic, Department of Rhode Island, G-A-R, February 2nd, 1889. Providence: Head-Quarters, Department of Rhode Island, 1899.

Journal of the Twentieth Annual Session of the National Encampment, Grand Army of the Republic, San Francisco, California, August 4th, 5th, and 6th, 1886. Washington, DC: Gibson Bros., 1886.

Journal of the Twenty-Eighth National Encampment, Grand Army of the Republic, Pittsburgh, Pa. September 12th and 13th, 1894. Boston: E. B. Stillings, 1894.

Journal of the Twenty-Sixth National Encampment, Grand Army of the Republic. Albany: S. H. Wentworth, 1892.

Keiley, A.M. *In Vinculis or The Prisoner of War.* New York: Blelock & Co., 1866.

Keiley, Charles Russell. *The Official Blue Book of the Jamestown Ter-Centennial Exposition: The Only Authorized History of the Celebration.* Norfolk: Colonial Publishing Co., 1909.

Kellogg, Robert H. *Life and Death in Rebel Prisons.* Hartford: L. Stebbins, 1867.

Kent, Charles Nelson. *History of the Seventeenth Regiment, New Hampshire Volunteer Infantry, 1862–1863.* Concord, NH: Seventeenth New Hampshire Veteran Association, 1898.

Kimball, Edward P., ed. *Brimley Hall Album and Post 10 Sketch Book.* Worchester, MA: F. S. Blanchard & Co., ca. 1896.

LaBree, Benjamin, ed. *Campfires of the Confederacy.* Louisville: Courier-Journal Job Printing Co., 1898.

Ladd, David, and Audrey Ladd, eds. *The Bachelder Papers.* 7 vols. Dayton, OH: Morningside Bookshop, 1994.

Lathrop, D. *The History of the Fifty-Ninth Regiment Illinois Volunteers.* Indianapolis: Hall & Hutchinson, 1865.

Law, E. M. *The Confederate Revolution: An Address Delivered before the Association of the Army of Northern Virginia, Richmond, Va., May 28, 1890.* Richmond: W. Ellis Jones, 1890.

Lee, Fitzhugh. "The Unveiling of the Monument to the Confederate Dead of Alexandria, Va." In *Speeches of Capt. Raleigh T. Daniel and Gov. Fitzhugh Lee, May 24th 1889.* N.p., ca. 1889.

Lee Robert E., Jr. *Address of R. E. Lee, Jr. to the Veterans: Delivered During the Confederate Reunion Held at Richmond, Virginia, 1907.* N.p., ca. 1907.

Lewis, George. *The History of Battery E, First Regiment Rhode Island Light Artillery in the War of 1861 and 1865 to Preserve the Union.* Providence: Snow & Farnham, 1892.

Lewis, Oseola. *History of the One Hundred and Thirty Eighth Pennsylvania Volunteer Regiment.* Norristown: Wills, Iredell & Jenkins, 1866.

Locke, William Henry. *The Story of the Regiment.* Philadelphia: J. B. Lippincott & Co., 1868.

Loehr, Charles T. *War History of the Old First Virginia Infantry Regiment.* Richmond: Wm. Ellis Jones, 1884.

Logan, John A. *The Volunteer Soldier of America.* Chicago: R. S. Peale, 1887.

Loring, George B. *An Oration Delivered at the Dedication of the Soldiers Monument in North Weymouth, Mass. on July 4th, 1868.* Weymouth, MA: C. G. Kasterbrook, 1869.

Maine at Gettysburg: Report of the Maine Commissioners. Portland: Lakeside Press, 1898.

Marshall, John A. *American Bastille.* Philadelphia: Thomas W. Hartley & Co., 1881.

McClure, Alexander K. *Old Time Notes of Pennsylvania.* 2 vols. Philadelphia: Fulton Publishing, 1876.

McElroy, John L. *Andersonville: A Story of Rebel Military Prisons.* Toledo, OH: T. R. Locke, 1879.

McGuire, Hunter. *The Confederate Cause and Conduct of the War Between the States.* Richmond, VA: L. H. Jenkins, 1907.

McKim, Randolph Harrison. *The Motives and Aims of Soldiers of the South in the Civil War.* N.p.: ca. June 1904.

McMorries, Edward Young. *History of the First Regiment Alabama Volunteer Infantry, C.S.A.* Montgomery: Brown Printing Co., 1904.

McMurray, W.J. *History of the Twentieth Tennessee Regiment Volunteer Infantry, C.S.A.* Nashville: W. J. McMurray, Deering J. Robert, & Ralph J. Neal, 1904.

McPherson, Edward. "Address of Edward McPherson." In *Michigan at Gettysburg, July 1st, 2nd, 3rd, 1863, June 12th 1889.* Detroit: Winn & Hammond, Printers and Binders, 1889.

Michigan at Gettysburg, July 1st, 2nd, 3rd, 1863. June 12th 1889. Proceedings Incident to the Dedication of the Michigan Monuments upon the Battlefield of Gettysburg, June 12th 1889. Detroit: Winn & Hammond, Printers and Binders, 1889.

Military Papers and Recollections: Papers Read Before the Commandery of the State of Illinois, Military Order of the Loyal Legion of the United States. 8 vols. Chicago: Dial Press, 1899.

Military Essays and Recollections of the Pennsylvania Commandery of the Loyal Legion of the United States. 2 vols. 1890; reprint, Wilmington, NC: Broadfoot, 1995.

Minutes of the First Annual Meeting and Reunion of the United Confederate Veterans Held in the City of Chattanooga, Tenn, July 3rd, 1890. New Orleans: Hopkins' Printing, 1891.

Minutes of the Ninth Annual Meeting and Reunion of the United Confederate Veterans Held in the City of Charleston, S. C. May 10th, 11th, 12th, & 13th, 1899. New Orleans: Hopkins' Printing, 1900.

Minutes of the Sixth Annual Meeting and Reunion of the United Confederate Veterans Held in the City of Richmond, Va. June 30th & July 1st & 2nd, 1896. New Orleans: Hopkins' Printing, 1897

Monfort, E. R., H. B. Furness, and Fred. H. Alms, eds. *G.A.R. War Papers: Papers Read Before Fred. C. Jones Post, No. 401, Department of Ohio, G.A.R.* Cincinnati: Fred. C. Jones Post, No. 401, 1891.

Monroe, Nelson. *The Grand Army Button: A Souvenir.* Boston: Rockwell & Churchill Press, 1893.

Moore, Frank, ed. *The Rebellion Record: A Diary of American Events.* New York: D. Van Nostrand, 1869.

Morgan, William Henry. *Personal Reminiscences of the War of 1861–5.* Lynchburg, VA: J. P. Bell Co., Inc, 1911.

Morton, Joseph W. *Sparks from the Campfire or Tales of the Old Veterans.* Philadelphia: Keeler & Kirkpatrick, 1899.

Murray, J. Ogden. *The Immortal Six Hundred: A Story of Cruelty to Confederate Prisoners of War.* Roanoke: Stone Printing and Manufacturing Co., 1911.

Neill, Edward D., ed. *Glimpses of the Nation's Struggle: Papers Read Before the Minnesota Commandery of the Loyal Legion of the United States, 1889–1892.* New York: D. D. Merrill Co., 1893.

Nevin, Alfred. *Men of Mark of Cumberland Valley, Pa. 1776–1876.* Philadelphia: Fulton Publishing, 1876.

New York Monuments Commission for the Battlefields of Gettysburg and Chattanooga—Final Report of the Battlefield of Gettysburg. 2 vols. Albany, NY: J. B. Lyon, Printers, 1900.

Newlin, Thomas H. *A History of the Seventy-Third Regiment of Illinois Volunteers.* N.p., 1890.

Observances of the Centennial Anniversary of the Birth of Abraham Lincoln, February Twelfth, 1909. N.p.: National Committee, GAR, 1909.

Official Manual Grand Army of the Republic: New York City, 1887. N.p., ca. 1887.

Official Proceedings of the Fifth Annual Reunion of the Missouri Division United Confederate Veterans, Springfield, Mo., August 8, 9, and 10, 1901. St. Louis: C. C. Rainwater, 1901.

Parker, Bowdoin S. *What One Grand Army Post Has Accomplished: History of the Edward W. Kinsley Post No. 13, Department of Massachusetts.* Norwood, MA: Norwood Press, 1913.

Parker, Thomas H. *History of the 51st Regiment of P.V. and V.V.* Philadelphia: King & Baird, 1869.

Paul, James Laughery. *Pennsylvania's Soldiers' Orphan Schools.* Harrisburg, PA: James Hart, 1877.

Pennsylvania at Gettysburg: Ceremonies of the Dedications of Monuments. 2 vols. Harrisburg, PA: E. K. Meyers, 1893.

Personal Recollections of the War of the Rebellion: Addresses Delivered Before the Commandery of the State of New York, Military Order of the Loyal Legion of the United States. 4 vols. New York: Published by the Commandery, 1891.

Proceedings at the Dedication of the Soldiers' and Sailors' Monument in Providence. Providence, RI: A. Crawford Greene, 1871.

Proceedings in Congress on the Occasion of the Reception and Acceptance of the Statue of General Ulysses S. Grant Presented by the Grand Army of the Republic, May 19, 1900. Washington, DC: Government Printing Office, 1901.

Proceedings of the 32nd Annual Encampment Department of Maryland, Grand Army of the Republic, April 9 and 10, 1908. Baltimore: Press of N. C. Killam, 1908.

Proceedings of the 39th Annual Encampment, Department of Pennsylvania, Grand Army of the Republic, June 7 and 8 1905. Harrisburg, PA: Harrisburg Publishing Co., 1905.

Proceedings of the 43rd Annual Encampment, Grand Army of the Republic, Gettysburg. Harrisburg, PA: C. E. Aughinbaugh, 1909.

Proceedings of the 43rd National Encampment, Department of Pennsylvania, Grand Army of the Republic, Jan 9 and 10, 1909. Harrisburg, PA: C. E. Aughinbaugh, 1909.

Proceedings of the 56th Annual Encampment, Department of Pennsylvania, Grand Army of the Republic. Harrisburg, PA: J. L. L. Kuhn, Printer to the Commonwealth, 1922.

Proceedings of Annual Encampment G.A.R. Department of New York, 1907. New York: State of New York, 1907.

Proceedings of the Conference for Educations in the South Held at the University of Virginia on April 25th 1903. N.p., ca. 1903.

Proceedings of the First to Tenth Meetings, 1866–1876 (inclusive) of the National Encampment, Grand Army of the Republic. Philadelphia: Samuel P. Town, 1877.

Proceedings of the Sixth Annual Meeting and Reunion of the United Confederate Veterans Held at Richmond Virginia, June 30 and July 1st and 2nd, 1896. New Orleans: Hopkins' Printing Office, 1897.

Proceedings of the Thirty-Fourth Annual Encampment Department of Maryland, Grand Army of the Republic, April 8th and 9th, 1910. Baltimore: Press of J. G. Leake & Co., 1910.

Proceedings of the Thirty-Sixth Annual Encampment Department of Maryland, Grand Army of the Republic, April 9th and 10th, 1912. Baltimore: Press of J. G. Leake & Co., 1912.

Proceedings of the Twenty-Second Annual Encampment Department of Maryland, Grand Army of the Republic, February 21 and 22. Baltimore: John R. Shane & Co., 1898.

Proceedings of the Twenty-Third Annual Encampment Department of Maryland, Grand Army of the Republic, February 21 and 22, 1899. Baltimore: John R. Shane & Co., 1899.

Quinn, J. S. *The History of the City of Fredericksburg, Virginia.* Richmond, VA: Hermitage Press, 1908.

Reid, Jessie Watson. *History of the Fourth Regiment of S.C. Volunteers, from the Commencement of War to Lee's Surrender.* Greenville: Shannon & Co., 1892.

Remlap, L. T. *General U.S. Grant's Tour Around the World.* Chicago: J. Fairbanks, 1879.

Riddle, Albert Gallitin. *Recollections of War Times: Reminiscences of Men and Events in Washington.* New York: G. P. Putnam's Sons, 1895.

Robins, Richard, ed. *Toasts and Responses at Banquet Given Lieut. Gen P. H. Sheridan by the Military Order of the Loyal Legion of the United States, Commandery of the State of Illinois.* Chicago: Knight & Leonard, 1883.

Robson, John S. *How a One-Legged Rebel Lives.* Durham, NC: Educator Co., 1898.

Roosevelt, Theodore. *Addresses and Presidential Messages of Theodore Roosevelt.* New York: G. P. Putnam's Sons, 1904.

Russell, Charles Theodore, Jr., ed. *Speeches and Addresses of William E. Russell.* Boston: Little, Brown, and Co., 1894.

Rutherford, Mildred Lewis. *Four Addresses.* Birmingham: Mildred Rutherford Historical Circle.

Schofield, John M. *Forty-Six Years in the Army.* New York: The Century Co, 1897.

Schurz, Carl. *The Reminiscences of Carl Schurz.* 3 vols. New York: McClure, 1907.

Services for the Use of the Grand Army of the Republic. Toledo, OH: Headquarters of the Grand Army of the Republic, 1884.

Sheldon, Winthrop D. *"The Twenty-Seventh" (Connecticut): A Regimental History.* NewHaven, CT: Morris & Benham, 1866.

Shepard, H. N. *The Record of the Processions and of the Exercises of the Dedication of the Monument Erected to the People of Pembroke, Mass.* Plymouth, MA: Avery & Doten, 1890.

Sherman, John. *John's Recollections of Forty Years in the House, Senate and Cabinet: An Autobiography.* Chicago: Warner Co., 1895.

Sherman, William T. *Memoirs of William T. Sherman,* 2 vols. London: Henry S. King, 1875.

Simon, Ezra D. *A Regimental History: The One Hundred and Twenty-Fifth New York State Volunteers.* New York: Ezra D. Simons, 1888.

Sketches of War History 1861–1865 Papers Read Before the Ohio Commandery of the Military Order of the Loyal Legion of the United States 1883–1886. 9 vols. Cincinnati: Robert Clarke & Co., 1888.

Snowden, Yates. *History of South Carolina.* Chicago: Lewis Publishing Co., 1930.

State of New Jersey, Final Report of the Gettysburg Battle-field Commission, 1891. Trenton, NJ: John L. Murphy, 1891.

Stephens, Alexander H. *A Constitutional View of the Late War Between the States: Its Causes, Character, Conduct, and Results.* 2 vols. Chicago: Ziegler, McCurdy & Co., 1868–1870.

Stephenson, Mary Harriet. *Dr. B. F. Stephenson, Founder of the Grand Army of the Republic.* Springfield, IL: H. W. Rokker Printing House, 1894.

Stewart, Robert Laird. *History of the One Hundred and Fortieth Pennsylvania Volunteers.* N.p.: Franklin Bindery, 1912.

Stonebraker, Jos. R. *A Rebel of '61.* New York: Wynkoop Hallenbeck Crawford Co., Printers, 1899.

Storrs, John W. *The "Twentieth Connecticut": A Regimental History.* Ansonia, CT: Press of the Naugatuck Valley Sentinel, 1886.

Stuart, Taylor. *Official Manual, Grand Army of the Republic: New York City, 1887.* N.p., 1887.

Sutherland, Daniel E. *Reminiscences of a Private: William E. Bevens of the First Arkansas Infantry.* Fayetteville: University Press of Arkansas, 1992.

Thomas, Henry W. *History of the Doles-Cook Brigade, Army of Northern Virginia, C.S.A.* Atlanta: Franklin Printing and Publishing Co., 1903.

Todd, William, ed. *History of the Ninth Regiment (Eighty-Third N.Y. Volunteers) 1845–1888.* New York: J. S. Oglevie, 1889.

——. *The Seventy-Ninth Highlanders, New York Volunteers in the War of the Rebellion.* Albany, NY: Press of Brandow, Barton & Co., 1886.

Townsend, Luther Tracy. *History of the Sixteenth Regiment, New Hampshire Volunteers*. Washington, DC: Norman T. Elliott, Printer and Publisher, 1897.

Tregaskis, John. *Souvenir of the Re-Union of the Blue and Gray on the Battlefield of Gettysburg, July 1,2,3, and 4, 1888* [sic 1887]. New York: American Graphic, 1888.

Tucker, John Randolph. *The Old and New South: Baccalaureate Address Before the South Carolina College, Commencement, 1887*. Columbia: Presbyterian Publishing House, 1887.

Unveiling and Dedication of Monument to Hood's Texas Brigade on the Capitol Grounds at Austin, Texas, Thursday, October Twenty-Seven, Nineteen Hundred and Ten and Minutes of the Thirty-Ninth Annual Reunion of Hood's Texas Brigade Association Held in Senate Chamber at Austin, Texas, October Twenty-Six and Twenty-Seven, Nineteen Hundred and Ten, Together With a Short Monument and Brigade Association History and Confederate Scrapbook. Houston: F. B. Chilton, 1911.

Vermont War Papers and Miscellaneous State Papers and Addresses for the Military Order of the Loyal Legion of the United States. 1915; reprint, Wilmington, NC: Broadfoot, 1994.

Walcott, Charles Folsom. *History of the Twenty-First Regiment Massachusetts Volunteers in the War for the Preservation of the Union*. Boston: Houghton, Mifflin, 1882.

Walker, William Carey. *History of the Eighteenth Regiment Conn. Volunteers in the War for the Union*. Norwich, CT: Published by the Committee, 1895.

War Papers Being Read Before the Commandery of the District of Columbia Military Order of the Loyal Legion of the United States. 4 vols. 1906; reprint, Wilmington, NC: Broadfoot, 1993.

War Papers Read Before the Michigan Commandery MOLLUS. 2 vols. Detroit: James H. Stone & Co., 1898.

War Papers Read Before the Commandery of the State of Maine, Military Order of the Loyal Legion of the United States. 2 vols. Portland, ME: Lefavor-Tower Co., 1902.

War Papers Read Before the Commandery of the State of Wisconsin, Military Order of the Loyal Legion of the United States. 4 vols. Milwaukee, WI: Burdick & Allen, 1914.

War Talks in Kansas. Kansas City, MO: Franklin Hudson Publishing Co., 1906.

Ward, William H. *Records of Members of the Grand Army of the Republic*. San Francisco: H. S. Crocker & Co., 1886.

Washburn, George H. *A Complete Military History and Record of the 108th Regiment N.Y. Volunteers from 1862 to 1864*. Rochester, NY: E. R. Andrews, 1894.

Wilson, Thomas A. *Sufferings Endured for a Free Government; or, A History of the Cruelties and Atrocities of the Rebellion*. Washington, DC: Thomas A. Wilson, 1864.

Periodicals

American Mercury
Atlanta Journal-Constitution
Atlantic Monthly
Augusta (GA) Evening Sentinel
Baltimore American
Baltimore Sun
Beaver Falls (PA) Tribune
Brooklyn Eagle
Charleston (SC) News and Courier
Chicago Daily Tribune
Chicago Sun Times
Confederate Veteran
Congressional Record
The Daily Inter Ocean
The Evening Star
Grand Army Record
Grand Army Sentinel
Jet
The Land We Love
The Living Age
National Tribune
New England Magazine
New York Times
New York Tribune
News Blaze
North American Review
Republican Vindicator
Richmond (VA) Dispatch
Richmond (VA) Times
Richmond (VA) Times-Dispatch
Rolling Stone
Sabbath Recorder
Scribner's Magazine
Seattle Times
Southern Bivouac
Southern Historical Society Papers

The State
Variety
Virginia Dispatch
Washington Post
Wisconsin Democrat

SECONDARY SOURCES

Books

Anderson, Benedict. *Imagined Communities: Reflections on the Origins and Spread of Nationalism.* 1983; reprint, London: Verso, 1991.

Andrews, Matthew Page. *History of the United States.* Philadelphia: J. B. Lippincott, 1914.

Appleby, Joyce, Lynn Hunt, and Margaret Jacob. *Telling the Truth about History.* New York: W. W. Norton & Co., 1994.

Ayers, Edward L., *The Promise of the New South: Life after Reconstruction.* New York: Oxford University Press, 1992.

Ayers, Edward L., Gary W. Gallagher, and Andrew J. Torget, eds. *Crucible of the Civil War: Virginia from Secession to Commemoration.* Charlottesville: University of Virginia Press, 2006.

Basler, Roy P., ed. *The Collected Works of Abraham Lincoln.* 8 vols. New Brunswick, NJ: Rutgers University Press, 1953.

Blair, William. *Cities of the Dead: Contesting Memory of the Civil War in the South, 1865–1914.* Chapel Hill: University of North Carolina Press, 2004.

———. *Why Didn't the North Hang Some Rebels? The Postwar Debate over Punishment for Treason.* Milwaukee, WI: Marquette University Press, 2004.

Blair, William, and William Pencak, eds. *Making and Remaking Pennsylvania's Civil War.* University Park: Pennsylvania State University Press, 2001.

Blight, David W. *Frederick Douglass' Civil War: Keeping Faith in Jubilee.* Baton Rouge: Louisiana State University Press, 1989.

———. *Race and Reunion: The Civil War in American Memory.* Cambridge, MA: Harvard University Press, 2001.

Bodnar, John. *Remaking America: Public Memory, Commemoration, and Patriotism in the Twentieth Century.* Princeton, NJ: Princeton University Press, 1992.

Bowers, Claude. *The Tragic Era: The Revolution after Lincoln.* New York: Blue Ribbon Books, 1929.

Brodsky, Alyn. *Grover Cleveland: A Study in Character.* New York: Truman Talley Books, 2000.

Brown, Peter A. *Take Sides with the Truth: The Postwar Letters of John Singleton Mosby*. Lexington: University Press of Kentucky, 2007.

Brundage, Fitzhugh. *The Southern Past: A Clash of Race and Memory*. Cambridge, MA: Harvard University Press, 2005.

——. *Where These Memories Grow: History, Memory, and Southern Identity*. Chapel Hill: University of North Carolina Press, 2000.

Buck, Paul H. *The Road to Reunion, 1865–1900*. Boston: Little, Brown, 1937.

Calhoun, Charles W. *From Bloody Shirt to Full Dinner Pail: The Transformation of Politics and Governance in the Gilded Age*. New York: Hill & Wang, 2010.

Caudill, Edward, and Paul Ashdown. *Sherman's March in Myth and Memory*. Lanham, MD: Rowman & Littlefield Publishers, 2008.

Collins, Donald E. *The Death and Resurrection of Jefferson Davis*. Lanham, MD: Rowman & Littlefield, 2005.

Campbell, Ballard C., ed. *The Human Tradition in the Gilded Age and Progressive Era*. Wilmington: Scholarly Resources Inc., 2000.

Campbell, Jacqueline Glass. *When Sherman Marched North from the Sea: Resistance on the Confederate Home Front*. Chapel Hill: University of North Carolina Press, 2003.

Catton, Bruce. *A Stillness at Appomattox*. Garden City, NY: Doubleday, 1953.

Confino, Alon, and Peter Fritzsche, eds. *The Work of Memory: New Directions in the Study of German Society and Culture*. Urbana: University of Illinois Press, 2002.

Connelly, Thomas L., *The Marble Man: Robert E. Lee and His Image in American Society*. Baton Rouge: Louisiana State University Press, 1977.

Connelly, Thomas L., and Barbara L. Bellows. *God and General Longstreet: The Lost Cause and the Southern Mind*. Baton Rouge: Louisiana State University Press, 1982.

Coski, John M. *The Confederate Battle Flag: America's Most Embattled Emblem*. Cambridge, MA: Harvard University Press, 2005.

Cosmas, Graham A. *An Army for Empire: The United States Army and the Spanish American War*. Columbia: University of Missouri Press, 1971.

Cox, Karen L. *Dixie's Daughters: The United Daughters of the Confederacy and the Preservation of Confederate Culture*. Gainesville: University of Florida Press, 2003.

Cozzens, Peter, and Robert L Girardi, eds. *The Military Memoirs of General John Pope*. Chapel Hill: University of North Carolina Press, 1998.

Cullen, Jim. *The Civil War in Popular Culture: A Reusable Past*. Washington, DC: Smithsonian Institution Press, 1995.

Davies, Wallace Evans. *Patriotism on Parade: The Story of Veterans' Hereditary Organizations in America*. Cambridge, MA: Harvard University Press, 1955.

Davis, William C. *Cause Lost: Myths and Realities of the Confederacy*. Lawrence: University Press of Kansas, 1996.

Dearing, Mary R. *Veterans in Politics: The Story of the G.A.R.* Baton Rouge: Louisiana State University Press, 1952.

Desjardin, Thomas A. *These Honored Dead: How the Story of Gettysburg Shaped American Memory.* Cambridge, MA: DeCapo Press, 2003.

Dixon, Thomas. *The Clansman: An Historical Romance of the Ku Klux Klan.* 1905; reprint, New York: A. Wessels, 1907.

——. *The Leopard's Spots: A Romance of the White Man's Burden, 1865–1900.* New York: Doubleday, 1903.

Donald, David Herbert. *Lincoln.* New York: Simon & Schuster, 1995.

Douglass, Frederick. *The Life and Times of Frederick Douglass Written by Himself.* Hartford, CT: Park Publishing, 1881.

Du Bois, W. E. B. *Black Reconstruction in America, 1860–1880.* 1935; reprint, New York: Free Press, 1998.

Fahs, Alice, and Joan Waugh. *The Memory of the Civil War in American Culture.* Chapel Hill: University of North Carolina Press, 2004.

Faust, Drew Gilpin. *The Creation of Confederate Nationalism: Ideology and Identity in the Civil War South.* Baton Rouge: Louisiana State University Press, 1988.

——. *The Republic of Suffering: Death and the American Civil War.* New York: Knopf, 2008.

Fellman, Michael. *The Making of Robert E. Lee.* New York: Random House, 2000.

Fishwick, Marshall W. *Lee after the War.* Westport, CT: Greenwood Press, 1963.

Foner, Eric. *Free Soil, Free Labor, Free Men: The Ideology of the Republican Party before the Civil War.* London: Oxford University Press, 1970.

Foster, Gaines M. *Ghosts of the Confederacy: Defeat, the Lost Cause, and the Emergence of the New South.* New York: Oxford University Press, 1985.

Freehling, William W. *The Road to Disunion, Volume II: Secessionists Triumphant 1834–1861.* New York: Oxford University Press, 2007.

Gallagher, Gary W. *Causes Won, Lost, & Forgotten: How Hollywood and Popular Art Shape What We Know about the Civil War.* Chapel Hill: University of North Carolina Press, 2008.

——. *Fighting for the Confederacy: The Personal Recollections of General Edward Porter Alexander.* Chapel Hill: University of North Carolina Press, 1989.

——. *The Union War.* Cambridge, MA: Harvard University Press, 2011.

Gallagher, Gary W., and Alan T. Nolan, eds. *The Myth of the Lost Cause and Civil War History.* Bloomington: Indiana University Press, 2000.

Gannon, Barbara A. *The Won Cause: Black and White Comradeship in the Grand Army of the Republic.* Chapel Hill: University of North Carolina Press, 2011.

Gilmore, Glenda, Bryant Simon, and Jane Daily, eds. *Jumpin' Jim Crow: Southern Politics from Civil War to Civil Rights.* Princeton, NJ: Princeton University Press, 2000.

Goff, Tim. *Under Both Flags: Personal Stories of Sacrifice and Struggle during the Civil War*. Chicago: C. R. Graham, 1896.

Goldfield, David. *Still Fighting the Civil War*. Baton Rouge: Louisiana State University Press, 2002.

Gordon, Armistead C. *William Gordon McCabe: A Brief Memoir*. Richmond, VA: Old Dominion Press, 1920.

Grant, Susan-Mary. *North over South: Northern Nationalism and American Identity in the Antebellum Era*. Lawrence: University Press of Kansas, 2000.

Grant, Susan-Mary, and Peter J. Parish, eds. *Legacy of Disunion: The Enduring Significance of the Civil War*. Baton Rouge: Louisiana State University Press, 2003.

Grimsley, Mark. *The Hard Hand of War: Union Military Policy toward Southern Civilians, 1861–1865*. Cambridge: Cambridge University Press, 1995.

Hale, Grace Elizabeth. *Making Whiteness: The Culture of Segregation in the South*. New York: Vintage, 1999.

Hall, James R. *Den of Misery: Indiana's Civil War Prison*. Gretna: Pelican Publishing Co., 2006.

Haney-Lopez, Ian. *White by Law: The Legal Construction of Race*. New York: New York University Press, 1997.

Hartwig, D. Scott, and Anne Marie Hartwig. *Gettysburg: The Complete Pictorial of Battlefield Monuments*. Gettysburg, PA: Thomas Publications, 1995.

Hershock, Martin J. *The Paradox of Progress: Economic Change, Individual Enterprise, and Political Culture in Michigan, 1837–1878*. Athens: Ohio University Press, 2003.

Hesseltine, William B., ed. *The Civil War Prisons*. Kent, OH: Kent State University Press, 1962.

Hinkle, Don. *Embattled Banner: A Reasonable Defense of the Confederate Battle Flag*. Paducah, KY: Turner, 1997.

Holt, Michael F. *By One Vote: The Disputed Election of 1876*. Lawrence: University Press of Kansas, 2008.

———. *The Political Crisis of the 1850s*. New York: W. W. Norton, 1978.

Holzer, Harold. *Emancipating Lincoln: The Proclamation in Text, Context, and Memory*. Cambridge, MA: Harvard University Press, 2012.

Horigan, Michael. *Elmira: Death Camp of the North*. Mechanicsburg, PA: Stackpole Books, 2002.

Jabbour, Alan, and Karen Singer Jabbour, *Decoration Day in the Mountains, Traditions of Cemetery: Decorations in the Southern Appalachians*. Chapel Hill: University of North Carolina Press, 2010

Janney, Caroline E. *Burying the Dead but Not the Past: Ladies' Memorial Associations & the Lost Cause*. Chapel Hill: University of North Carolina Press, 2008.

——. *Remembering the Civil War: Reunion and the Limits of Reconciliation.* Chapel Hill: University of North Carolina Press, 2013.

Joslyn, Mauriel Phillips. *The Biographical Roster of the Immortal 600.* Shippensburg, PA: White Mane Publishing, 1992.

——. *States Prisoner of War Policy.* Shippensburg, PA: White Mane Publishing, 1996.

Kammen, Michael. *Mystic Chords of Memory: The Transformation of Tradition in American Culture.* New York: Knopf, 1991.

King, Spencer B., Jr. *Darien: The Death and Rebirth of a Southern Town.* Macon, GA: Mercer University Press, 1981.

Lawson, Melinda. *Patriot Fires: Forging a New American Nationalism in the Civil War North.* Lawrence: University Press of Kansas, 2002.

Levin, Kevin. *Remembering the Battle of the Crater: War as Murder.* Lexington: University Press of Kentucky, 2012.

Linderman, Gerald F. *Embattled Courage: The Experience of Combat in the American Civil War.* 1987; reprint, New York: New York Free Press, 1989.

Linenthal, Edward Tabor. *Sacred Grounds: Americans and Their Battlefields.* Urbana: University of Illinois Press, 1991.

Litwicki, Ellen M. *America's Public Holidays 1865–1920.* Washington, DC: Smithsonian Institution Press, 2000.

Lowenthal, David. *The Past Is a Foreign Country.* London: Cambridge University Press, 1985.

Manning, Chandra. *What This Cruel War Was Over: Soldiers, Slavery and the Civil War.* New York: Knopf, 2007.

Marshall, Anne E. *Creating a Confederate Kentucky: The Lost Cause and Civil War Memory in a Border State.* Chapel Hill: University of North Carolina Press, 2010.

McConnell, Stuart *Glorious Contentment: The Grand Army of the Republic, 1885–1900.* Chapel Hill: University of North Carolina Press, 1992.

McEyla, Micki. *Clinging to Mammy: The Faithful Slave in the Twentieth-Century America.* Cambridge, MA: Harvard University Press, 2007.

McPherson, James M. *Battle Cry of Freedom: The Civil War Era.* New York: Oxford University Press, 1988.

——. *Drawn with the Sword: Reflections on the American Civil War.* New York: Oxford University Press, 1996.

——. *For Cause and Comrades: Why Men Fought in the Civil War.* New York: Oxford University Press, 1997.

Mitchell, Reid. *The Vacant Chair: The Northern Soldier Leaves Home.* New York: Oxford University Press, 1993.

——. *What They Fought For: 1861–1865.* 1994; reprint, New York: Doubleday, 1995.

Neely, Mark E., Jr. *The Civil War and the Limits of Destruction*. Cambridge, MA: Harvard University Press, 2007.

Neely, Mark E., Jr., Harold Holtzer, and Gabor S. Boritt, eds. *The Confederate Image: Prints of the Lost Cause*. Chapel Hill: University of North Carolina Press, 1987.

Neff, John R. *Honoring the Civil War Dead: Commemoration and the Problem of Reconciliation*. Lawrence: University Press of Kansas, 2005.

Nichols, James L. *General Fitzhugh Lee: A Biography*. Lynchburg, VA: H. E. Howard, 1989.

Nolan, Alan T. *Lee Considered: General Robert E. Lee & Civil War History*. Chapel Hill: University of North Carolina Press, 1991.

Oates, Stephen B. *To Purge This Land with Blood: A Biography of John Brown*. Amherst: University of Massachusetts Press, 1984.

Osborne, Charles C. *Jubal: The Life and Times of General Jubal A. Early, CSA, Defender of the Lost Cause*. Chapel Hill, NC: Algonquin Books, 1992.

Osterweis, Rollin G. *The Myth of the Lost Cause: 1865–1900*. Hamden, CT: Archon Books, 1972.

Page, Thomas Nelson. *Robert E. Lee: Man and Soldier*. New York: Scribner's, 1911.

Painter, Nell Irvin. *Standing at Armageddon: The United States, 1877–1919*. New York: W. W. Norton, 1987.

Patrick, Jeffrey L., ed. *Three Years with Wallace's Zouaves: The Civil War Memoirs of Thomas Wise Durham*. Macon, GA: Mercer University Press, 2003.

Peterson, Merrill D. *Lincoln in American Memory*. New York: Oxford University Press, 1994.

Phillips, Jason. *Diehard Rebels: The Confederate Culture of Invincibility*. Athens: University of Georgia Press, 2007.

Piston, William Garrett. *Lee's Tarnished Lieutenant: James Longstreet and His Place in Southern History*. Athens: University of Georgia Press, 1987.

Platt, Barbara L. *"This is Holy Ground": A History of the Gettysburg Battlefield*. Harrisburg, PA: Barbara L. Platt, 2001.

Pressly, Thomas J. *Americans Interpret Their Civil War*. Princeton, NJ: Princeton University Press, 1954.

Pucci, Kelly. *Camp Douglas: Chicago's Civil War Prison*. Charleston: Arcadia Publishing, 2007.

Rable, George C. *Fredericksburg! Fredericksburg!* Chapel Hill: University of North Carolina Press, 2002.

Ramage, James A. *Grey Ghost: The Life of John Singleton Mosby*. Lexington: University Press of Kentucky, 1999.

Reardon, Carol. *Pickett's Charge in American Memory*. Chapel Hill: University of North Carolina Press, 1997.

Royster, Charles. *The Destructive War: William Tecumseh Sherman, Stonewall Jackson, and the Americans.* New York: Knopf, 1991.

Rydell, Robert W. *All the World's a Fair: Visions of Empire at American International Expositions, 1876–1916.* Chicago: University of Chicago Press, 1984.

Rydell, Robert W., John E. Finding, and Kimberly D. Pelle, eds. *Fair America: World's Fairs in the United States.* Washington, DC: Smithsonian Institute Press, 2000.

Shackel, Paul A. *Memory in Black and White: Race Commemoration, and the Post-Bellum Landscape.* Lanham, MD: Rowman & Littlefield, 2003.

Shaffer, Donald R. *After the Glory: The Struggles of Black Civil War Veterans.* Lawrence: University Press of Kansas, 2004.

Silber, Nina. *Daughters of the Union: Northern Women Fight the Civil War.* Cambridge, MA: Harvard University Press, 2005.

———. *The Romance of Reunion: Northerners and the South.* Chapel Hill: University of North Carolina Press, 1993.

Silber, Nina, and Mary Beth Sievens, eds. *Yankee Correspondence: The Civil War Letters between New England Soldiers and the Home Front.* Charlottesville: University of Virginia Press, 1996.

Simpson, John A. *Edith D. Pope and Her Nashville Friends: Guardians of the Lost Cause in the Confederate Veteran.* Knoxville: University of Tennessee Press, 2003.

———. *S. A. Cunningham and the Confederate Heritage.* Athens: University of Georgia Press, 1994.

Skocpol, Theda. *Protecting Soldiers and Mothers: The Political Origins of Social Policy in the United States.* Cambridge, MA: Harvard University Press, 1995.

Stokes, Melvyn, and Richard Malyby. *American Movie Audiences: From the Turn of the Century of the Early Sound Era.* London: British Film Institute, 1999.

Tise, Larry E. *Proslavery: A History of the Defense of Slavery in America, 1701–1840.* Athens: University of Georgia Press, 2004.

Toplin, Robert Brent, ed. *Ken Burns's "The Civil War": Historians Respond.* New York: Oxford University Press, 1996.

Towns, W. Stuart. *Enduring Legacy: Rhetoric and Ritual of the Lost Cause.* Tuscaloosa: University of Alabama Press, 2012.

Trachtenburg, Alan. *The Incorporation of America: Culture and Society in the Gilded Age.* New York: Hill & Wang, 1982.

Trask, David F. *The War with Spain in 1898.* Lincoln: University of Nebraska Press, 1981.

Trueau, Noah Andre. *Gettysburg: A Testing of Courage.* New York: HarperCollins, 2002.

Underwood, J. L. *The Women of the Confederacy.* New York: Neale Publishing Co., 1906.

Ward, Geoffrey C., and others, eds. *The Civil War: An Illustrated History.* New York: Knopf, 1990.

Waugh, Joan, and Gary W. Gallagher, eds. *Wars Within a War: Controversy and Conflict over the American Civil War.* Chapel Hill: University of North Carolina Press, 2009.

Wert, Jeffry D. *General James Longstreet: The Confederacy's Most Controversial Soldier.* New York: Touchstone, 1993.

White, Ronald C. *Lincoln's Greatest Speech: The Second Inaugural.* New York: Simon & Schuster, 2006.

White, William W. *The Confederate Veteran.* Tuscaloosa, AL: Confederate Publishing, 1962.

Wiley, Bell Irvin. *The Life of Johnny Reb: The Common Soldier of the Confederacy.* Indianapolis, IN: Bobbs-Merrill, 1943.

Williams, Burton J. *Senator John J. Ingalls: Kansas' Iridescent Republican.* Lawrence: University Press of Kansas, 1972.

Williams, George W. *History of the Negro Race in America 1619–1880.* 2 vols. New York: G. P. Putnam's Sons, 1883.

Wilson, Charles Reagan. *Baptized in Blood: The Religion of the Lost Cause.* Athens: University of Georgia Press, 1980.

Woodward, C. Vann. *Origins of the New South.* Baton Rouge: Louisiana State University Press, 1951.

Yarsinske, Amy Waters. *Jamestown Exposition: American Imperialism on Parade.* 2 vols. Charleston: Arcadia, 1999.

Articles

Bradley, Ed. "The House, the Beast, and the Bloody Shirt: The Doorkeeper Controversy of 1878." *Journal of the Gilded Age & Progressive Era* 3 (January 2004): 15–34.

Collins, Bruce. "Confederate Identity and the Southern Myth since the Civil War." In *Legacy of Disunion: The Enduring Significance of the Civil War,* edited by Susan-Mary Grant and Peter J. Parish, 30–47. Baton Rouge: Louisiana State University Press, 2003.

Cook, Robert. "Unfinished Business: African American and the Civil War Centennial." In *Legacy of Disunion: The Enduring Significance of the Civil War,* edited by Susan-Mary Grant and Peter J. Parish, 48–64. Baton Rouge: Louisiana State University Press, 2003.

Drinkwater, Ray. "War and Reconciliation in the 19th-Century American South: The Personal Journey of William Gordon McCabe." *Southern Historian* 15 (Spring 1994): 5–23.

Faust, Drew Gilpin. "Battle over the Bodies: Burying and Reburying the Civil War Dead." In *Wars within a War: Controversy and Conflict over the American Civil*

War, edited by Joan Waugh and Gary W. Gallagher, 184–201. Chapel Hill: University of North Carolina Press, 2009.

Fields, Barbara J. "Who Freed the Slaves?" In *The Civil War: An Illustrated History,* edited by Geoffrey C. Ward and others, 176–181. New York: Knopf, 1990.

Fleche, Andre. "'Shoulder to Shoulder as Comrades Tried': Black and White Union Veterans and Civil War Memory." *Civil War History* 51 (June 2005):175–201.

Gallagher, Gary W. "Jubal A. Early, the Lost Cause, and Civil War History: A Persistent Legacy." In *The Myth of the Lost Cause and Civil War History,* edited by Gary W. Gallagher and Alan T. Nolan, 35–59. Bloomington: Indiana University Press, 2000.

Gannon, Barbara A. "Sites of Memory, Sites of Glory: African-American Grand Army of the Republic Posts in Pennsylvania." In *Making and Remaking Pennsylvania's Civil War,* edited by William Blair and William Pencak, 163–88. University Park: Pennsylvania State University Press, 2001.

Gillispie, James M. "Postwar Mythmaking: Popular Writings on the Treatment of Prisoners, 1865–1920." In *North & South: The Official Magazine of the Civil War Society* 6, no. 3 (March 2003): 40–49.

Grant, Susan Mary. "The Charter of Its Birthright: The Civil War and American Nationalism." In *Legacy of Disunion: The Enduring Significance of the Civil War,* edited by Susan-Mary Grant and Peter J. Parish, 188–206. Baton Rouge: Louisiana State University Press, 2003.

Hale, Grace Elizabeth. "The Lost Cause and the Meaning of History," *OAH Magazine of History* 27 (January 2013): 13–17.

Harris, M. Keith. "Slavery, Emancipation, and Veterans of the Union Cause: Commemorating Freedom in the Era of Reconciliation, 1885–1915." *Civil War History* 53 (September 2007): 264–90.

Hesseltine, William B. "The Propaganda Literature of Confederate Prisons." *Journal of Southern History* 1 (February 1935): 56–66.

Janney, Caroline E. "Written in Stone: Gender, Race, and the Heywood Shepard Memorial." *Civil War History* 52 (June 2006):117–41.

Johnson, Mary. "An 'Ever-Present Bone of Contention': The Heywood Shepard Memorial." *West Virginia History* 56 (January 1997): 1–26.

Jordan, Brian Matthew. "'Living Monuments': Union Veteran Amputees and the Embodied Memory of the Civil War." *Civil War History* 57, no. 2 (June 2011): 121–52.

Keely, Karen A. "Marriage plots and national reunion: The trope of romantic reconciliation in postbellum literature[a]. *Mississippi Quarterly* 51 (Fall 1998): 621–48.

Kelly, Patrick K. "The Election of 1896 and the Restructuring of Civil War Memory." In *The Memory of the Civil War in American Culture,* edited by Alice Fahs and Joan Waugh, 180–212. Chapel Hill: University of North Carolina Press, 2004.

Krowl, Michelle A. "In the Spirit of Fraternity: The United States Government and the Burial of Confederate Dead at Arlington National Cemetery." *Virginia Magazine of History and Biography* 3 (2003): 151–86.

Lee, Susanna Michelle. "Reconciliation in Reconstruction Virginia." In *Crucible of the Civil War: Virginia from Secession to Commemoration,* edited by Edward L. Ayers, Gary W. Gallagher, and Andrew J. Torget, 189–208. Charlottesville: University of Virginia Press, 2006.

Madison, James H. "Civil War Memories and 'Pardnership Forgittin,' 1865–1913." *Indiana Magazine of History* 99, no. 3 (September 2003): 198–230.

McPherson, James M. "Long-Legged Yankee Lies: The Southern Textbook Crusade." In *The Memory of the Civil War in American Culture,* edited by Alice Fahs and Joan Waugh, 64–78. Chapel Hill: University of North Carolina Press, 2004.

Moser, Bob. "Conflicts Arise over Lincoln Statue in Richmond Va. Cemetery." *Southern Poverty Law Center Intelligence Report* 110 (Summer 2003).

Smith, Adam I. P., and Peter J. Parish. "A Contested Legacy: The Civil War and Party Politics in the North." In *Legacy of Disunion: The Enduring Significance of the Civil War,* edited by Susan Mary Grant and Peter J. Parish, 81–99. Baton Rouge: Louisiana State University Press, 2003.

Stokes, Melvyn. "The Civil War in the Movies." In *Legacy of Disunion: The Enduring Significance of the Civil War,* edited by Susan Mary Grant and Peter J. Parish, 65–78. Baton Rouge: Louisiana State University Press, 2003.

Taylor, Robert T. "The Jamestown Tercentennial Exposition of 1907." *Virginia Magazine of History and Biography* 65 (April 1957): 169–208.

Waugh, Joan. "Pageantry of Woe: The Funeral of Ulysses S. Grant." Civil War History 51 (June 2005): 151–74.

———. "Ulysses S. Grant: Historian." In *The Memory of the Civil War in American Culture,* edited by Alice Fahs and Joan Waugh, 5–38. Chapel Hill: University of North Carolina Press, 2004.

FILMS

Burns, Ken, and Ric Burns. *The Civil War.* PBS Home Video, 1990.

Griffith, D. W. *The Birth of a Nation.* 1915; reprint, Kino Video, 2002.

Maxwell, Ron. *Gods and Generals.* Warner Brothers Home Video, 2003.

Zwick, Edward. *Glory.* Tristar Home Video, 1989.

WEB SITES

Address of Franklin Delano Roosevelt, Gettysburg, Pennsylvania, July 3, 1938, www .gettysburgdaily.com/?p=1482, February 8, 2009.

Alexander H. Stephens's Cornerstone Speech, www.teachingamericanhistory.org/library/index.asp?documentprint=76, March, 20, 2009.

AmericaBlog.com, www.americablog.com/2008/01/huckabee-gave-speech-to-white.html, March 22, 2009.

The Arkansas Division of the Sons of Confederate Veterans, arkansasscv.com/, March 22, 2009.

Message of Jefferson Davis to the Provisional Congress of the Confederate States of America, sunsite.utk.edu/civil-war/jdmess.html, March 20, 2009.

MySpace.com, Sons of Confederate Veterans, profile.myspace.com/index.cfm?fuse action=user.viewprofile&friendID=389874616, March 22, 2009.

Sons of Confederate Veterans Weblog, sonsofconfederateveterans.blogspot.com/, March 22, 2009.

Sons of Confederate Veterans General Headquarters, www.scv.org/, March 22, 2009.

INDEX

Abolition, 116, 125; and the cause of the war, 120–21, 125; northern association with, 127, 129, 130–31, 136

Abolition Crusade and Its Consequences, 125

Acton, Lord John Dalberg, 69

Adams, Clarendon E., 62

Adams, John G. B., 24–25

African Americans: marginalization of, 5; as prisoners of war, 27; as prison guards, 28, 29, 30; GAR units, 91; as soldiers, 108; protection by former Confederates, 136

Alabama units: 20th Infantry Regiment, 74–75; 1st Infantry Regiment, 129; 5th Cavalry Regiment, 131

Alcott, Louisa May, 123

Alderman, Edwin A., 88

Allen, William, 124

Alton prison, 30

American Bar Association, 71

American Legion, 56

Andersonville prison, 16, 21, 23, 26–27, 28, 35, 36; monuments at, 98

Antietam, battle of, 98; and emancipation, 103, 110

Appomattox, surrender at, 15, 18, 62, 98–99; and Grant's magnanimity, 110

Arkansas units: 11th Infantry Regiment, 127

Arlington National Cemetery, 24

Army of Northern Virginia, 15; veterans of, 36; II Corps, 72

Army of the Cumberland, 62

Association of Confederate Soldiers and Sailors of Maryland, 75

Association of the Army of Northern Virginia (AANVA), 19–20, 30, 77

Association of the Army of Tennessee, 20

Association of the Survivors of Rebel Prisons, 24

Atlanta, Georgia, burning of, 16, 32

"Atrocities narrative," 12, 15, 21, 23, 34

Baker, Alan C., 57

Ballew, W. W., 37, 83

Ball's Bluff, battle of, 53

Banes, Charles H., 21

Barhydt, T. L., 101

Beard, John S., 74, 77–78

Beaver, James Addams, 40

Bebe, L. H. B., 53

Belle Isle prison, 25, 36

Berkeley, William, 70

Beveridge, John L., 107

Bevier, Robert S., 131

bin Laden, Osama, 140

Black, Richard A., 139

Blaine, James G. 23

Bloody shirt, 5

Blue-Gray reunions, 9, 70, 95–96, 111; 1913 Gettysburg, 8–9; 1938 Gettysburg, 9. *See also* Gettysburg, battlefield

Booth, George Wilson, 126

Booth, John Wilkes, 140–41
Bowling, Bradgon, 139
Bradwell, Gordon, 120
Brainard, Mary Genevie Green, 23
Breckinridge, William C. P., 36
Brimley Hall, 26
Brinski, George, 56
Brooklyn Eagle, 104
Brooklyn Post (New York GAR), 57–58
Brooks, Red Emerson, 113
Brown, John, 116
Buchannan, James, 56
Burnell, H. L., 35
Burns, Ken, 4
Burnside, Ambrose, 31
Butler. Benjamin F., 42, 93–94
Butterfield, Daniel, 110

Calhoun, William L., 83
Campfires of the Confederacy, 28
Cannon, John Stephen, 139
Cannon, Le Grand B., 108
Cave, Robert C., 132–33
Chambersburg, Pennsylvania, burning of, 16, 34–35
Chancellorsville, battlefield, 10
Chandler, Thomas Coleman, 28
Chandler, William E., 105
Charleston, South Carolina, siege of, 28
Christian, George, L. 37–38, 73
Churchill, Winston, 141
Cincinnati Commercial, 32
City Point prison, 27
Civil History of the Government of the Confederate States, 131
The Civil War (1990 documentary), 4
Clairborne, John Herbert, 74
Clark, Charles, 22
Cleveland, Grover, 56–57, 125
Cold Harbor, battle of, 24
Collier's Weekly, 55
Collins, W. T., 1, 2, 51

Columbia, South Carolina, burning of, 16, 31; prison at, 24, 36
Commemoration: traditions of, 4, 7, 13, 16, 20, 84, 116; and the national ethos, 7, 10–11, 17, 25, 28, 43, 114, 117, 142, 143–44, 146n6; and veteran leadership, 8; emancipation and, 13–14, 91, 96–97; Union culture of, 23, 46, 47, 93, 107, 117, 142; Confederate culture of, 27, 28, 32, 66–67, 76, 80, 87, 89, 114–15, 117, 119, 121, 125–26, 127, 129, 138, 169n4; nonveterans, 41, 97; border state, 60–61; "defense of home" theme, 117–19, 121; waning Confederate influence, 141–42
Confederate Battle Abbey (Richmond), 134
Confederate cause, 13; slavery, 13, 109; condemnation of, 106; U. S. Grant on, 110–11; distance from slavery 125–26
The Confederate Cause and Conduct in the War Between the States, 72–73
Confederate flags, 65, 138, 141, 142, 166n42; return controversy, 56–57; condemnation of, 64; modern controversy, 142
Confederate Military History, 77
Confederate Relief and Historical Association of Memphis, 19
Confederate States Cavalry (veterans' organization), 20
Confederate Survivors' Association, 77
Confederate Survivors' Association of South Carolina, 19
Confederate Veteran, 11, 30, 81–82, 86–88, 118, 120, 123, 124, 134, 136
Connecticut units: 27th Infantry Regiment, 21, 47; 20th Infantry Regiment, 50
Constitutional Convention (1787), 81
Cooke, Giles B., 88
Copperheads, 92
Crane, N. M., 101
Cravath, I. M., 63
Curry, J. L. M., 124, 131–32
Curry, Manly B., 122

Daniel, Ferdinand, Eugene, 127
Daniel, John Warwick, 70–71, 78
Daniel, Raleigh T., 79
Danks, John A., 100
Darien, Georgia, burning of, 16, 31
Davis, Jefferson, 64, 80, 131, 141; praise for,
    43, 53, 81; condemnation of, 54, 55
Davis, William Watts Hart, 21
Decoration Day, 105. *See also* Memorial
    Day
*Defending the Southern Confederacy: Men in
    Gray,* 133
Democratic Party, 42, 56, 120, 121
Devens, Charles, 52
Dick, Charles, 63
Dickerson, L. T., 28
Dinkins, James, 31
Dodge, Theodore Ayrault, 110
Doorkeeper Controversy, 42
Doubleday, Abner, 110
Douglas, Stephen A., 134
Duffy, Ross C., 48
Dunaway, Wayland Fuller, 84, 126–27
Durham, Thomas Wise, 92

Early, Jubal A., 19, 35, 67–68, 69, 124;
    tributes to, 73
Eclectic History of the United States, 124
Edgerton, H. K., 141
Ellis Island, 58
Ellyson, James Taylor, 118
Elmira prison, 16
Emancipation, 13–14; commemorations of,
    91, 95, 97, 103, 106, 111–12: as a Union
    cause, 92, 95, 97, 104, 107–8, 123, 124,
    129, 131, 173n7; Confederate dismissal
    of, 117; as a Union war measure, 120, 137;
    Union dismissal of, 134–35
Emancipation Proclamation, 91, 95, 103–4,
    109–10, 130, 134
Ennis, B. William, 57
Eternal Light Peace Memorial (Gettysburg), 9

Evans, Clement A., 77
Ex-Prisoner of War Association, 24

Fairchild, Charles Bryant, 110
Fairchild, Lucius, 56
Fair Oaks, battle of, 61
Fallows, Samuel, 107
Fiske, John, 124
Flag Day, 47
Flower, Mark D., 60–61
Foote, Shelby, 4, 5
Foraker, J. B., 82, 95
Ford's Theatre, 141
Forrest, Nathan Bedford, 36
Fort Delaware prison, 28
Fort Pillow, massacre at, 36
Fort Sumter, 43, 107
Founding generation (Revolutionary era),
    3, 16, 17, 36, 41, 43, 82, 108; as a theme in
    commemorative literature, 45, 133–34,
    143–44; and connections to the Civil
    War, 47–48; Confederate connections to,
    67, 71, 76–77, 78–79, 87–88, 135
Fred C. Jones Post (Ohio GAR), 95, 112
Fredericksburg, battlefield, 10, 31; battle of,
    24, 30, 31, 34, 40
Freedmen's Bureau, 135–36
Free labor ideology, 100–101, 120
French, David, 140
Fuller, Charles, A. 90

Garrison, William Lloyd, 125, 137
Georgia units: 42nd Infantry Regiment, 83;
    31st Infantry Regiment, 120–21
Gettysburg: battlefield, 8–10, 60–62; battle
    of, 24, 43; monuments at, 60–61, 98–99,
    100; reunions at, 90. *See also* Blue-Gray
    reunions
Gettysburg Address, 99. *See also* Lincoln,
    Abraham
Glenny, William, 61
Goode, Virgil, 140

Goolrick, John T., 70
Gordon, John Brown, 116
Grand Army Button, 105
Grand Army of the Republic (GAR), 18, 24, 48, 82, 93, 153n6; in comparison to Confederate counterparts, 30; Department of Maryland, 45, 47; Department of Nebraska, 48; Department of New York, 48–49, 105; Department of Minnesota, 53, 58; Department of Pennsylvania, 56; Department of Wisconsin, 59, 112; African Americans in, 91; Department of the Potomac, 104
Grand Army Record, 54, 55
Grant, Ulysses S., 15, 32, 104, 110; blame for prison privations, 27; in comparison to Lee, 55
Grant's Tomb (General Grant National Memorial), 113
Green, Robert M., 48, 110
Grimm, J. L., 47
Ground Zero (Manhattan), 140

Hallowell, Edward N., 28, 29
Hamden, Henry, 112
Hamilton, North Carolina, burning of, 31
Hanby, William R., 1
Harding, R. J., 33, 34, 81
Hard war, 16
Harnden, Henry, 92
Harris, G. B., Jr., 72
Harris, Joel Chandler, 33
Hartford Convention (1814), 69
Harvard University, 124
Hay, John, 111
Hayes, Rutherford B., 107
Henry, Patrick, 13, 133
Herbert, Hilary A., 125
High Water Mark, 62–63, 98–99. *See also* Gettysburg
Hill, B. H., 85

Historic Fredericksburg: The Story of an Old Town, 70
Hollywood Cemetery (Richmond), 141
Holstein, Charles L., 45–46
Hood's Texas Brigade Association, 33, 66, 81
Howard, McHenry, 29
Hunter, R. M. T., 86

Illinois units: 11th Cavalry Regiment, 94
Immortal 600. *See* the Society of the Immortal 600
Indiana units: 11th Infantry Regiment (Wallace's Zouaves), 92
Ingalls, John J., 90–91
Ingersoll, Robert Green, 42, 94
Isham, Asa B., 54, 101

Jackson, Thomas Jonathan (Stonewall), 43, 72, 124
Jackson, W. Huntington, 107
Jamestown Tercentennial Celebration, 7
Jefferson, Thomas, 13, 69, 133
John G. Foster Post (New Hampshire GAR), 105
Johnson, Bradley T., 17, 19, 75
Johnson, George W., 44–45
Jones, Benjamin Washington, 119–20, 121
Jones, Charles C., 83
Jones, Joseph, 19

Kaine, Tim, 140
Kemper, James L., 130
Kimball, Edward P., 26
Kissick, Robert, 56
Kline, Robert, 140

Lafayette Post (New York GAR), 48–49, 50, 63–64. *See also* Mills, Abraham Gilbert
Lamb, John, 40, 134
The Land We Love, 11, 84, 118
Law, Evander M., 79

Lee, Fitzhugh, 5, 36, 70–71, 79

Lee, Robert E., 10, 15, 94, 124; death of 19; as American hero, 19, 71; praise for, 43; condemnation of 54–56; conciliatory public image of, 69; private reflections of, 69–70; surrender of, 98–99

Lee, Robert E., Jr., 76

Lee Camp #1, UCV, 20, 132

Lee Monument (Richmond), 132

Lewis, George, 22

Lewis, Osceola, 21

Libby prison, 16, 21, 23, 24, 26, 36, 58

The Liberator, 125

Lincoln, Abraham, 3, 9, 32, 51, 77, 99, 134; blame for atrocities, 34; image as emancipator, 39, 92–93, 104, 107, 108; tributes to, 53; Confederate impressions of, 81, 82, 88; image as abolitionist, 121, 130; Tredegar Iron Works monument, 139–40, 141; Washington, D. C. memorial, 139

Lincoln, Thomas (Tad), 139–40

Locke, William Henry, 21

Loeher, Charles T., 27

Logan, John A. 23, 110; General Order No. 11, 24

Longstreet, James, 69

Loring, George B., 96

Lost Cause, 13, 102, 152n18; rejection of, 13, 72, 73–75, 85; modern uses of, 183n6

Low, Seth, 97

Lucius Fairchild post, GAR, 39

Lundt, George, 124

Manassas (Bull Run), battlefield, 10

Maryland Line (veterans' organization), 72

Massachusetts units: 15th Infantry Regiment, 53; 2nd Infantry Regiment, 91–92

Maury, Dabny, 84

Maxwell, John H., 49

Maxwell, John S., 105

McCabe, William Gordon, 3, 118–19

McGlashan, P. A., 78

McGrady, Edward, 120

McGuire, Hunter, 72–73

McKee, James Harvey, 22

McKee, Thomas, 64

McKim, Randolph Harrison, 137

McMorries, Edward Young, 129–30

McMurry, W. J., 127–29

McPherson, Edward, 42–43

Meade George Gordon, 103

Medal of Honor, 24

Memorial Day, 39, 51, 53, 94; origins of, 24, 50; Confederate, 50, 74, 80; and commemoration of emancipation, 105, 113

Memory: and sectionalism, 1, 7; perceptions of, 3, 146n2; and reconciliation, 4, 6, 9; national, 6, 150n11; sentimentalization of, 7; veterans' preservation of, 12, 18, 31, 40, 126, 168n3; of prisons, 24; of battles, 36, 101; of treason, 42, 43, 59, 143; of slavery and emancipation, 114–15, 116, 119, 142; modern battles over 143–44

Michigan units: Wolverine Brigade (cavalry), 54; 7th Cavalry Regiment, 101; 24th Infantry Regiment, 102; 10th Cavalry Regiment, 102

Miles, Nelson, 104

Military Order of the Loyal Legion of the United States (MOLLUS), 18, 106–7; "War Papers," 26, 106–7; commanderies, 26

Millan prison, 25

Mills, Abraham Gilbert, 48–49

M'Neilly, James H., 81–82

Monroe, Nelson, 105–6

Monuments: Confederate state, 10

Moorman, George, 78

Morgan, John T., 137

Morgan, William Henry, 130

Morris Island prison, 24, 28, 29

Morton, Joseph W., 14
Morton, O. P., 103
Mosby, John Singleton, 116
Mullan, James M., 82
Munford, B. B., 86
Murray, John Ogden, 29
Museum of the Confederacy, 140

National League of Professional Baseball
    Clubs, 49
The National Tribune, 11, 22, 25, 38, 44, 54,
    94, 111
Neo-Confederates, 141, 142
New Hampshire units: 15th Infantry
    Regiment, 45
New Jersey units: 8th Infantry Regiment,
    100; 13th Infantry Regiment, 100
Newlin, William Henry, 47
New York Times, 85, 103
New York units: 125th Infantry Regiment,
    22; 5th Infantry Regiment (Duryea's
    Zouaves), 49; 84th Infantry Regiment,
    97; 108th Infantry Regiment, 100; 76th
    Infantry Regiment, 101

Oakwood Cemetery (Chicago), 51
Ohio units: 12th Infantry Regiment, 43;
    31st Infantry Regiment, 93
The Origin of the Late War, 124

Palmer, John, 58
Parker, Thomas H., 21
Parsons, Cornelius R., 100
"Patriotic Instruction," 39
Pea Patch Island prison, 28
Pegram Battalion Association, 68
Pelham, Peter, 136
Pennsylvania units: 126th Infantry Regi-
    ment, 21; 104th Infantry Regiment, 21;
    124th Infantry Regiment, 48; 90th
    Infantry Regiment, 99–100
Personal Memoirs of U. S. Grant, 110–11

Phil Sheridan Post 10 (Wisconsin GAR), 112
Phillips, John W., 99
Pickens, Francis Wilkinson, 64
Pickett, George, 130
Pickett's Charge, 62–63. *See also* Gettysburg
Point Lookout prison, 27, 28
Pope, John, 110
Porter, Horace, 104
Potter, Orlando, 59
Potts, James H., 101–2
Prisoner of war camps, 12, 15. *See also* Al-
    ton; Andersonville; Belle Isle; City Point;
    Columbia; Elmira; Fort Delaware; Libby;
    Millan; Morris Island; Pea Patch Island;
    Point Lookout; Sandusky

Racism, 5, 35–36, 95
Rand, Arnold, 107
Reagan, John H., 82, 116
Ream's Station, battle of, 40
Recollection of War Times, 108
*Recollections and Letters of General
    Robert E. Lee*, 76
Reconciliation: promotion of, 1, 4, 40, 42,
    50; addresses concerning, 1; definition
    of, 2, 14; general views of 3, 145n2;
    monuments to, 5; spirit of, 5; racism and,
    6; Confederate culture of, 10, 64–65, 89;
    conditional, 11; national, 11, 43, 101, 126,
    129; sectional, 11, 16–17, 91, 116; impli-
    cations of 12; earliest incarnations of,
    15–16; Union culture of, 64, 96, 101–2,
    149n10; Confederate culture of, 68, 78,
    110, 115
"Reconciliation Premise," 5, 13, 148n8
Reconstruction Era, 77, 83: politics, 21
Regimental Histories, 11–12, 20, 22–23,
    109, 126
Republican Party, 111, 146n4
Reunion, definition of, 2
Richmond Howitzers, 118
Riddle, Albert Gallitin, 108

Rogers, John Henry, 88
Rome, Georgia, burning of, 31
Rood, Hosea, W., 39
Roosevelt, Franklin Delano, 9
Roosevelt, Theodore, 57, 63
Rosser, Thomas Lafayette, 5

Sandusky prison, 28
Schiebert, J., 120
Schofield, John McAllister, 110
Schurz, Carl, 110
Sears, William, 57
Sectionalism: memory of, 1, 6, 123, 127, 131; commemorative culture, 11; bitterness, 12. *See also* Memory; Reconciliation; Veterans
Sellers, A. J., 99–100
Sheldon, Winthrop D., 21, 47
Shenandoah Valley, actions in, 34–35. *See also* Early, Jubal; Sheridan, Phillip
Sheridan, Phillip, 107; Shenandoah Valley campaign, 32, 34, 123
Sherman, William T., 41, 95, 141; Georgia campaign, 31–32, 33; in the Carolinas, 31; Confederate perceptions of, 32–33, 142
Shields, James, 42
Simons, Ezra D., 22, 110
Slavery, as cause of war, 39, 90, 92, 95, 102, 103, 112–13, 115–16, 121, 128; and Confederate commemorative culture, 114, 117–18, 119, 126–27, 130, 133; as a positive good, 122; in southern literature, 122; as an inherited northern institution, 132, 134
Smith, Edward, 140
Snowden, Yates, 29
Social media, 141, 142, 184n7
Society of the Army of Northern Virginia, 19
Society of the Army of the Cumberland, 18
Society of the Army of the James, 18
Society of the Army of the Potomac, 18
Society of the Army of the Tennessee, 18

Society of the Burnside Expedition, 18
The Society of the Immortal 600, 28, 29–30
Soldiers and Sailors Monument (Richmond), 132
Soldiers and Sailors National Union League, 18
Sons of Confederate Veterans (SCV), 40, 94, 139; Virginia Division, 139, 141
South Carolina College, 81
The Southern Bivouac, 11
Southern Historical Society (SHS), 19, 84
Southern Historical Society Papers, 11, 31, 33, 84–85, 86, 118, 134, 136
Southern States and Constitution, 124
Spanish-American War, 5, 17, 85, 147n7
Spencer, Clinton, 61–62
Spotsylvania, battle of, 24, 28, 73
Stanton, Edwin M., 27, 29; biography of, 64
Steele, S. A., 133–34
Stephens, Alexander H., 38, 93, 32
Stevens, J. W., 66
Stewart, Robert Laird, 99
Stewart, Lucy S., 51
Stiles, Robert, 118
Storrs, John W., 50
Stowe, Harriet Beecher, 91, 122
Sumbardo, C. L., 43
Survivors of Rebel Prisons (veterans' organization), 24
Sutherland, George E., 93

Taylor, Benjamin F., 101
Taylor, Stuart, 113
Tennessee units: 20th Infantry Regiment, 127–28
Textbooks, 12, 55, 123–25
Thalheimer, M. E., 124
Thayer, Joseph W., 51
Thomas, George H., 62
Thornton, Matthew, 98
Towbridge, Luther Stephen, 102
Townsend, Luther Tracy, 45

Tredegar Iron Works, 139
Tucker, John Randolph, 71–72, 81, 135
Tyler, D. Gardner, 79
Tyler, John ,79

Uncle Remus, 33
Uncle Tom's Cabin, 91, 121, 122–23
Underwood, John Levi, 74–75
Union cause, 12; emancipation, 13–14
Union ex-Prisoners of War Association, 17–18
Union Soldiers' Alliance, 18
Union Veteran Legion, 18
Union Veterans' Union, 18
United Confederate Veterans (UCV), 11, 19–20, 30, 52, 59, 116, 118, 125; Department of Georgia, 77
United Daughters of the Confederacy, 94, 123
United States Army Corps: XV, 23
United States Colored Troops (USCT), 35–36, 149n9
United States Marine Corps, 52
Unreconstructed Rebels, 5

Van Sant, Samuel, R., 104
Veterans: Confederate message, 2, 22, 38, 40–41, 73, 143, 80; Union message, 2, 22–23, 41, 44, 61, 108, 113; leadership, 8, 25; reunions, 9–10, 25, 30, 44; commemorative efforts, 10, 20; speeches, 17; written recollections 21–22, 75, 104; attitudes toward former enemies, 36, 123, 124; objections to sectionalism, 37;

sectionalism 37–38; and the passage of time, 40, 45, 112–13, 137–38, 143–44, 151n15
Virginia Military Institute (VMI), 28
Virginia units: Tyranny Unmasked Artillery, 28; 11th Cavalry Regiment, 29; Surrey Light Artillery, 37; Surry Light Artillery, 119; 47th Infantry Regiment, 126–27

Walker, Ivan N., 58–59
War Between the States, 38. *See also* Stephens, Alexander
Washington, George, 13, 69, 78, 79, 133
Washington and Lee University, 71, 80–81
Washington Post, 103
Waul, Thomas Neville, 66
Wheeler, Joseph, 5, 85, 133
Wilcox, Cadmus M., 69
Wilcox, Lymon G., 39
Wilderness, battle of, 24, 63
Williamsburg, North Carolina, burning of, 31
Wilson, Dan J., 36
Wilson, Woodrow, 9, 56
Wirz, Henry, 41
Wisconsin units: 12th Infantry Regiment, 39
Wise, Henry A., 85
Women, and Confederate commemorations, 19, 75, 123, 154n8
Woodruff, Thomas M., 95
World War I, 50
World's Columbian Exposition, 6, 22